# EMERGE

God's Biblical Blueprint for True Masculinity

Jürgen Matthesius

Copyright © 2024 by Jürgen Matthesius

**v.1**

# CONTENTS

| | | |
|---|---|---|
| **CHAPTER ONE:** | MAN | 5 |
| **CHAPTER TWO:** | PRAYER | 21 |
| **CHAPTER THREE:** | FATHER | 37 |
| **CHAPTER FOUR:** | BROTHER | 60 |
| **CHAPTER FIVE:** | HUSBAND | 70 |
| **CHAPTER SIX:** | FRIEND | 96 |
| **CHAPTER SEVEN:** | KING | 115 |
| **CHAPTER EIGHT:** | PRIEST | 131 |
| **CHAPTER NINE:** | WARRIOR | 144 |
| **CHAPTER TEN:** | PRODUCER | 169 |
| **CHAPTER ELEVEN:** | LEADER | 186 |
| **CHAPTER TWELVE:** | CHAMPION | 202 |
| **CHAPTER THIRTEEN:** | ALPHA | 221 |
| **CHAPTER FOURTEEN:** | DISCIPLE | 232 |
| **REFERENCES** | | 245 |

**EMERGE**

CHAPTER ONE: **MAN**

CHAPTER ONE

# MAN

## *Adam*

*Noun:* An Adult Male. Masculine. Seed Bearer.

*"What is man that you are mindful of him?
You have made him a little lower than Elohim."
Psalm 8:5 NKJV*

*And God said, let us make man in our image, and in our likeness
in the image of God, he created him in the likeness of God
he created them male and female.
Genesis 1:26-27 NKJV*

# EMERGE

## QUOTES

*"I mean to make myself a man, and If I succeed in that,
I shall succeed in everything else!"*
- James Garfield

*"It was men who stopped slavery. It was men who ran up the stairs in the
Twin Towers to rescue people. It was men who gave up their seats on the
lifeboats of the Titanic. Men are made to take risks and
live passionately on behalf of others."*
- John Eldredge

*The ultimate measure of a man is not where he stands
in moments of comfort and convenience, but where he stands at
times of challenge and controversy.*
- Rev. Martin Luther King

## IS MASCULINITY TOXIC?

"Toxic" (Tok-Sik) adj. "poisonous, harmful, malicious, causing unpleasant feelings"

Is masculinity, the way God designed it, "poisonous, harmful, malicious and the cause of unpleasant feelings?" This is the question we must ask ourselves if we are to defend masculinity against the spirit that is currently the most dominant and pervasive influence in our culture. One of my 'go to' voices is Paul Joseph Watson out of the UK. He is a prophetic voice to our time. This is what he says in response to all the claims that masculinity is in itself "toxic!"

*"First of all, there's this implied idea out there that masculinity itself is a natural, organic, innate concept, or that 'being tough' is automatically a negative trait that has to be socially engineered out of young men! As if God and thousands of years of human development somehow just got it wrong. Masculinity isn't toxic by nature; it's a fundamental human necessity that builds societies and protects communities and families. By automatically maligning it, we coerce young men into feeling ashamed of their own gender!"*
- Paul Joseph Watson

# CHAPTER ONE: MAN

Before we criticize or defend "masculinity," it would greatly benefit us to define it. The best definition I have heard so far is this: *"Masculinity is that which is least feminine, and femininity is that which is least masculine!"*

God created the two genders completely different yet totally complementary to one another. When God created man, He created the one who would carry and portray that which is masculine. He created the female to espouse, carry, and portray all that is feminine.

> *"So God created man in His own image; in the image of God He created him; male and female He created them."*
> *Genesis 1:27 NKJV*

## WHAT IS A MAN?

What is a *man*? Up until very recently, this question would have been superfluous, but in the current godless age in which we live, it requires us to do a deep dive into the various aspects of what we have come to mean by the term *"man!"*

Man carries the masculine expression of God. The world in which we live has a spirit that loves to invert, pervert, and confuse everything, especially the things of God. We have all heard the adage, *"Real Men don't cry!"* So what do *"real men"* do then? Do they sing? Do they compose? Do they like art? Do they sail? Do they design? Are they allowed to enjoy fashion? Do they struggle? Do they fight? Or are they ONLY men if they win? Do *"real men"* never lose? Do they admit weakness? Do they have weaknesses? Is a *"real man"* identified by sporting a muscular physique and a six pack? Is a *"real man"* defined by how many women he can bed? What the heck is a *"real man?"*

## CULTURE WARS

Matt Walsh produced a magnificent documentary highlighting the stupidity of our depraved and ignorant times, called *"What is a Woman?"* In this extraordinary film, he travels throughout the United States seeking an answer to what should be an elementary question. His travels even take him to a remote village in Africa where he gets a much clearer and more precise answer from tribal nomadic folk living in mud hut villages than all of the professors and therapists in our left-wing, modern cities and institutions of academia.

**EMERGE**

*"What is a woman?"* The documentary reveals a departure from basic science and biology, and one could argue common sense (sadly, it's not too "common" anymore), especially among those who would proclaim themselves as our "intellectual elites." As a viewer, you sat watching awkwardly as they dodged, deflected, and tried everything they could not to give a direct answer to a question that, just a few years ago, any toddler in preschool could have clearly answered! *What is a Woman?*, is a must watch exposé of the incredulous stupidity of our times. As Romans 1:22 declares, *"Professing to be wise they became utter fools!"*

The Bible asks this question for us in the eighth Psalm, fourth verse;

*"What is MAN that you are mindful of him?"*

Great question. What is *man* that God is mindful of him, and what is/was the Creator's intention behind *man's* design? Did God have a plan, a design, a purpose for him when He created MAN in His image and likeness? Our godless education system has been teaching the bankrupt "theory of evolution" to our students for almost a century, in which they tell us that, *"We came from nothing, we are going nowhere, and there is no point, purpose or reason for us to be here!"* Is it any wonder we have a generation lost in a sea of hedonistic, self-pleasing, pleasure-seeking, empty pursuits, using each other and any substances they can to achieve their next high or hit? YOU were created with purpose, intention, and design. You are not a monkey who got lucky, but a man-made to reflect the Almighty in the earth!

For a book written to address the issues of our times, it is essential that we begin by clearly defining what it means to be a man! To do this, we will dive into the etymology and origin of the term "man." We will use the Bible, specifically the Torah written in Hebrew, one of the most ancient languages, to bring clarity, revelation, and understanding. After all, if you cannot define something, how can you become it?

We have all heard the saying, "Come on, behave like a man!" or "Act like a man!" or "You need to grow up and be a man!" But what does it mean to be a man? What is a man? In this book, I endeavor to unveil what the Bible says about masculinity and manhood. We have heard of toxic masculinity, but here, we're going to find God's divine design and biblical blueprint for "terrific masculinity."

## YOU WILL HAVE NO UNCERTAINTY ABOUT WHAT IT IS TO BE A MAN!

The ultimate measure of a man and masculinity is Jesus Christ. There is no one greater. He is the highest benchmark. God looked down from heaven and said, "You are

## CHAPTER ONE: MAN

My Son in whom I am well pleased." It was God in the beginning who created man in His image and in His likeness. When Adam fell, so did God's heart. When Jesus came, He was the last Adam, sometimes referred to as the second Adam. He is the one in whom God delights. He is the one in whom God takes great joy. He is the penultimate of masculinity not just for what He suffered, not just for what He accomplished, but the entire way that He lived His life. I am very nervous about pointing to people who don't believe that and using the data or their revelations. I think the more we look at Jesus Christ, and who He was, and who He is, the more we will discover He was the perfect man.

We see in Jesus Christ many aspects of masculinity, described throughout the Bible. Everything in the Bible is a shadow and a type of Jesus Christ. I don't have time to expound on that fully; however, you will find me expounding on many of the principles related to Jesus Christ. He is the delight of the Father. He is the joy of the Divine Creator. He is the heartbeat and the passion of God himself. Jesus is a hunter-warrior. He is redeemer and Savior. He is kind and caring. He is compassionate, and at the same time, he is a destroyer of all things evil.

I have a hard time with many of the Hollywood depictions of Jesus Christ. Even *The Chosen*, which arguably has the best depiction of Christ, I still believe falls far short of depicting the masculinity Christ possessed, both physically as well as psychologically. It wasn't "Toxic Masculinity" when Jesus flipped the tables of the money changers in the temple, made a whip out of cords, and drove out the corrupt merchants in the temple; it was "Terrific Masculinity!"—biblically based, divinely designed masculinity.

Jesus grew up as the son of a carpenter. The wood He made into tables, chairs, beams, and other structures; he had to cut from trees *by hand*. He then had to plane that wood to remove barbs and knots, saw the wood to usable dimensions, and then, by hand, He would have to chisel that wood and nail it into a useful structure, all with His bare hands! There were no transportation systems in those days, so when He finished the table or a piece of furniture for somebody, He would've had to carry it to the person's home—possibly on the back of a mule, but no doubt He would've had to unload, load, and carry it upstairs Himself.

His hands were not soft, but calloused. His arms were not skinny, but strong and muscular. Jesus possessed great physical strength that's lost on most because He didn't rely on or depend upon it. Jesus was strong. When He died on the cross, the Bible says that when the soldiers spread the news, Pontius Pilate marveled that Jesus had died

## EMERGE

so quickly. This is written with an understanding that he thought Jesus was physically stronger. It is helpful to note here that it wasn't the crucifixion that killed Christ so much as it was the wrath and judgment of God upon the sins, yours and mine, that Jesus bore when He hung on the cross!

My biggest battle growing up was grappling with whether or not I was a man. I remember that even many years into my marriage, after I had fathered a child and was living in a foreign country, I was plagued with self-doubt and the persistent thought that I didn't have what it took, that I was still a boy and not a man. Part of that thinking was the damage I sustained growing up in my home. I was told my grandfather on my father's side, whom I had never met, was a violent, abusive, alcoholic man. My father ran away from home, but because he despised his father, he became the very epitome of the things he despised—a violent, abusive, alcoholic man. I remember an altercation when I was about fifteen or sixteen. My father was drunk and had gotten into an argument with my mother that then became violent. He choked her on the kitchen table. My brother and I were fear-stricken, as you can imagine. I panicked and felt like I had to save my mother's life. I thought he was going to kill my mother, so I ran to my mother's aid, only to find my father then striking me in the face with his fist, knocking me to the ground, picking up a chair, and threatening to break it over my head. As he brought the chair down, thank God the legs of the chair hit the wall before me, disrupting the altercation.

My mother did not get choked out, but I remember crying in my room, feeling like I failed my mother, that my father was too strong for me, and that I wasn't a man. The strength of a man was not able to protect my mother. How could I call myself a man? The trauma from this event plagued me for many years. In fact, even into my senior pastoring years here in San Diego, I had to have deliverance. I had to find forgiveness. I had to release my father and deal with the trauma. The thoughts that "I don't have what it takes. I'm not strong enough. I'm not big enough. I'm not tall enough. I'm not masculine enough. I'm not warrior enough" were so persistent, dominating the landscape of my mind. So many men live under the disqualifying cloud of trauma, whether that's from childhood or the failures of past mistakes. In this book, strap yourself in, put on your seatbelt, and put your helmet and your pads on because you're about to go through a radical transformation. The real you, the real man in you, is about to emerge.

CHAPTER ONE: **MAN**
# THE FIVE STAGES OF
# A MAN'S VALUES DEVELOPMENT

## STAGE 1: MIMICKING AND COPYING AGES 0 - 1

When we are infants, we learn through mimicking and copying what we hear and see. *"Can you say, Dad-dah?"* To which baby responds, *"Dad, Duh!"* And then is showered with praise, delight, and shouts of acclamation! Infants watch, listen, and develop, perhaps even fine-tune, their communication skills to connect and engage with the world around them. Interestingly, children in orphanages or homes starved of human interaction develop their communication and speech abilities at a much slower rate!

## STAGE 2: IMPRINT BY OBSERVATION AGES 1 - 7

In the very early formative years of a human being's life, we learn through imprint and observation. That means our home environment creates what we come to believe is our normal and ground zero. If we see and hear parents fighting or siblings name-calling, we believe this is normal behavior. We may not deem it right or wrong. This is a process of discovery. We soon learn that tantrums and throwing our food from our high chairs are egregious transgressions and behaviors that must be curtailed. It's a case of "Children *see*, Children *do!*"

I remember some of the most joyous moments with Jordan, my firstborn. When Daddy would mow the lawn, he would come out and "help" me with his plastic lawn mower. When we were in the car, and Daddy was driving, he was in his car seat sporting a fake toy steering wheel, horn, blinkers, and stick shift— driving just like Daddy, except I'm sure I didn't sound the horn as often as he did! In church, he would stand at the front with his little buddies, Joel and Brett, and their electric toy guitars, rocking out to the praise and worship. In the car, we would hear him singing the songs from church, but it seemed we were singing the wrong lyrics: *"You turn my morning into dancing again, you lifted my so-what..."* was apparently the lyrics to the song! Whatever we did, he did.

## STAGE 3: MODELING BY HEROES AGES 8-13

In this stage of our development, we look out a little further than our immediate family circle to all the voices around us as we start forming our own key, crucial values,

11

**EMERGE**

many of which stay with us for the rest of our lives. This is perhaps the most significant period of value development as we form heroes and role models who inspire our ideals and who we want to become. It is *not* uncommon for children at this age to tell you they want to be *"An astronaut, "firefighter, policeman, superhero, or a pastor like daddy,"* etc. Young boys at this age love action toys and action figures. They play lots of role-playing games with guns, swords, and spears, imagining themselves as the heroes who save the town from evil villains and so forth.

It is *not* uncommon to see people pursuing careers in alignment with who they identified as their heroes when they were ten years old—nurses, doctors, firefighters, policemen, missionaries, pastors, etc. I had a conversation with someone at church. They told me how, at age ten, they saw a movie where the firefighters not only fought a blazing inferno threatening to engulf an entire block of apartments, but one of the firefighters heard whimpering screams from inside and raced in to save a mother and her baby infant, rescuing them just as the building was about to collapse. From that moment on, he idolized firefighters and said his dream was to become one ever since.

*Who was your hero when you were ten?*

Can you still remember? Your life's direction today was heavily shaped by who you wanted to be back then!

## STAGE 4: SOCIALIZING BY PEERS OR SIGNIFICANT OTHERS AGES 14 - 20

*"But everybody else is doing it!"*

Suppose you are a parent to a teenager. In that case, you will have had these words used against you as a form of manipulation to coerce you into giving permission for your child to experience a freedom beyond his or her current maturity level! If we were really honest, we could remember when we used that phrase on our parents when we wanted to do something or attend a party!
This age is when "socialization" takes precedence, and parenting takes the backseat. It can be MOST troubling and unsettling for parents because "mom and Dad's" values are now being TESTED in the marketplace of ideas and among the collective of their friends and peers! Teenagers are better described as "Between-Agers" because this is the period between childhood and adulthood. In this stage, we make strong

CHAPTER ONE: **MAN**

decisions about our hair, clothing style preferences, and music tastes. Why? Because while still living under Mom and Dad's roof, we realize that we indeed have a level of autonomy over these areas. Because of this, Mom and Dad feel the pushback and usually give in, allowing their kids to make decisions within certain parameters based on their values.

Parenting here is *massively* essential, particularly when defining and reinforcing which *boundaries* are the necessary hills to die on. For example, we may "give in" to our child's request to grow long hair or color their hair, but we say *no* to a tattoo that we know will be a permanent fixture from a phase they are currently going through. We may say you can listen to rock music, but satanic, thrash metal bands are not going to be permitted. We may say you can dress in weird or baggy clothes too big for you, giving you that "homeless vagrant" look, but a piercing is *out* of the *question*!

*At this age, they are testing everything* you taught them at home by bouncing it off their peers to see if what you taught them has any significance, traction, stickability, or efficacy. It's in these years where parents are made to "feel" like they don't know *anything* and are "*so lame*" and "*totally not cool*!"

> "When I was a boy of 14, my father was so ignorant I could hardly stand to have the old man around. But when I was 21, I was astonished at how much he had learned in just seven years!"
> - Walter M Schirra Sr.

I think we have all been here!

## STAGE 5: SIGNIFICANT EMOTIONAL EVENT OR BY CHANGING OR REPLACING VALUES AGES 21+

After twenty-one, our values are pretty firmly set and established. They can still be adapted, shifted, or completely changed, but only through what sociologists label "A significant emotional event!" For example, An encounter with God will do this and has done so repeatedly throughout human history. From Saul of Tarsus "getting knocked off his high horse," to Moses at the Burning Bush, to Gideon in a wine press,

## EMERGE

to myself on a beach at a Christian Surfers event. A near-death experience, the death of a loved one, bankruptcy, betrayal, the ugliness of divorce or infidelity—there are many moments that change our course because of a resetting of our core values!

## TEACHING

In the book of Genesis, Isaac and Rebekah have two sons, twin boys. Esau is the firstborn. Jacob is the younger. When Esau was born, he came out red and hairy. Jacob came out clasping Esau's heel and was named Jacob, which literally means "heel grabber" in Hebrew. These boys grew up in the same house, with the same parents, but could not have been more different. The Bible says Isaac loved Esau because he ate the game of the food Esau would hunt and kill. The Bible says Esau was a hunter, a hairy man, a real man, a man of the field.

In contrast, Jacob was smooth-skinned and domestic. The Bible says Isaac loved Esau, but Rebecca loved Jacob. Not all men are born jocks. You don't have to be a hairy hunter to be a real man. God did not choose an effeminate man. God did not select a lesser man. God chose a man by the name of Jacob to be the father of His people, Israel.

Apparently, only about 6% of men are not born jocks. They are not born as warriors, fighters, or hairy hunters. They are the creatives, the musicians, the artists, the prophets, the seers, the innovators, the creators, and the inventors. Are they any less masculine? Does their seeming lack of desire for hunting, killing, dominating, or controlling make them less of a man? The answer, of course, is an emphatic no!

Imagine where we would be without Beethoven, Leonardo da Vinci, Johan Sebastian Bach, Steven Spielberg, Elton John, Michael Jackson, and Elon Musk. These are the creative types of people who have made our lives better. These are the people who have given themselves to their creative and innovative side and have made life so much more beautiful and pleasant by adding color, texture, splendor, and joy to our lives. Thank God for the 6% who are not born linebackers!

Several years ago, I watched a documentary about some of the gangs in New York. I remember seeing gangs from the Bronx and gangs from Brooklyn. These were tough gangbangers. Many of them had taken the life of other men. They lived by the sword, and many of them died by the sword. It was remarkable to hear the commentary of these men who idolize Michael Jackson. Saint Michael Jackson was the man. Michael Jackson was a hero. He was the real deal. He was bad. I remember thinking,

## CHAPTER ONE: **MAN**

"Michael Jackson? Effeminate Michael Jackson? The Michael Jackson? Do these guys think he's the real deal? That he's bad?"

Then I began to realize that even the strong among us, the warriors among us, the hunters and killers among us long for the creative. Our lives are enhanced by the creatives. We need some. We need color. We need art. We need beauty in our lives. It doesn't make us less manly; rather, it fulfills all the expressions of masculinity and manhood.

These creative, more sensitive men are the prophetic seers. When England suffered the national tragedy of losing Lady Diana, aka "the People's Princess," Elton John was called to minister in song during the funeral service at Westminster Abbey. If you get a chance to watch it on YouTube, it is so moving. You can literally feel the anointing of God upon the song as he sang to honor memory and legacy while comforting a nation.

I remember attending a Michael Jackson concert in Auckland, New Zealand. As he sang the song, "Heal the world," thirty thousand people in attendance held hands, then lifted them as we all sang the chorus, *"Heal the world, make it a better place, for you and for me and the entire human race. There are people dying, if we care enough for the living, make it a better place for you and for me!"* The *same* artist, Michael Jackson, spoke so powerfully into race tensions with his song "Black or White":

*"For gangs, clubs, and nations*
*Causing grief in human relations*
*It's a turf war on a global scale*
*I'd rather hear both sides of the tale*
*See, it's not about races*
*Just places, faces*
*Where your blood comes from*
*Is where your space is*
*I've seen the bright get duller*
*I'm not going to spend my life being a color."*

He then goes on to declare that it doesn't matter if you're black or white!

# EMERGE

How about, *"I'm starting with the man in the mirror. I'm asking if he'll make a change. If you want to make the world a better place, then take a look at yourself and make the change!"* BOOM! *(Michael Jackson, "Man in the Mirror")*

## MEN ARE FROM MARS; WOMEN ARE FROM VENUS?

Well, then, let's dive into what God designed at the beginning in the book of Genesis. The Bible says the Lord God formed the man from the dust of the earth and breathed in the man's nostrils the breath of life. Man became a living being in Genesis chapter two. It's interesting to know that man was not created in the garden. He was not created in the tranquil, ordered, colorful, structured, perfumed fragrances of a garden. Man was created in the wilderness, in the ragged, untamed wild. Then, he was placed in the garden to tend and to keep it. Eve, on the other hand, was created in the garden. Her first experience with her senses was beauty and structure— the most explicit design, fragrance, and splendor. Everywhere she looked was spectacular. There were all kinds of animals, birds, fruits, trees, plants, and budding flowers. Is it any wonder that the woman longs for these things and brings much taming to a man who can wear the same jocks without a spouse asking him if it's the third day he's still wearing the same underwear? (To which he will often respond, "I turned them inside out.")

I get very nervous and skeptical about much of the data used in a lot of men's books that say a man is like an ape. A recent study on the Bonobo apes tells a story of men who have given themselves over to the pleasure of having multiple spouses at the expense of being alpha, at the expense of being a leader and allowing gangs of women to dominate the culture of the tribe. This is presented in a number of books[1], as well as a number of pieces on the Internet, as a systematic evolutionary solution to shift culture away from the patriarchy, from misogyny, and from a male-dominated world.

The first problem I have with all of this is that the argument is built on the presupposition that evolution is a fact. Evolution is not a fact; it's a nineteenth-century theory that was destroyed by twenty-first-century science. The more science discovers about the complexity of the single cell; the more macro-evolution becomes an impossibility. Man did not evolve up from the ape. Man did not evolve up from the animal kingdom at all. The Bible says man descended down from God. Psalm 8:1 (NKJV) says, "Oh, Lord, our Lord, how majestic is your name in all the Earth what is man that you are mindful of him the son of man that you think of him for surely you have created him a little lower than Elohim."

# CHAPTER ONE: MAN

God created man in His image and in His likeness. When Adam sinned, he fell short of the standard set by God. This is important because many biologists and evolutionists will try to justify reprehensible behavior by saying, "Well, you're just an evolved monkey. You're just an evolved animal, a mammal from the animal kingdom, and therefore, reprobate behavior is acceptable."

I was watching a documentary about evolution on BBC that justified infanticide, abortion, murder, and rape. I even heard the justification of a man eating his own offspring because the animals do it. The apes do it. The gorillas do it. My dog will go and poop in somebody else's yard. If I were to poop in someone's front lawn and then say, "Well, my dog does it. I'm just an animal. I'm just doing what animals do," I don't think that will fly really well. We don't evolve up from the animal kingdom, but sadly, we have fallen down from God's standard.

In this book, you will not only discover what God's standard is, but you'll receive power and principles to enable you to live up to all God has designed for you, allowing you to have the very best and the very greatest of life. The Bible says in Isaiah 55:8 NKJV (God speaking), "My thoughts are not your thoughts, nor my ways, your ways, for the heavens are higher than the earth so, on my way, is higher than your ways and my thoughts higher than your thoughts." In this book, you will discover how to walk in God's ways by learning to think His thoughts after Him.

## WHAT THE CULTURE SAYS

*"Toxic masculinity is a set of certain male behaviors associated with harm to society and men themselves. Traditional stereotypes of men as socially dominant, along with related traits such as misogyny and homophobia, can be considered "toxic" due in part to their promotion of violence, including sexual assault and domestic violence. The violent socialization of boys often normalizes violence, such as in the saying "boys will be boys" about bullying and aggression."*
*- Wikipedia*

I want you to notice how the writers of Wikipedia confuse strength with violence. They confuse masculinity with harm. Century after century of human history shows that the strength of men does not harm the tribe, society, family, or community; rather, it is because of the strength of men that the tribe, society, family, and community are kept safe, are able to thrive, and are able to enjoy great peace and great prosperity. It is the strength of man that overcomes the wilderness. It is the strength of man that causes him to endure in harsh climates. It has been the strength of men that has enabled women and children—who are weaker, more feeble, more susceptible to laments, and therefore at greater risk—to survive. Because of the sacrifices of the strong men in our societies, they were not only able to survive but also able to thrive!

We must stop attacking the strength of men. We need to be championing manhood, masculinity, and strength. We need to build up the warriors, the fighters, the protectors, and the leaders the Divine Creator designed men to be among us and for us!

Man is *not* an evolved ape. Man is a fallen being created in the image and likeness of the Divine Creator of the universe.

If we wonder why men are concerned or uncertain today, it's precisely because of the mixed signals and double-standard hypocrisy given to them by our "intellectual elites!" On the one hand, they say, "Masculinity is toxic" and seek to make men more effeminate. On the other hand, they justify the most reckless, perverted, irresponsible behavior by having us look to the animal kingdom as our origin!

The Animal Kingdom is *not* your origin. *"But we share 99% of the same DNA… the same Biology…"* is the retort we hear over and over from many of these secular biologists. It does *not* prove evolution. On the contrary, it supports the idea that the *same* Creator who created them is the same Creator who created us! It's His signature, His watermark.

You are *not* to *live down* to your basest instincts, proclivities, and vices. You are to *live up* to the standard of God! This standard was originally revealed to mankind through Moses on Mt. Sinai and is now available to one and all through the Holy Scriptures. God's moral standards are *not* there to condemn so much as they are a wonderful challenge to shape, guide, redirect, and even diminish many of our destructive impulses to keep us from significant harm, pain, and misery. God's magnificent laws provide excellent guidance to our bents and biases, taming and redirecting our physical appetites and carnal impulses so that instead of falling short of God's absolute best for our lives, we can live up to the Creator's divine standard and absolutely *thrive*!

*Emerge* from the primordial mud into the magnificent *Son* of the Most High God like you were intended and created to be!

## CHAPTER ONE: MAN
# THE HUMAN CONDITION

The struggle is very real. I certainly don't want to minimize the battle every man faces in what can appear to be my very simple and almost naive "idealistic" statements above. On the contrary, I wanted to state the truth and then climb into the dilemma at hand, journeying with you toward the ideal. We're programming our desired destination into our GPS navigation system before we reverse out the garage.

Why did God's law come down to us on Mt Sinai? The answer is very simple. I know I have probably just offended many scholars, rabbis, and philosophers with such a rudimentary statement, but my intention is *not* to dazzle you with "superior" knowledge. I want to empower you with simple truths.

The first truth is this: *your brain* is *amoral*.

It is neither immoral nor moral according to God's laws. Oh, how often I wish it was, but alas, it isn't. Your brain processes "good and bad" not based on God's divine laws but on experience and the brain's pleasure centers. God designed us to live with Him in a paradisiacal garden, where euphoria would have been the daily norm. Adam no doubt would have had great depths of gratitude, love, and affection for God, leading into the most jubilant and exuberant worship. When Adam sinned, the wiring in the brain remained the same, but a knowledge of good and evil entered the fray. We were *only* meant to experience good. Evil was never on God's menu for us. Just like my children, I do not want them to suffer evil. I desire to see them continually enjoy the good that life offers. God wants the same for us.

Because the brain secretes endorphins and dopamine every time we experience pleasure, the brain processes this as "*good*" and desires more. This is the major factor contributing to all addictions. The brain doesn't realize that this drug, that porn, or that substance is doing great harm to you and will eventually ruin your life. It doesn't process long-term gain. It only processes through the lens of immediate gratification!

As Freddie Mercury sang so brazenly before tragically dying of AIDS at the young age of forty-one, *"I want it all, I want it all, I want it all, and I want it now!"* He was literally singing an external echo of what his internal brain was saying. Hedonism is the pursuit and worship of pleasure. No society or civilization that has given itself over to hedonism has survived to tell about it. The essence and danger of a pleasure-centric society is the focus solely on self. It elevates personal happiness and experience

**EMERGE**

above that of others or the community. It always ends in self-destruction. Always. From Sodom and Gomorrah to Ancient Greece to Ancient Rome under Caligula. Hedonism is the undoing of lives, family, society, community, and civilization.

When God gave Moses the Ten Commandments, it was so the heart and head could engage in a thorough debate and human beings could chart their destinies, enjoying life and experiencing pleasure without destroying themselves in the pursuit. Think of it as a fire burning in the fireplace in your living room. It warms the house and creates a romantic ambiance. The same fire, not in the fireplace but in the curtains, carpet, walls, or flooring, will, without intervention, burn the house to the ground and cause great harm.

God is *not* anti-pleasure (or anti-fire). He just says, "Hey, this fire is best in this setting and in this context!" (Namely, a fireplace!) In the same way, God's moral laws given through the Ten Commandments seek to govern our sexuality, money, possessions, desires, worship, justice, etc., so we live in the ambient joy of the fireplace and not in the destruction of our house. The brain that is used to immediate gratification or has become given to entitlement will *not* like this one bit. Not at all. It will go to great lengths to get around it or even seek to kill those who *dare* tell it to restrain those pleasure hits!

Worship is choosing God's laws to guide and govern your pleasures. God's law came down to Moses on Sinai, and while they immediately created a conflict between what the sinful flesh wants and craves, they were given to us so that we might have life! See this magnificent Psalm:

*"You make known to me the path of life; you will fill me with joy in your presence, with eternal pleasures at your right hand."*
*Psalm 16:11 NIV.*

God is *not* anti-pleasure. He is *against* the destruction and demise of your house. Obey His laws and live!

*"See, I have set before you today life and good, death and evil, in that I command you today to love the Lord your God, to walk in His ways, and to keep His commandments, His statutes, and His judgments, that you may live and multiply; and the Lord your God will bless you in the land which you go to possess."*
*Deuteronomy 30:15-16 NKJV*

CHAPTER TWO: **PRAYER**

# CHAPTER TWO
# PRAYER

## מדא

*Full potential - Communes with God*

## ORIGINS & ETYMOLOGY

The Hebrew language, often regarded as the language of God, is unlike other languages. Each letter carries a sound, a value, a picture reference, and even a numeric standard known as a gematria. The closest language we have that I can use to describe Hebrew would be that of the periodic table. For example, we know that H2O is water because it's made of two hydrogen molecules and one oxygen. This is the same with Hebrew. The letters that make up the word are NOT the phonetic spelling used in the West to sound out the word. Instead, they describe the intrinsic design and composite of each word.

## EMERGE

Let's dive in a little deeper. In the book of Genesis, the first book of the Bible, 1:26, God says, *"Let Us make man in Our image and in Our likeness."* The word "man" in Hebrew is the word *"Adam."* There are no vowels in Hebrew, so the word *Adam* is made up of three letters: אדמ

The Alef - א
The Dalet - ד
And the Mem - מ

The literal translation to English would be *ADM*. The last two letters, *'DM'* (The dalet and the Mem), are translated as *DAM*. This word is very significant as, in Hebrew, it means *Blood*. The first letter of *Adam*, the 'A,' is the *Alef* - א.

*Alef* is where we get the Greek letter *Alpha*. The Aleph is ALWAYS connected to, and throughout scripture, it is used in reference to God. He is the Alpha, the Alef, the beginning, the first. Elohim, Adonai, El Shaddai—all begin with the letter *'Alef.'* In ancient Hebrew, the *'Alef' was* represented by the Ox, depicting *strength!*

## ORIGINS

Science is discovering more and more that mankind did not evolve from the apes. Apes are not evolving into men today and did *not* evolve over billions of years. How do we know this? Without going down a proverbial rabbit hole, it's quite simple. Evolution says things began in the crude primordial slime and gradually improved over time, perfecting errors via natural selection, the survival of the fittest, yada yada yada. However, think about it for a moment. Man is made of several highly complex systems, such as the *skeletal, muscular, nervous, endocrine, cardiovascular, lymphatic, respiratory, digestive, urinary, and reproductive systems.* When we are sick and go to the doctor, the doctor will first see which of these systems is compromised and causing the breakdown.

How many of these systems had to be perfectly operational on day one, or man could not/would not be able to survive, let alone exist? The answer is *"all of them!"* Without a digestive system, man would have starved to death and died out. Without a respiratory system, he would have suffocated and died out. Unless, of course, men did not eat while simultaneously holding their breath for millions of years... the whole evolution "myth" breaks down entirely! If your cardiovascular system wasn't operating perfectly from the start, you would not survive. You would die. If your respiratory system wasn't perfectly operating from the start, you would die. If both the male and female reproductive systems were *not* perfectly wired and operating from the start, there would be no babies and, therefore, *no mankind*! Evolutionists use language like "billions of years" to cloak the theory's fatal faults, shrouding and burying them into

## CHAPTER TWO: **PRAYER**

something beyond the grasp of the human mind. They use *"billions of years"* so the lie can survive on the premise of *"well, I guess anything can probably happen over billions of years!"*

Man did *not* evolve. He was created—not just designed, but divinely designed! As the Psalmist says, "When I consider my frame, I realize that I am fearfully and wonderfully made!" Psalm 139:14 (the Paraphrase is mine.) You bear the markings of divine design and the image of the Almighty God!

The Bible teaches as an absolute that man is primarily the son of God. Bearing the *imago Dei*—The Image of God! But, to *truly* discover the identity of man, one must look at not only his origin but also the *intent* around his origin. As stated above, this is because there is *nothing* in existence that wasn't created with purpose and intent. Our history books have long referred to the age of revolutions and discovery with things like fire, the wheel, or irrigation systems! We know that for hundreds of years, mankind was basically nomadic, limited to living close to water sources. Nomadic meant that man's biggest quest was to find water. Water was (and still is today) essential to life.

The greatest empires were built next to rivers like the Tigris (ancient Babylon) and the Nile (ancient Egypt). Both ruled the Earth for several hundred years and had riches, wealth, and opulence so abundant it would be difficult to imagine even in today's material world. The abundance of water by these rivers meant that crops, cattle, livestock, and, yes, even human beings would thrive. There came a day, however, when man, with his innate wiring to subdue/overcome, discovered how to "move the water," relocating it to him via aqueducts and canals. Today, we know this as irrigation systems! Then, man began to conquer previously uninhabitable terrains!

Man is an overcomer. Wired to be fruitful, innovative, creative, and a problem solver. Man invented the automobile when "faster horses" would no longer suffice. Now, man could travel in comfort from one place to another with ease. Planes were invented to bridge continents... you get the picture. *You* were created for a purpose—a divine purpose. Until you discover that purpose, you are not *living* but merely existing! Before you get to the end of this book, you will have discovered your purpose in life!

## THE LAW OF "FIRST"

There are a number of laws that the rabbis use to interpret scripture. One of these is "The Law of first mentions." When something is first mentioned in scripture, that initial introduction frames the rest of the interpretations for subsequent mentions. For example, in Genesis chapter three, we are introduced to the "serpent'" as cunning and ultimately satanic. From that time on, throughout the scripture, the serpent is

## EMERGE

associated with satanic power, control, and influence.

The *first* thing we notice about the creation of man is that man was formed from the ground. The Hebrew word for ground is "Adamah!" God formed "Adam" out of the "Adamah." He literally took the "Adam" out of the "Adamah." That would leave just the "Ah" behind. The "Ah" is what God put into Abram's and Sarai's name to bring forth life. It is the ה (heh) of God. It is the wind or breath of God. Just as the Earth is a living organism producing life, in the same way, God then takes the "Adam" (Man) and breathes into his nostrils the breath of life, the ה (heh), so that man would become a living, life-producing being!

The word "Adamah" in Hebrew refers to the female gender. Out of the earth/ground, God brought forth man, much like how all life proceeds and is born into this world out of a woman's womb. We read in the scriptures that *"Out of the ground the LORD God made all the trees grow..." Genesis 2:9* The devil has been swift to create so many earth-worshiping cults revering Gaia, Maya, and even "mother earth" itself because he knows the interrelation of the ground (Adamah) to life. The earth/ground (Adamah) receives "seed" and, in turn, produces life.

> *"And He said, "The kingdom of God is as if a man should scatter seed on the ground, and should sleep by night and rise by day, and the seed should sprout and grow, he himself does not know how. For the Earth yields crops by itself: first the blade, then the head, after that the full grain in the head. But when the grain ripens, immediately he puts in the sickle, because the harvest has come.""*
> Mark 4:26-29 NKJV

Even though Adam (man) was taken from the ground, he was given authority to rule over the ground. Man was brought forth from the Earth, yet because he was born of the will of Heaven, his identity was not to be defined as the offspring of the Earth but rather the son of the creator God of Heaven. He was born a prince. The Earth he proceeded from would not rule over him; rather, he was born and crowned to rule over the Earth.

## EMERGE

The genesis for the name of our men's ministry, *Emerge*, came from a vision God gave me almost twenty years ago. It was man "emerging" from the mud of the ground, only to find his life fraught with the battle over his base, earthly, sensual lusts, appetites, and inclinations. In the vision, God showed me that the preaching of Heaven's truth, the

## CHAPTER TWO: PRAYER

Word of God, caused men to rise, to *emerge*, and become sons of Heaven, sons of God, reflecting Christ in the Earth.

> *"For [even the whole] creation [all nature] waits eagerly for the children of God to be revealed."*
> *Romans 8:19 AMP*

It's vital that you know *you* were created, designed, and given authority to *rule* over your environment and circumstances and not live under or subject to them. Adam's identity was not of the Earth but that of the son of Heaven. It would be his battle as it is our battle today. All men face the struggle of believing their identity is tied to and associated with their conception, their birth, and their earthly biology. The scripture, however, makes it clear that even though you may have been born into a family of alcoholism, abuse, poverty, generational welfare, or a certain ethnicity, you are called to be born again of Heaven's seed and live your life ruling over and conquering these things.

Identity is *every man's* battle. I was conceived out of wedlock, born to an East German escapee who fled the communist regime of the USSR (United Socialist Soviet Republic). I was born into poverty. Due to severe economic challenges facing my family and my mother being pregnant with my little brother, we migrated to Australia just before my third birthday. I was also an economic migrant, a German kid growing up in a land that is harsh in its elements and also was not friendly to "immigrants." They certainly let us know, reminding me often as a young child, that it was indeed the Germans who "lost the war!" I was called Nazi, Hitler, Kraut, and a few other derogatory terms I don't want to mention in this book. Even though these were the issues surrounding my origin (my coming into this world), these would *not* be the significant governing forces of my life. When I received Christ, His word and Spirit came into my heart. I was born again and restored to ruling over, no longer controlled by, restrained to, or subject to the details of my past and origin.

> *"He has made us more than conquerors in Christ Jesus!"*
> *Romans 8:37 NKJV*

In Christ, you are empowered to live above your past circumstances. My battle has been that all my memory cells attempt to hijack my thoughts and reduce me to being «*no better than my fathers*» (1 Kings 19:4). Often, I have to choose to believe the truth of what God has said about me, over the chorus of my flesh, my failures, and my memories telling me that I am no better than my past.

**EMERGE**

# YOU EMERGE AS YOU BELIEVE

*"See, I have made you as God to Pharaoh!"*
*Exodus 7:1*

I am convinced that all of us, left unto ourselves, will not reach our fullest potential but live far below God's created and intended purpose for our lives. We *need* to encounter God in our lives. We need His word and Spirit to permeate every part of our lives: heart, mind, and body. At eighty years of age, God appears to Moses and tells him that his life assignment is to be a deliverer of God's people, Israel. He reminds Moses of the promises He made in times past to Abraham and his descendants, to which Moses belonged. He was of the tribe of Levi.

Moses, however, does *not* feel qualified for the call, task, or assignment God is presenting to him. Instead, Moses glosses over all his frailties and disqualifications, drawing from his eighty years of history. Moses was born in perhaps one of the most aggressive abortion and infanticide decrees ever uttered by the lips of men and put into law. He was then adopted by an Egyptian princess, who named him Moses (meaning "drawn out") because she *drew him out of the Nile* after placing him in a basket and sent down this crocodile-infested Egyptian waterway. He was the Hebrew kid. He never felt like he fit or belonged. He was adopted. He was different; no matter how hard he tried, he couldn't fit in.

At forty years of age, which is the acquisition of maturity according to Eastern wisdom, Moses wanders from the palace into the thoroughfare of community life in the Egyptian provinces. Here, he sees the mistreatment of the people of his origin at the hands of an Egyptian overlord. Incensed by the injustice, he murders the Egyptian and buries his body in the sand, thinking nobody will find out. The very next day, however, he sees two Hebrews fighting. As he attempts to intervene and play peacemaker, they jolt back at him, *"What are you going to do, kill us like you killed the Egyptian yesterday?"*

At this, Moses flees to the desert. A bounty is put upon his head, and he spends the next forty years living as a fugitive! Now, at eighty years of age, God comes to him and says, *"Behold, I am sending you back to Egypt, to Pharaoh to deliver my people out of his hand."* Moses, drawing in the rich tapestry of human error, misdeeds, and mishaps, reminds God of all of the reasons *why* he is unqualified for such a mission. Surely God had the wrong man! At that moment, God interrupts three chapters of Moses' negative whining to disrupt his self-perceptions and give him a much-needed reality check!

*"SEE, I have made you as God to Pharaoh!"*
*Exodus 7:1 NKJV*

# CHAPTER TWO: **PRAYER**

*You*, Moses, are *not* your past, your mistakes, or what the Earth has said about you. *You* are who I have made you to be. *You* are who Heaven says you are! *Quit* living down to your failures, mistakes, and human weaknesses. Instead, *live up* to who I have called you to be!

THIS is the same word for you today! Take a moment and let this transform from words on a page to an edict to your heart! No longer live down to all the weaknesses and transgressions of your past. Begin to live *up* to what God has said about you!

Have you ever been to the circus? You will see massive bull elephants tied to a stake in the ground with the flimsiest ropes. The elephant possesses more than the required strength to snap the rope like flax and scurry off, but it doesn't. It stays there, putting up little or no resistance. Why? Because when that elephant was a calf, it had an iron chain fixed to its leg, and as much as it tried to break the iron chain and get free, it couldn't. The iron was too strong. Now, as an adult, iron is no longer required; it is just the flimsiest of ropes. The elephant, though *more than powerful enough*, puts up no fight because it has been conditioned to think resistance is futile. It is a captive.

The devil does the same with you and me. He wants you to believe your past failures and mistakes are indicative of all future prospects and outcomes, diminishing hope that breeds faith. It is *by faith* we break through, break free, and break out of every limitation of our past. *Only* the word of God can expose to you all the false beliefs you hold concerning your future, your potential, and your destiny. Stop living under the false pretenses of *"It's no use. It's always going to be like this. There's no point trying. The odds are always stacked against me. I never win. It's in my genes to fail..."* The Bible makes it clear you *emerge* as you *believe!*

> *"And do not be conformed to this world, but be transformed by the renewing of your mind, that you may prove what is that good and acceptable and perfect will of God."*
> *Romans 12:2 NKJV*

Our lives are completely transformed as we believe differently. We have a choice before us: *conformity* to this world or *transformation* through believing God's promises. When babies are born, they should ideally come out head first. It's a symbolic gift from God to remind you that *all advancement and breakthroughs* must happen (in the) "head first!" Do you see the contrast here? The world (Adamah) versus Heaven. The world's power seeks to conform your life to your limitations, while the *Word's* power seeks to transform your life up to Heaven's design for you! Live **up**. Don't settle down. Transform and refuse to conform!

**EMERGE**

> *"So God created human beings in his own image. In the image of God, he created them; male and female he created them. Then God blessed them and said, "Be fruitful and multiply. Fill the Earth and govern it. Reign over the fish in the sea, the birds in the sky, and all the animals that scurry along the ground."*
> *Genesis 1:27-28 NLT*

God created, designed, authorized, and commissioned man to *rule over* his environment and not be subject to or mastered by it! Man was instructed to "tend and keep" the paradisiacal world God gave him. Man is both steward and master.

## OVERCOMER OF ENVIRONMENT

Man's commission to overcome his environment is *why* we have things like elevators, air conditioning, skyscrapers, airplanes, motor cars, freeways, refrigeration, microwave ovens, etc. These are all manifest evidence of God's intrinsic and innate programming for man to "exercise dominion" (rule over) his environment. Man has conquered the highest mountains. He has explored the depths of the great seas. He has conquered the skies, traveled into outer space, and even set foot on the moon. *Man was created to have dominion, to overcome, and to rule.*

I say all this to *remind* you that whatever environment you inherited or territory you were born into, *you* are wired to overcome it. Another great *lie* of Satan is that *your* environment rules over you. If you were born into poverty, then poverty will be your master all your days. If you grew up in a house of addiction, abuse, and dysfunction, these things will not only be predominant in your life, but the devil wants you to believe they will "Pre-Dominate" your life! LIE! Every human being is born with a predisposition to sin. Some babies are born with addiction to drugs already in their systems because their mothers were drug addicts while they were being formed in the womb. In Genesis chapter two, we read something *very powerful* the devil doesn't want you to see:

> *"And the Lord God formed man of the dust of the ground, and breathed into his nostrils the breath of life; and man became a living being. The LORD God planted a Garden eastward in Eden, and there He put the man whom He had formed."*
> *Genesis 2:7-8 NKJV*

## CHAPTER TWO: **PRAYER**

God breathed into Adam the breath of life—the very Spirit of God Himself. A Spirit that brings forth life. A Spirit of animation, of power, of divine function. Romans 8:11 tells us it was this very Spirit *that raised Christ from the dead and is even now working in our mortal bodies.* The Spirit of God hovers *over* creation because the Spirit is *not* subject to creation. God's spirit, His breath, causes things to live, thrive, and flourish. *You* were created to receive this Spirit. You were created to thrive, not just survive. You were created to conquer, to overcome, and to win. The Spirit of God is a gift you were created to receive, one the devil does his darndest to make sure you never hear about, let alone receive. He wants to keep you a slave of your past, your vices, your environment, your inclinations. God's Spirit, however, is not subject to the environment; rather, it is God's celestial, divine spark to give *you* power!

## SAVIOR PREDESTINED

Before I move on, I want to draw your attention to one last phenomenon in the Hebrew origin of the word "Man" (Adam). As we have done above, the three letters could be divided into two sections. The "alef" (Alpha) א and "dam" (Blood) דמ man by definition is "Alpha blood." To live a beta life is to live beneath God's wiring for your life. Come with me and look a little deeper. Isaiah 46:10 says:

> "Declaring the end from the beginning, And from ancient times things that are not yet done, Saying, 'My counsel shall stand, And I will do all My pleasure,'"
> Isaiah 46:10 NKJV

God *always* declares the end of a thing from the beginning. "Man," in Hebrew, comprises the Alpha and Blood. God, when He formed the man, had already pre-determined that His divine Alpha Blood would redeem man from sin and death. אדמ. God is so true to His word. He is **truth**. He doesn't possess truth; He is the very embodiment of truth. God also does not *see* as a man sees. (1 Samuel 16:7) Whenever God looks at man, He sees "Alpha-Blood" in him. As man sinned, rebelled, and turned from the LORD God and His commands, God had already declared His firstborn would come and shed His perfect Alpha Blood on the cross to redeem man!
On the sixth day of creation, God created man in His image and likeness, declared it good, and rested from all His work. On the sixth day, Jesus hung on a cross and

**29**

# EMERGE

removed mankind's sins by shedding His own Blood to redeem us, declaring once more that all who are in Him are "good!"

On the sixth day of creation, God created man in His image and likeness.

> "So God created man in His own image; in the image of God He created him; male and female He created them."
> Genesis 1:27 NKJV

*But*, on the sixth day (the Friday of Passover week), man created/presented God in "his" (man's) image upon the cross. How so? When Jesus hung on the cross, He hung between two thieves. He was declared a blasphemer, guilty, and sentenced to death, and He literally "became sin" upon that cross. (2 Corinthians 5:21) He (Jesus/God) was presented as a criminal, weak, subject to death, helpless. Do you see it? The first sixth day of the Old Testament saw *man* made in God's image and likeness. The last sixth day of what we call the Old Testament/covenant saw God created in man's image. It is a perfect depiction and warning that *everything* under the sun is prone to defilement and corruption, yet it was all foreseen by God. He executed the perfect exchange. A trade was made that day;

> "For He made Him who knew no sin to be sin for us, that we might become the righteousness of God in Him."
> II Corinthians 5:21 NKJV

That exchange was advantageous for mankind but came at a deadly cost to God. His pain literally became our gain! His death is temporal, our life eternal! My question is this: Are *you* living in your *alpha* state? You were born of God's will, wired with Alpha blood. This divine Alpha Blood redeemed you on the cross two thousand years ago. This Alpha blood restored you back to your original state, namely that of one destined to overcome, conquer, have dominion, and win. Is the breath of Heaven in your life? Have you received the Holy Spirit? Jesus referred to a baptism of *power* that He wants you to receive and walk in.

> "And He said to them, "It is not for you to know times or seasons which the Father has put in His own authority. But you shall receive power when the Holy Spirit has come upon you, and you shall be witnesses to Me in Jerusalem, and in all Judea and Samaria, and to the end of the Earth."
> Acts 1:7-8 NKJV

*Until you receive this baptism, you are incomplete.*

## CHAPTER TWO: **PRAYER**

There has been so much pressure on me over the years to retract or back up from that statement, but as I search the scriptures, I cannot find any way around it. I would be lying to you if I said otherwise! God didn't just form you; He ordained your life to receive empowerment so you can tend and keep all He has entrusted into your hands. *You* were created to rule over all that God has created!

> *"When I consider Your heavens, the work of Your fingers, The moon and the stars, which You have ordained, What is man that You are mindful of him, And the son of man that You visit him? For You have made him a little lower than the angels, And You have crowned him with glory and honor.* <u>You have made him to have dominion over the works of Your hands;</u> *You have put all things under his feet, All sheep and oxen— Even the beasts of the field, The birds of the air, And the fish of the sea That pass through the paths of the seas. O Lord, our Lord, How excellent is Your name in all the Earth!"*
> *Psalms 8:3-9 NKJV*

*You* have been made to have dominion over the works of God's hands! Wow, all of this is just from the Hebrew word for man. Trust me, this is only scratching the surface.

### WHOSE IMAGE?

How do we determine the value of a human life? Sociologists and scientists have developed various algorithms to answer this question. The best they have been able to come up with is that a man's life is worth the value of the life he is able to live. Euthanasia is the argument presented declaring that because someone's life has been greatly compromised by terminal illness, disease, or mental illness, its value is, therefore, greatly "diminished" and should be ended accordingly. In the late 1930s, the German National Socialist Democratic Party (Nazi's) developed a measure that valued a human life on what they were able to contribute to society. Before you quickly dismiss this as simply a Nazi heresy, this is what *most* professors in America believe. It is espoused and championed by the reprobates in the WEF (World Economic Forum) and throughout communist China right now!

Hitler referred to people who were elderly or disabled (mentally or physically) as "useless eaters" and fit for elimination from the gene pool. I remember walking through the mall with my German mother as a child. We would happen upon someone with severe cerebral palsy, writhing in an electric wheelchair, and my mother (who was born three years after the end of Adolf Hitler's reign) would remark, "Oh Gee, why

# EMERGE

didn't they give that person a needle when they were a baby, putting them to sleep?" So prevalent was that theology of the day that even after Hitler's demise, his philosophy carried on within the psyche of the next generation.

## What gives a man his worth?

Is it the "value" of the life he is able to live? Is it determined by what he can produce for the *state*? Is it quality, quantity, and production? What gives a man his value? Jesus, in the Gospel of Mark chapter twelve, is confronted with what His critics and rivals thought was a checkmate question. There was so much tension around the Roman occupation of the land God had sworn to give to Abraham and his descendants. Here in this land, they were not only conquered by the Roman Empire but also forced to pay taxes to Caesar for the privilege of living under his occupation of the Holy Land. They ask Jesus in front of the Chief Priests, lawyers, and the praetorian guard, *"Rabbi, is it lawful to pay taxes to Caesar or not?"*

They felt the noose already tightening around His neck simply for giving them an audience and His willingness to answer this question. Either way, Jesus would be done for, they schemed. To say "No" to paying taxes to Caesar and thereby declaring His faith and loyalty in the promises of their father Abraham would have him arrested for sedition. To say "Yes" was to dismiss any authenticity Jesus might claim as a rabbi teaching the truth of the Holy Tanakh(Law, prophets, wisdom books - scriptures.) Jesus, knowing their hypocrisy and scheme, does the following;

> *"Shall we pay, or shall we not pay?" But He, knowing their hypocrisy, said to them, "Why do you test Me? Bring Me a denarius that I may see it." So they brought it. And He said to them, "Whose image and inscription is this?" They said to Him, "Caesar's." And Jesus answered and said to them, "Render to Caesar the things that are Caesar's, and to God the things that are God's." And they marveled at Him."*
> Mark 12:15-17 NKJV

A denarius, like all coins, had two sides. One depicted the reigning monarch, much like Australian coins carried the head of Queen Elizabeth, now to be re-minted with the head of King Charles. However, that is *only* one side of the coin. The other side bore an image of their god. Jesus asked for something the Pharisees coveted daily: a Roman coin. I wouldn't be at all surprised if it even came from a Pharisee pocket to be presented to Jesus that day. How often can we humans not "see" the forest for the trees? Jesus, upon examining the coin, would have no doubt looked at both sides: Caesar's and the deities. *Render to Caesar*

## CHAPTER TWO: **PRAYER**

*the things that belong to Caesar and to God the things that belong to God!* Was the reply that shut their mouths and confounded their wicked ploy.

The depiction of the king is what gave the money its authority to be traded as currency. Its value came from the image on the coin. *You* carry the *imago dei (Latin)*—The Image of God. Your life's value is *not* based on what you do or have done. The value of your life is not determined by your contribution to society, your education, your skin color, your ethnicity, or your social or economic standing (though the current "diversity" and "equity" training philosophy of this world espouses exactly these demonic lies). *You* are of value because of whose image you bear.

What's the difference between a Rolex and a Seiko watch? Besides quality, the answer is price. *Both* tell the time. Both contribute to society. Both perform meaningful and valuable functions to their beneficiaries. Yet *one* is exceedingly more expensive than the other. You may say, "Well, one contains much more expensive materials." The price tag still does not reflect the cost differential in materials and accouterments. What makes the Rolex so much more expensive? You're correct. It's the name, the logo, and the trademarked image it bears.

One last example to drive the point home: what's the difference between a Bentley and a BMW? Both are considered luxury vehicles. Both boast of superior craftsmanship and engineering, yet one is almost ten times the price of the other. Both perform similar services. Both contribute comparative functions on the road. The Bentley, however, is more expensive because it bears that name. Name or logo determines worth. Logo is where we get the word "word" from. **«*A man›s word is his worth!*»** It is an old but very true saying.

*You* were created bearing God's Image and likeness. You literally carry the *logo* of God! Despite what you have done. Despite what you haven't done. No matter your skin color, height, weight, or ethnicity. Whether you were born in privilege, a king, a duke, a lord, a marquis, a peasant, or a farmer. Whether you were the product of rape, adoption, or a failed abortion, your value is in the fact that *you* bear His Image and His likeness. God's image imprinted on you makes you invaluable!

In real estate, realtors have a saying used during the rise and fall in market value: *"Something is only worth what someone is willing to pay for it!"*

33

## EMERGE

For this reason alone, the Gospel is vehemently attacked by the devil, the spirit of this age. Because John 3:16 NKJV tells us, *"For God so loved the world that he gave His only begotten Son, that whosoever believes in Him would not perish but have everlasting life!"*
Your life is of such infinite value that God Himself made the most powerful and expensive transaction in human history. Jesus was sold for thirty pieces of silver, but to *buy you back*, God spent that which was of the highest value in Heaven, His only begotten Son! How much are you worth? Priceless. Heaven bought your life back from sin, death, hell, and the devil with the life of Heaven's Prince! He would *not* have had to spend such a great treasure if your life was cheap. But *you are* that valuable. The problem right now, as you read this, is that you *don't believe it*! That's *ok*. I still grapple with the enormity of this truth. We live in a world whose culture is antithetical to all things kingdom. You are told your value is in your doing. Your self-worth has been shaped by the words, or too often the lack thereof, by those around you. "Hopeless," "useless," "good for nothing," "son of a ____," "loser," and "failure" are words that seek to cover the "Rolex" or "Bentley" logo you bear.

If I take a $100 bill, drop it into the mud, scrunch it into a ball, curse it, and tell it that it's no good when I go into the bank, is that $100 bill worth any less? Nope. It's still worth the description it has upon it. It's the same with you!

Take a moment right now to allow this truth to travel from your mind to your heart and soul. God's truth must be digested into the soul to be fully lived and experienced!

## MAN AND THE CURSE

As we have discovered, Adam was created from the ground (Adamah). Though he "came" from the ground, he was not to be mastered by it; rather, he was born to be "master" over it. However, when Adam sinned, God set into motion a reality that we must address here.

> *"Then to Adam He said, "Because you have heeded the voice of your wife, and have eaten from the tree of which I commanded you, saying, 'You shall not eat of it': "Cursed is the ground for your sake; In toil, you shall eat of it All the days of your life. Both thorns and thistles it shall bring forth for you, And you shall eat the herb of the field. In the sweat of your face you shall eat bread Till you return to the ground, For out of it you were taken; For dust you are, And to dust you shall return."*
> *Genesis 3:17-19 NKJV*

## CHAPTER TWO: **PRAYER**

God did *not* curse man. He cursed the ground. God cannot curse what He has blessed. Genesis 1:28 He blessed man. He is not bipolar. He doesn't bless one day and then curse the next. So God cursed the ground. The very ground that Adam was commissioned to rule over, the ground that would bring forth his food, the ground that would facilitate his prosperity and flourishing. The ground came under a curse because of Adam's sin. It would now be subject to blight, mildew, disease, and other harmful plant life that would sprout alongside the good seed placed into it—often choking, always competing for the nutrients in the soil. Adam's sin brought loss, struggle, and challenge through the curse proclaimed over the ground (Adamah).

*But,* God has given us His word from Heaven. The law *came down* from Heaven to Moses. He was high up upon Mt. Sinai when the Almighty gave him two stone tablets bearing the Ten Commandments, inscribed by the very finger of God Himself. What comes down from Heaven always breaks the curse of what's on the Earth. Because Heaven is more powerful than Earth. Jesus came down from Heaven and broke the curse on the Earth. Until Christ, sin and death reigned. Because Christ came, now death is swallowed up, and sin has been defeated. All who believe in Him have everlasting life! As the scripture says,

*"Whatever is born of God, overcomes the world!"*
*1 John 5:4 NKJV*

When we bring the tithe, God opens the windows of Heaven and pours out such a blessing that there isn't room enough to receive it. Because Heaven is greater than Earth, it is more powerful and overcomes the Earth. That's why we are instructed to pray *"on Earth as it is in Heaven."* Our assignment is to bring Heaven to Earth. As a man, *your* job is to bring Heaven into the Earth. You don't have to live according to the dictates of the Earth and the world around you. You can release Heaven into your life and transform impossibilities into possibilities and new realities.

YOU are a MAN.
YOU are infused with the divine alpha blood.
YOU are authorized to conquer, overcome, and rule over your environment and circumstances.
YOU are to bring Heaven to Earth.
YOU are transformed as you BELIEVE Heaven's word over the narrative of your history.
YOU are called to be a Son of God.
DIVINE WIRINGS
*(Understanding yourself)*

## EMERGE

*"So God created man in His own image, in the image of God He created him. Male and female, he created them. Then God blessed them, and God said to them, 'Be fruitful and multiply; fill the earth and subdue it; have dominion over the fish of the sea, the birds of the air, and over every living thing that moves on the earth!"*
*Genesis 1:27 NKJV*

In the following chapters, we will outline the Genesis of man in more detail, but from the above verse, I want to highlight some powerful realities you may not be aware of. Genesis, the first book of the Bible, literally means the book of the beginnings or origins—hence the word "genes" (genetics) being its core compound root. Man was made, as we have already established, in the image and likeness of God. Until he finds God, he will wander from place to place, wondering, "Who am I, and pondering, "Why am I here?" The Bible makes it clear you were created by God, for God, and He has divinely ordained, powerful plans for your life. Many search for the meaning of life, but the meaning of life is not such a mystery to the one who has found God. The meaning of life is simple; it is to give your life meaning and purpose.

Man was created not in the garden but in the wilderness. He is rugged. He doesn't require everything to be regulated, structured, perfumed, and orderly. Man was created to overcome, fight, win battles, and transform chaos into order. Man was created to bring peace through strength by subduing whatever disturbs or threatens that peace. His origins are in the untamed, but his peace is found in the beautiful and ordered.

Man is a warrior by nature. He was commissioned to have dominion over the created forces and landscapes around him, including the sky and seas. God created man to create, to solve enigmas, to innovate, to ask why, to generate and regenerate the Earth. From the highest mountains to the deepest seas and even outer space, you, as a man, are created to win battles, conquer obstacles, overcome the odds, and win no matter how many times you get knocked down.

*"Because there is very little honor left in American life, there is a certain built-in tendency to destroy masculinity in American men."*
*–Norman Mailer, American Novelist*

# CHAPTER THREE
# FATHER

## אבא

*Av/Ab/Abba*

"A coach teaches what he knows, but a father imparts who and what he is!"
- Paul Cole, President of Christian Men's Network

"One father is more than a hundred schoolmasters."
— George Herbert, English Poet

"Behold, I will send you Elijah the prophet before the coming of the great and dreadful day of the Lord. And he will turn The hearts of the fathers to the children, And the hearts of the children to their fathers, Lest I come and strike the Earth with a curse."
Malachi 4:5-6 NKJV

"A FATHER is the FIRST HERO your children will revere, for many for the rest of their lives. It is the most incredible of privileges and the weightiest of burdens!"

**EMERGE**

# THE WAR ON FATHERS

The last book of the Old Testament, the book of Malachi, finishes with the admonishment that the Spirit of the Prophet Elijah would be sent into the Earth to turn the hearts of the fathers to their children and the children to their fathers, lest the Earth be struck with a curse.

Satan loves curses. He operates and has power within them. He relentlessly seeks to create chaos, confusion, transgression, and rebellion to increase his power and activity on Earth.

As Christians, our assignment on the Earth is to bring blessing, to overthrow the curses—to transform, redeem, and restore biblical order, bringing the kingdom of God to Earth. The kingdom of God simply means the place where God is king and His word is final! When the Earth is in alignment with God's word, there is peace, prosperity, and power. Whenever it is out of alignment with God's word, there is strife, contention, confusion, chaos, destruction, hopelessness, and powerlessness.

After Malachi, God does not speak again for 400 years. Only as Christ was born in Bethlehem did God's Spirit begin to stir and visit once more. Prophetic words and visions begin to surface again. There is a sense that God the Father is about to send His only begotten Son into the world to bring about man's redemption and judgment upon the devil, his angels destroying their works (1 John 3:8). We see that the very thing preventing the curse from operating in the Earth is fatherhood! That's why there are such vehement, vitriolic attacks on manhood, masculinity, and especially fatherhood! It's no coincidence that over 70% of long-term prison inmates come from father-absent households.

1. Fatherhood is God's vehicle to bring Kingdom order, peace, and harmony in the Earth. The Roman Empire reserved its harshest of capital punishments for patricide, the murder of a father. The entire empire, which lasted almost six hundred years, was established upon the foundation that the family is the centerpiece of all civilization, and the father is the one who holds the family together. For centuries (literally), the Roman Empire flourished and gained so much wealth and strength that it became the world's most prosperous superpower. Its dominion extended around the globe, established upon almost every land that touched the seven seas—all built upon the strength of family and fatherhood!

# CHAPTER THREE: **FATHER**
## **ETYMOLOGY**

*The etymology of the Hebrew word for father is very interesting. It consists of two letters: Alef and Beit.*
*The Alef (א) in Hebrew denotes the OX or the STRENGTH.*
*While the Beit (ב) denotes the house.*

Therefore, it is correct to deduce that God designed the father to be the 'strength' of the house—to protect and provide. When the father is absent or removed, the house is weakened and becomes vulnerable to attack and plunder.

How many statistics show the devastation of father-absent households? Many books have been written on the crisis that fatherless households create in our society. One of the most brilliant I have read of late is "The Boy Crisis!" In their brilliant book, The Boy Crisis, Warren Farrell, PHD. and John Gray, PHD state that in the medical community, whenever they discover a new disease, one of the first steps to conquering it is to name it. They go on to state that today's world faces a crisis they have named "Dad deprived boys."

2. "Whether our children become financially rich or poor, or emotionally rich or poor depends increasingly on whether they grow up dad-rich or dad-poor!" There is no substitute for the power of a present, engaged, loving father in developing healthy sons, healthy adults, and healthy communities.

Studies show the significant impact of fatherlessness in our society and the damage it brings. One study of ISIS fighters concluded that almost all had in common "some type of an 'absent father' syndrome!"

*Did you know that mass shooters have one common ingredient? Father absent households. Suicide among teenagers is correlated more to father absence than any other factor. (The Boy Crisis, Chapter 12, pg 107.)*

We need fathers. When the disciples asked Jesus to teach them to pray, of all the introductions Jesus could have used to describe the author of life and the creator of the universe, he used the words, "Our FATHER!" God is the solution to society's ails! Notice I said, "God" not religion. Religion is often God-washed through the lens of man's (broken) ideals and interpretations. Only the Bible gives us a clear and precise picture of who God is. In fact, Jesus came to "show us the Father!"

**EMERGE**

> *"If you had known Me, you would have known My Father also; and from now on, you know Him and have seen Him." Philip told Him, "Lord, show us the Father, and it is sufficient for us." Jesus said to him, "Have I been with you so long, and yet you have not known Me, Philip? He who has seen Me has seen the Father; so how can you say, 'Show us the Father'? Do you not believe that I am in the Father, and the Father in Me? The words that I speak to you I do not speak on My own authority; but the Father who dwells in Me does the works. Believe Me that I am in the Father and the Father in Me, or else believe Me for the sake of the works themselves."*
> *John 14:7-11 NKJV*

If, like me, your childhood had significant damage in this area, the Bible and Christ bring us great news. God is our Father! It's no wonder the author and architect of chaos, pain, and disease (the devil) seeks to stop connections or encounters with God! Draw near to Him today and experience His incredible love, grace, and power. It has brought me incredible healing and the clearest depiction of what being a father could and should look like for my four children.

## THE POWER OF A FATHER

In my late teens, I was in an apprenticeship to become a mechanical engineer. I met a trades assistant on one of the many rotations they put us apprentices through to give us the complete experience of working in steel engineering. This trades assistant looked like he lived a pretty hard life. He had a disability, walked with a significant limp, and was covered in as many scars as he had tattoos (or as many tattoos as he had scars, it was hard to distinguish which one was the greater). He just looked like a guy who ran with the wrong crowds his whole life.

I discovered he used to be part of the Hells Angels motorcycle gang and had lived his life for many years as a reckless outlaw. He told me how there was a night when he'd been drinking and getting "totally stoned" at one of the many Hells Angels' parties. Against all wise judgment, he decided to get on his Harley Davidson and ride it at dangerously high speed. It had been raining on and off all day, and the roads were quite wet and slick. As he hit a sharp bend, his bike slid out from underneath him, hurtling him into a head-on crash with a power pole, destroying his motorcycle and almost destroying himself!

He was not expected to live, but after eight months of hospital care, countless surgeries,

## CHAPTER THREE: **FATHER**

and months and months of physiotherapy, he not only survived but also was able to regain some of his motor neuron functions. He had lived to ride again, was able to walk (with a cane), and even got a job. He certainly bore the scars from the horrific collision, and the disability served as evidence that he had indeed been in a horrific accident.

He was assigned to be my assistant for a week of maintenance projects. We struck up a conversation and started somewhat of a friendship. He would tell me about the Hells Angels and some of their criminal activities and exploits. I just listened without questioning whether or not his statement was completely true. I didn't want to offend him and endanger myself by being put on the hit list of this fierce motorcycle gang! I figured it couldn't hurt to listen, smile, and act impressed. I was certainly glad to have never crossed the Hells Angels based on some of the stories he was telling me of people who had and are no longer with us today (many of them meeting their end in the most unpleasant ways a man could die)!

He bragged about all of the drugs, parties, prostitutes, smuggling, fighting, and the other lawless antics these rebels got up to. Still, I couldn't help but notice the man I was talking to no longer ran with these people. He also didn't seem to hold their values. I knew from the continual F-bombs he was dropping that he hadn't yet given his life to Christ, but I was most intrigued as to what had caused the significant shift in his life. I thought it must have been the trauma of the motorcycle accident that left him fighting for his life and permanently disabled.

When I asked him about it, his answer shocked me and rocked me simultaneously. He said that, yes, the accident really shook him, but as soon as he was able to ride again, he returned right back to the reckless lifestyle he had before the accident. His life changed when he found out his girlfriend was pregnant with his child. He got the wake-up call of his life when she told him the news. He said he liked sex but had never given any thought to being a dad. He hadn't thought of anything beyond the sexual act and never put sex and the potential for fatherhood together!

He then went on to tell me his own dad abandoned him before he could even walk. His drug-addicted mother hooked up with abusive man after abusive man, living only to feed her addiction. At the same time, he was reduced to inconvenient collateral. Because of this, he was beaten and abused regularly by her and her boyfriends. Some of them taught him how to smoke a bong when he was only four years old, and he was drinking hard spirits at age five. He then painfully recalled living for weeks on the streets when he was seven be-

# EMERGE

cause the guy his mom hooked up with didn't want a kid in the picture. He ate out of trash cans, hanging out behind restaurants so he could pounce on the trash as they often threw out good food that had hardly been touched!

Being a physically smaller kid, he was beaten up a lot on the streets as well as at home. When he had the chance to join the Hells Angels, he said he wouldn't have done anything they asked of him just to be accepted and feel a sense of belonging. They became his "family," and he would kill for them if that's what they asked of him! But the man telling me this didn't seem like the same man he was describing. Something had changed, and I was absolutely puzzled. I wanted to know what it was!

He told me that everything changed when he watched the birth of his son, "at that moment, my life was never the same again!" While he wasn't religious, he said that when he looked at his son's face as he came into the world and held this helpless, little life he created, he could only describe it "as a miracle!"

At the time of our conversation, he had three sons, and each birth confirmed that life is a miracle and a gift. It permanently changed him. He left the Hells Angels gang and lifestyle behind to start a new life with his family. He then said, "That's **when I got me this job, a regular job.»** He wanted to give his kids what he never had himself. I could see from his vulnerability that he had a genuine heart and life change. He told me, "There is nothing in the world so amazing as being a father! No drug, no high, no bike, no woman..." He was a changed man from the power of witnessing one of God's most precious miracles—the blessing of becoming a father.

*Few things in my life are more wonderful than being a father!*

## THE ATTACK ON FATHERS.

Findings published in the 2017 Pediatrics journal concluded that by nine years of age, children who grew up without a father have significantly shorter telomeres. The telomeres in our cells keep our genes from being deleted as our cells divide. As the National Academy of Sciences reports, telomere length in early life predicts lifespan! How much damage to life expectancy is created by dad deprivation? The science is still unfolding, but what is certain is that having a present father increases not only the quality of your life but also the health of your life.

The telomeres of children with father loss by age nine are 14% shorter than children with present dads. However, when compared to girls, telomere damage from father loss is 40% greater for boys. Dads—like moms, air and water—are essential to our lives. Sadly, in today's culture, we've tried to believe we can live without dads, even

## CHAPTER THREE: **FATHER**

though we haven't tried to live without moms, air, or water. Dad-deprived boys are more likely to either drown in their purpose void or fill it with a destructive sense of purpose, which usually ends up being violent and extreme behavior!

A recent study of ISIS fighters concluded that almost all of these men had one thing in common: some type of "absent father syndrome." This made them vulnerable to recruitment because they longed for masculine meaning, acceptance, purpose, and belonging! At age nineteen, Anthony Simms' participation in a gun battle led to him slaying a young mother in Oakland, California. Anthony's final Facebook post before his arrest was, "I wish I had a father!"

Fatherlessness is the primary and common hole in the heart of boys who are vulnerable to gangs and targeted by sexual predators. It was also the common denominator for the boys targeted and recruited by Hitler for the Hitler Youth! Canadian soldiers said these boys would run at tanks and machine gun fire, only able to be stopped by being shot. They battled fiercely as if the Fuhrer's affection, approval, and acceptance depended upon it!

In 2015, Warren Farrell, PhD, author of The Boy Crisis, did a Ted talk in which he concluded that "dad-deprived" boys and school shootings were powerfully connected. Adam Lanza—Sandy Hook, Elliot Rodgers—UC Santa Barbara, and Dylann Roof—Charleston church, all shooters committed suicide and multiple homicides. They also came from homes where no father was present in their childhood.

In the film Spotlight, it was revealed that 6% of Catholic priests who molested children honed in on dad-deprived boys. It was as if the priests could "smell" these boys' desperation for a father's attention, love, and guidance. While the film exposed the church's cover-up, it didn't expose what made the priest so desperate for celibacy. Was it their own "dad deprivation" or something else? I believe that the absence of a father (provision and protection) subconsciously communicated to these priests that these kids were "unprotected" and, therefore, safe, vulnerable, and easy to abuse!

Sadly, our juvenile detention centers across the USA are filled with "dad-deprived" boys. A US Department of Justice report found that 7.7% of boys in these centers reported being sexually abused by adult staff. There were two major distinctions between this abuse and the male Catholic priests' abuse: 89% of the juvenile detention staff perpetrators were female, and once uncovered, the systemic sexual abuse

## EMERGE

by male priests became a worldwide scandal. The systemic abuse by the female staff goes largely uncovered by the Department of Justice and is still largely ignored today! It's as if kids from "dad-deprived" homes emit a signal that they have no guardian or protection. It's sad. It's evil!

*"A COACH IMPARTS WHAT HE KNOWS, A FATHER IMPARTS WHO HE IS!"*
*- Paul Cole, Christian Men's Network*

*One day, two crabs came out of their home to take a stroll on the sand. The father said to the son, "You are walking very ungracefully. You should accustom yourself to walking straight forward." The son told the Father, "If you set the example yourself, then I will follow you!"*
*- Aesop Fable - The Two Crabs*

In this Aesop fable, a child crab is berated by the parent crab for walking awkwardly. The child crab points out to the parent that he should set the example. Example is the best precept.

## FATHERS ARE EXAMPLE SETTERS!

We have all heard the saying, "Children see, children do!" There is nothing more true than this. While we want our children to "Do as we say," they will always return to "Do as we did!" Indeed, setting an example is the role of fathering!

*The apostle Paul said it this way;*
*"Follow my example, as I follow the example of Christ."*
*- 1 Corinthians 11:1*

*The Apostle Paul also said this;*
*For though you might have ten thousand instructors in Christ, yet you do not have many fathers; for in Christ Jesus I have begotten you through the gospel.*
*- 1 Corinthians 4:15*

## CHAPTER THREE: **FATHER**

We are living in the day of what I call "the coach phenomenon." Life coaches, business coaches, sports coaches, fitness coaches, marriage coaches— the list seems endless. Now, while I'm all for having mentors and people helping us in our journeys, nothing has made me more apprehensive of embracing the coaching phenomena than the fact that many of these coaches don't have the "fruit" in their own lives, yet they want to teach others! For a while, anyone who was unemployed could become a "life coach." Lord, have mercy on the poor saps who hired these guys to "life coach" them.

The Apostle Paul said his day was much like ours. There were ten thousand instructors (life coaches), but there was a severe drought and a lack of fathers. Young men need fathers.

A coach can point the way, but fathers lead the way. A coach can guide you, but only a father can affirm, validate, and connect with you on a legacy level. A coach receives remuneration for his wisdom, whereas a father receives satisfaction as his reward, knowing he is setting up his son for the future.

## BUT WHAT IF I DON'T FEEL QUALIFIED TO BE A FATHER?

Welcome to my biggest battle for almost two decades of being a father. It wasn't until I had a significant breakthrough encounter with God at our EMERGE conference in 2019 that I realized all of my "disqualifications" were actually my "qualifications" for leading my sons, my men, and my church! I had made some strong inner vows when I was 16 and tried to defend my mother when my father was abusing her; he knocked me to the ground and then tried to smash a chair over my head. I felt so weak. I was a skinny teenager, and this only accentuated the issue that I was scrawny, lacking muscle and strength, heck, lacking the courage to protect my mother from the abuse. So, I gave in to the idea that I didn't have what it takes to be a man!

> *The Apostle Paul said He rejoiced NOT in his strengths but in his weaknesses because in his weakness God's power is made perfect!*
> *(2 Corinthians 12:9)*

If your sons never see your weaknesses, you don't inspire them; you intimidate them. Many men from these homes feel they could never live up to the standards of their fathers. Experiencing multiple exhausting failures causes them to give up. One of the most profound things Jesus said while hanging on the cross was simply, "I thirst." (Christ made seven statements on the cross; as you may know, seven is the number of completion and perfection.)

**EMERGE**

Why is "I thirst" so profound? Because here is the Son of God—sinless, powerful enough to calm storms, able to raise the dead and cleanse lepers, destroying the works of the devil while simultaneously saving mankind from sin and death—modeling perfect vulnerability in the middle of his struggle as he asks for a drink. With parched lips, he cried out, "I thirst!" It's stunning, profound, and powerful. All discipleship begins at the place of weakness, at the place of struggle.

I once heard a preacher say, "If you preach on your weaknesses and struggles, you'll never run out of material!" This is true for both the preacher and the father. One of the things that makes Superman so special is the fact that he is Clark Kent, a mild-mannered reporter for The Daily Planet! A father must show his son both the man who is invincible and the man who suffers and struggles with Kryptonite. We all have our Kryptonite. For some, it's porn; for others, it's fear. It may also be inadequacy, anger, or rejection. Superman models to us (like Christ does) that our struggle with Kryptonite doesn't make us any less Superman; it makes us even more relatable because we will all struggle with something at each level of life. It's not a question of "Do I struggle?" It's a question of "How well do I struggle?"

When Moses and Joshua were on the mountain receiving the Torah, the Ten Commandments from Almighty God, unbeknownst to Moses, the children of Israel abandoned him. They beckoned Aaron, Moses's brother, to make gods they could worship and follow. Aaron made them a golden calf. No sooner had they departed from the worship of the one true God that they had also departed into all kinds of base revelry and debauchery. Joshua comments to Moses on the descent;

> "And when Joshua heard the noise of the people as they shouted, he said to Moses, "There is a noise of war in the camp." But he said: "It is not the noise of the shout of victory, Nor the noise of the cry of defeat, But the sound of singing I hear." So it was, as soon as he came near the camp, that he saw the calf and the dancing. So Moses' anger became hot, and he cast the tablets out of his hands and broke them at the foot of the mountain. Then he took the calf they had made, burned it in the fire, and ground it to powder; he scattered it on the water and made the children of Israel drink it. And Moses said to Aaron, "What did this people do to you that you have brought so great a sin upon them?"
> Exodus 32:17-21

## CHAPTER THREE: **FATHER**

Moses laments to Joshua that this isn't the sound of war in the camp. He said it is "neither the noise of the shout of victory, nor is it the noise of the cry of defeat, but it's the sound of singing that I hear!" It's not a matter of if you're fighting and warring. It's only a question of WHAT you're warring against. There will be days where you will be weeping and other days where you will be rejoicing and shouting. But the Israelites in this story were partying with the world instead of warring for truth, righteousness, and justice!

As a father, you are a model to your children—especially your sons. Don't feel you need to feign or pretend perfection to be respected by your children. They look to you. They need to see how you model weakness, failure, need, and struggle just as much as they need to see you modeling strength, courage, virtue, and victory. Being a good father is being a role model to your children.

*"Leadership is example!"*

## THE POWER OF FATHERING

*"If a father kisses his son, his son will never kiss another man!"*
*- Leading Psychologist*

When we began our EMERGE men's ministry, we identified a massive need within the development of men—a rite of passage where a young man could clearly define the moment he was no longer a boy but had crossed that line into manhood. The inspiration for this came largely from Zack Snyder's blockbuster film 300. It tells of the development of the Spartan Warrior, which starts when boys are ten years old. Whether or not the narration is fact, fiction, or a combination of both is not one hundred percent clear; however, from the few available historical accounts, the concept is absolutely true. Every Eastern culture has some form of the rite of passage, delineating the time when the child is no longer a boy but is now accepted and considered part of the men!

In the Jewish tradition, this happens at around thirteen years of age, when a young man goes through his Bar-Mitzvah (Son of the Law). Upon completion of the ceremony, he is now considered a man responsible to God and His divine laws. He can buy property, hold title, start a business, and take out a loan. It's a clearly defined line.

We have nothing like this in the Western world. In the movie 300, young boys are sent

## EMERGE

into the wilderness at just ten years old, where they must survive the harsh elements. They cannot return home until they bring the hide of a wolf with them. It's hard to imagine any mother being excited, or even supportive, of a ritual of this kind, but it makes for a great movie script. In the movie, we see a young Leonidas (who becomes the king and hero of the movie) using himself as bait to lure an alpha wolf into a quagmire trap, a narrowing crevice between two cliff faces high up on a mountain. The boy knows even an apex predator cannot resist the opportunity to feast on the flesh of an easy kill, and thus the trap is set. As the wolf lunges toward the young boy, the boy hastily draws backward into the narrow crevasse. The advancing wolf, driven by the surge of adrenaline pumping through its veins, ignores the enclosing walls for the prospect of the kill and the reward of a full belly. It gets stuck in the enclosing walls as the young Leonidas reaches for a weapon he has hidden, thrusting it through with a spear he has carefully hidden in the recess of the cave.

The young Leonidas returns home with the hide of his would-be assassin and is immediately received with joy and recognized as a real man, a warrior, who would one day take his place as the king of Sparta. It's a magnificent idea. History shows that the weak are always at the mercy of the strong and the violent. As a king, he will have to protect his kingdom and its citizens from the barbaric and violent nations seeking to plunder his lands, his people, and their wealth.

The Western world has eliminated much of the need for such things, and we certainly don't send our ten-year-olds off into the harsh wilderness to kill or be killed by wild predators. However, there is still a need for a rite of passage. When am I no longer a boy? When do I become recognized as a man? In my own life, my broken and fractured relationship with my father made this almost impossible to distinguish. Doubts about whether I had what it takes to be a man followed me well into my marriage and fathering years. I would often become overwhelmed as a shudder of anxiety and fear coursed through my body with the thought, "You don't have what it takes to provide, to lead, to father, to solve problems, or to win!"

We decided to create a rite of passage where young males between the ages of twelve and eighteen would face three obstacles:

1. They would have to "fight a giant." We have a few 6'4" MMA fighters they would have to size up to.
2. They would have to push their body weight on a sled across a distant line to show they could carry their weight, endure, and be responsible for themselves!

## CHAPTER THREE: **FATHER**

3. Finally, they have to "run the gauntlet" as adult men with football pads bearing words like "failure," "rejection," "addiction," "loser," (and many other such negative adjectives) would use said pads/words to knock them down to the ground—taunting them with the words they were holding, threatening to knock them down again, and telling them they don't have what it takes to get past them! Upon completion, fathers meet their sons at the finish line where, in a ceremonial atmosphere filled with the cheering of hundreds of men, they present their sons with a medal or dog tag and place it over their heads while hugging them, kissing them, and telling them they are proud of them. It's probably one of the most powerful moments I have ever experienced. The raw, palpable emotion felt between father and son is inexpressible. You can literally witness generational curses replaced by the blessings of a father's affirmation, validation, and affection.

My three sons went through this process, my youngest son did it three years in a row. I was never able to speak coherently to my boys at the finish line. My heart burst with pride and joy as shudders of sheer delight pulsated through my body. My son's chest heaved from exhaustion and adrenal fatigue. Tears sat on their cheeks, testifying to the very real internal struggles they faced and overcame against the insurmountable, very "unfair" situations of grown men bullying them, knocking them to the ground, and chanting demeaning words at them, all while Dad observed from the sideline, forbidden to intervene. It was raw masculinity. It was terrific masculinity. It was, and is sheer magnificence.

## **THE ANOMALY**

One year, as my youngest son, Tommy, was going through the gauntlet, I watched him pass several boys who were older and more physically developed, lying on the ground. They were unable to get up or at least were very slow and hesitant to keep trying to break through. I didn't want to take my eyes off my son or stop cheering for him, but I was bewildered by why some of these "stronger," bigger kids were lying there while Tommy kept picking himself back up and would run again and again. One kid, who was about seventeen years old, burst into tears and cried repeatedly, "I can't, I can't do it!"

The Holy Spirit asked me, "Do you see what's happening here?" I was about to say, "No, I don't!" Then, He revealed to me that the boys who were unable to get back up (or were hesitant to get back up) had one thing in common. It wasn't that they were physically weaker or had some disability. In every case, these boys had no father present in their lives! Just then, I heard a taunt from one of the fathers on the sideline jeer, "Is that all you've got? Come on, hit him harder!" Startled, I looked over to

# EMERGE

see who the heck would be chanting "for" the bullies and "against" his own kid. It was none other than high school football coach Andre Johnson, whose son "Champ" was running the gauntlet. The contrast could not have been more glaring or spectacular. I had kids with no father's voice on the sidelines, unable or slow to rise, while I had a father cheering for the oppressors against his own son!

As I watched, Champ would get knocked backward to the ground. His father would cheer for the bullies, "Come on, you hit like a girl. Hit him harder! Is that all you got?" As I watched Champ's face, something unexpected happened. Instead of seeing a kid who thought his dad was against him, he looked at his dad as a determined smile formed on his face. His eyes glazed over with a growing determination and confidence. Each time he got back up, he would run even harder at the bullies. After getting knocked to the ground at least four or five times by the physically larger (and much stronger) men, with his father seemingly cheering for his enemies, I watched Champ pick himself up and run once again with fervent pace at the men with the pads. As they squinted, closing their eyes and bracing for impact, Champ modified his approach with a sidestep, easily passing by, knocking one of the adults off balance to the ground. As he passed by, he looked back and yelled, "See ya later, losers!" He darted with ease to the finish line.

Champ, who could hear his father cheering for the bullies, came to the realization that "My father sees more strength in me than I can currently see!" The contrast could not have been more dazzling. Physically strong and capable kids who didn't have fathers doubted themselves and gave up, whereas the presence of a father's voice gave immeasurable strength, resilience, and confidence!

> *"And a voice came from heaven;*
> *"You are my beloved son, in whom I am well pleased!"*
> *- Mark 1:11*

How many men never had a father's voice present on the sideline? How many men fell short of their potential, or even their destinies, because of the absence of a father's voice? Even Jesus Christ, after getting baptized by John in the Jordan River, had his Heavenly Father affirmingly declare, "You are my beloved Son, in whom I am well pleased!"

When a father's voice is absent from the sidelines of our lives, when a father's caress, affection, and kiss are absent, men struggle with same-sex attraction, looking to fill an unmet longing in their souls. Women turn to promiscuity, seeking to fill the void of their father's affection, embrace, and approval.

# CHAPTER THREE: **FATHER**

The late Sy Rogers once told our congregation that in our sexual development through adolescence, "we cannot effectively bond to the opposite sex if we have never learned in our formative years to bond with our same sex." Boys who never bonded with their fathers are most susceptible and vulnerable to sexual predators (like we saw with the so-called "celibate" Catholic priests) and falling into homosexual sins in a desperate attempt to secure that deep longing and missing bond.

The largest organ in the human body is not "in the body" so much as it is "on" it. Skin. Why? Because we were created with a need to be touched, held, caressed, and receive a pat on the back echoed by the words, "Well done, you did good!" Touch is essential and powerful. Holding hands. Kissing the face and lips. Adolf Hitler discovered this inadvertently when he commissioned his diabolical doctor, Josef Mengele, to help him create a "super army" who would obey orders without question—killing without pity or remorse. He began the process by giving each Hitler Youth a German Shepherd pup they had to care for and bond with for a year. Then, on the one-year anniversary, they were required to kill the pet they had bonded with and come to love and care for. (Unbelievably cruel. That's why the devil is also called 'The cruel one' - Proverbs 5:9). As you can imagine, the turmoil in these young kids was so great that many did not kill their dogs. Those who did had severe trauma and emotional distress afterward, rendering them almost inoperative for warfare.

Not to be defeated, Hitler then commissioned his diabolical quack, Mengeles, to begin earlier, from the time of birth. They conducted studies where little boys were not held, nursed at the breast, and comforted when they cried or cuddled to go to sleep. The agenda, according to the evolutionary lie that both Darwin and Nietzsche had propagated, was that a "superhuman" (German "uber-mensch") race would evolve— one who saw compassion and pity as weakness. One who would kill on reflex because compassion for the weak, the infirmed, the disabled, and even the elderly is against the evolutionary theory of natural selection and survival of the fittest.

The results of this heinous experiment were devastating, cataclysmic, and ended up being completely scrapped, but not before significant damage had been done to the children. Instead of developing a "superhuman" race who could kill on reflex without mercy or regret, most of these children died before their fourth birthday. Almost all of them developed severe mental trauma, anguish, and retardation. Many couldn't speak or communicate and would sit for hours in their own excrement and urine, almost lifeless, like listless zombies. Their immune systems became so debilitated that their bodies could not fight off even the slightest infections. Human beings need

# EMERGE

touch. As a father, there are few more vital and healthy activities you can do than cuddle, kiss, and wrestle your child!

The Bible states that Moses was the meekest of all men. Most men today confuse the word "meekness" with "weakness," but don't let our current perverted culture distort the truth of that word. Meekness actually means "Strength harnessed, or strength under control/command!" After all, it was Moses who "like a boss" commanded Pharaoh to "Let My People Go!" He delivered Israel from 400 years of bondage, negotiated the total surrender of the superpower of his time, and defeated the mightiest military army of his day when he drowned the Egyptian army with their Iron chariots in the Red Sea. He was not a weak man, but he was a meek man. He could receive correction from his father-in-law despite being the most powerful man on planet Earth at that time. He would intercede before God for the stubborn and rebellious Israelites because he loved and cared deeply for them and God's reputation.

God has put strength into fathers for two purposes:
1. to excite and
2. to protect.

Playing with Dad should be like being on a roller coaster. The kids are excited because they feel safe yet are overwhelmed by the strength and power. In this environment, they develop the confidence to take risks because they know the Clark Kent they're playing with can change into Superman in the blink of an eye, even without a telephone booth being present. Dads are meant to be meek. They are endowed by God to have physical strength and dominance in the home so they can protect and develop their children. Fathers are meant to operate with strength under control and power at their command as they toss their children high into the air.

When I would come home from work, there was nothing I looked forward to more than roughhousing with my boys! We would wrestle for hours on the lounge room floor, many lamps bearing the casualty of "too good of a time," much to Mom's chagrin! Sometimes, it would result in a hole in the wall or scuffed paint, but we would wrestle away anyway. Even when one child hurt themselves, accidentally bumping their head on the coffee table or falling awkwardly off my back attempting a WWE "jump off the ropes" move, the pause was only temporary.

*"Stop it! You're being way too rough with them!"*
*-Every Mom!*

## CHAPTER THREE: **FATHER**

The child would run to their mother, who would console them and then demand we stop such a frivolous misuse of our time. No sooner had Mom turned her back, and it was ON again! Wrestling on the living room floor, throwing them across the sofas, smashing them in the head with Mom's carefully placed pillow cushions, lifting them up over my head, and spinning them around until they thought they would throw up.

It was the highlight of my day. My sons, Jordan, Ash, and Tommy, would literally wait and then bait the activity and games! Even while Mom was yelling in the background, "Stop it, you're being too rough," my boys would yell out even louder, "More, Daddy, more!" The bond between myself and my boys today is as strong as ever. I can't help but wonder if the times when Mom would say, "Okay, time to put the kids to bed, so we (husband and wife) can have some peace and quiet and spend some time together!" I would carry the kids to bed, and then "round two" would take place. I became the "Orh way Orh" monster, with Mom having to scold us no less than a dozen times, touting that the kids would not sleep if I continued to stir them up. I remember smiling and kissing my boys on their beetroot-red, sweaty, overheated little heads and saying, "Good night. Daddy loves you so much, but I better go before Mommy makes me sleep outside!"

I watched a National Geographic program about lions in Africa and saw this exact saga: The young lion cubs tested and developed their strength by wrestling and roughhousing with pop! Fathers, don't let the world shame you into thinking you can raise your kids without touch, affection, and roughhousing! The statistics show you can't.

## **THE LIFE COACH PHENOMENON**

I wonder if our modern-day obsession with 'life coaches' is not the backlash of father-absent households. Maybe, like me, you had a father who was home but was not present to inject his voice affirmingly into your world, your trials, and especially your challenges. I'm not sure of the connection between life coaching and fatherlessness, but I'm sure a deeper study would provide interesting data. But what I do know is that the apostle Paul says that 10,000 life coaches doesn't equal one father;

> *"For you can have 10,000 instructors in Christ, but you can't have many fathers. For I became your father in Christ Jesus through the gospel."*
> *- 1 Corinthians 4:15 - Holman Christian Standard Bible*

**EMERGE**

# OUCH!

There is a popular song that wrecks me every time I hear it. I'm sure you are familiar with it. It's called "Cat's in the Cradle" by Harry Chapin. I first heard this song at the Wollongong Church of Christ after I got saved when the very talented associate pastor Wes Beavis performed it live. It so rocked me that it became a catalyst for much soul searching, healing, and many many encounters with God as 'father!'

*Here are the words:*
*My child arrived just the other day*
*He came to the world in the usual way*
*But there were planes to catch, and bills to pay*
*He learned to walk while I was away*
*And he was talking 'fore I knew it, and as he grew*
*He'd say "I'm gonna be like you, Dad"*
*"You know I'm gonna be like you."*

*And the cat's in the cradle, and the silver spoon*
*Little boy blue and the man in the moon*
*"When you coming home, dad?" "I don't know when"*
*But we'll get together then*
*You know we'll have a good time then*

*My son turned ten just the other day*
*He said, thanks for the ball, Dad, come on let's play*
*Can you teach me to throw, I said, not today*
*I got a lot to do, he said, that's okay*
*And he, he walked away, but his smile never dimmed*
*It said, I'm gonna be like him, yeah*
*You know I'm gonna be like him*

*And the cat's in the cradle, and the silver spoon*
*Little boy blue and the man in the moon*
*"When you coming home, dad?" "I don't know when"*
*But we'll get together then*
*You know we'll have a good time then*

## CHAPTER THREE: **FATHER**

*Well, he came from college just the other day*
*So much like a man, I just had to say*
*Son, I'm proud of you. Can you sit for a while?*
*He shook his head, and they said with a smile*
*What I'd really like, Dad, is to borrow the car keys*
*See you later, can I have them please?*

*And the cat's in the cradle, and the silver spoon*
*Little boy blue and the man in the moon*
*"When you coming home, son?" "I don't know when"*
*But we'll get together then, dad*
*You know we'll have a good time then*

*I've long since retired, my son's moved away*
*I called him up just the other day*
*I said, I'd like to see you if you don't mind*
*He said, I'd love to, Dad, if I can find the time*
*You see, my new job's a hassle, and the kids have the flu*
*But it's sure nice talking to you, dad*
*It's been sure nice talking to you*

*And as I hung up the phone, it occurred to me*
*He'd grown up just like me*
*My boy was just like me*

*And the cat's in the cradle, and the silver spoon*
*Little boy blue and the man in the moon*
*"When you coming home, son?" "I don't know when"*
*But we'll get together then, dad*
*We're gonna have a good time then*

*- Harry F. Chapin/Sandy Chapin - Warner Chappell Music Inc.*

It still moves me to tears and gives me a healthy dose of the 'fear of God' every time I listen to it. I would encourage you to download this song and put it into your playlist. Listen to it regularly, or at the very least annually. Its words and message are haunting, in a good way!

**EMERGE**

# FATHER FAIL

No father on Earth could stand up to the scrutiny of not failing in the area of fatherhood. I am the last to throw stones in judgment as I look back upon my failures and regrets of moments missed while raising my children. However, through the Bible, God has intentionally exposed the mistakes of others so we can learn from them and avoid the same pitfalls. One such story is of the Priest of Israel, Eli, and his sons, Phinehas and Hophni. These two corrupt men inherited the position of "priest" in Israel, but they had no heart for the God of Israel. They seduced and slept with the women who were seeking to come nearer to God, and they exploited the offerings of the people to make themselves fat. Caring only for the pleasures and wealth their positions afforded them, they completely neglected their priestly, and thereby godly, duties.

> "Then a man of God came to Eli and said to him, "Thus says the Lord: 'Did I not clearly reveal Myself to the house of your father when they were in Egypt in Pharaoh's house? Did I not choose him out of all the tribes of Israel to be My priest, to offer upon My altar, to burn incense, and to wear an ephod before Me? And did I not give to the house of your father all the offerings of the children of Israel made by fire? Why do you kick at My sacrifice and My offering which I have commanded in My dwelling place, and honor your sons more than Me, to make yourselves fat with the best of all the offerings of Israel, My people?' Therefore, the Lord God of Israel says: 'I said indeed that your house and the house of your father would walk before Me forever.' But now the Lord says: 'Far be it from Me; for those who honor Me I will honor, and those who despise Me shall be lightly esteemed. Now this shall be a sign to you that will come upon your two sons, on Hophni and Phinehas: in one day they shall die, both of them. Then I will raise up for Myself a faithful priest who shall do according to what is in My heart and in My mind. I will build him a sure house, and he shall walk before My anointed forever. And it shall come to pass that everyone who is left in your house will come and bow down to him for a piece of silver and a morsel of bread, and say, "Please, put me in one of the priestly positions, that I may eat a piece of bread."
> I Samuel 2:27-30, 34-36

Eli failed terribly. His inability to father his wayward sons in the laws, statutes, and commandments of God lost not only their lives but also their house, the place God designated for His priests in Israel. The Bible says Eli was aware of his sons' sinful and corrupt behavior but did nothing about it. There is a sin that is most egregious before God—the sin of indifference. What is indifference? It's the sin of not caring either way, not taking a side, or, in this situation, not taking the Lord's side seriously. Eli didn't measure his son's behavior in the light of the scriptures and God's commandments. God's commandments are life. They always have been, and they always will be. When we transgress, we don't so much "break God's laws" as we break ourselves against them! Eli refused to confront his children about their destructive, immoral behavior, which was a huge fail.

Too many fathers don't confront or correct their children because of shame. They feel disqualified from past transgressions and failures, or they want to protect a sense of being "The Sugar Daddy" who is the "best dad in the world" because they always give the kids whatever they want! Both are devastating. Both end up with the same result: the desolation of the children and their future.

> *"Chasten your son while there is hope,*
> *And do not set your heart on his destruction."*
> *Proverbs 19:18*

Learn from the best example set out in the holy Scriptures, namely the father-son relationship between David and Solomon:

> *"My son, hear the instruction of your father, And do not forsake the law of your mother; For they will be a graceful ornament on your head, And chains about your neck. My son, if sinners entice you, Do not consent. If they say, "Come with us, Let us lie in wait to shed blood; Let us lurk secretly for the innocent without cause; Let us swallow them alive like Sheol, And whole, like those who go down to the Pit; We shall find all kinds of precious possessions, We shall fill our houses with spoil; Cast in your lot among us, Let us all have one purse"— My son, do not walk in the way with them, Keep your foot from their path; For their feet run to evil, And they make haste to shed blood. Surely, in vain the net is spread In the sight of any bird; But they lie in wait for their own blood, They lurk secretly for their own lives. So are the ways of everyone who is greedy for gain; It takes away the life of its owners."*
> *Proverbs 1:8-19*

## EMERGE

Your parenting is literally the power that determines your children's destiny! Let them learn from your mistakes. Don't hide them. Lament them. Share the regret, the pain, and the destruction that ensued. Also, share the victories, lessons learned, and triumphant moments. Impart wisdom, knowledge, and understanding. Your greatest investment in this life is not in gold, Bitcoin, or property; it's in your wife and children. Fathering is the greatest threat to the devil. Your fathering yields the greatest bounty and harvest that lasts generationally.

As we have seen above, failing as a father has dire and devastating consequences. If you struggle to father your children properly, go to your Heavenly Father and receive the healing and the strength that He so graciously bestows upon us so you can be the best father your children need!

> "A father is a man who expects his son to be as good a man as he meant to be."
> — Frank A. Clark, American Politician

*I looked at you and smiled the other day*
*I thought you'd see me, but you didn't*
*I said, "I love you," and waited for what you would say*
*I thought you'd heard me, but you didn't*
*I asked you to come outside and play ball with me*
*I thought you'd follow me, but you didn't*
*I drew a picture just for you to see*
*I thought you'd save it, but you didn't*
*I made a fort for us back in the woods*
*I thought you'd camp with me, but you didn't*
*I found some worms for fishing if we could*
*I thought you'd want to go, but you didn't*
*I needed you just to talk to, my thoughts to share*
*I thought you'd want to, but you didn't*
*I told you about the game, hoping you'd be there*
*I thought you'd surely come, but you didn't*
*I asked you to share my youth with me*
*I thought you'd want to, but you didn't*
*My country called me to war; you asked me to come home safely*
*But I didn't.*
*- Stan Gebhardt*

## CHAPTER THREE: **FATHER**
# JESUS CAME TO REVEAL THE FATHER

*"Jesus said to him, "I am the way, the truth, and the life. No one comes to the Father except through Me. "If you had known Me, you would have known My Father also; and from now on you know Him and have seen Him." Philip said to Him, "Lord, show us the Father, and it is sufficient for us." Jesus said to him, "Have I been with you so long, and yet you have not known Me, Philip? He who has seen Me has seen the Father; so how can you say, 'Show us the Father'? Do you not believe that I am in the Father, and the Father in Me? The words that I speak to you I do not speak on My own authority; but the Father who dwells in Me does the works. Believe Me that I am in the Father and the Father in Me, or else believe Me for the sake of the works themselves."*
*John 14:6-11*

Jesus' greatest objective was to reveal the Father to the world. God is a perfect father. If you parent with God, you will experience the power of having your shortcomings covered by your most perfect Heavenly Father. It was always meant to be a partnership. Your children are a gift from God. They belonged to Him before He entrusted them to you. Why try to parent them alone? You should be fathering with your perfect Father in heaven!

*He is a good, good Father! He forgives. He provides. He leads. He delivers, and He restores:*

*"Our Father in heaven, Hallowed be Your name. Your kingdom come. Your will be done On Earth as it is in heaven. Give us this day our daily bread. And forgive us our debts, As we forgive our debtors. And do not lead us into temptation, But deliver us from the evil one."*
*Matthew 6:9-13*

## CHAPTER FOUR
# BROTHER

## אח

*(Ack)*

"We must live together as brothers or perish together as fools."
-Martin Luther King

"Brotherhood is the very price and condition of man's survival."
- Carlos Romulo

"Trying to build the brotherhood of man without the fatherhood of God is like trying to make a wheel without a hub."
- Irene Dunne

## CHAPTER FOUR: BROTHER
# WHAT THE BIBLE SAYS ABOUT BROTHERHOOD

*"A friend loves at all times, and a brother is born for times of adversity!"*
*- Proverbs 17:17*

*"A man who has friends must himself be friendly,*
*But there is a friend who sticks closer than a brother."*
*- Proverbs 18:24*

*"Therefore, if food makes my brother stumble,*
*I will never again eat meat, lest I make my brother stumble."*
*-I Corinthians 8:13*

## WHAT IS THE BIBLE'S DEFINITION OF A BROTHER?

*"What am I, my brother's keeper?"*
*- Cain, First brother/First Murderer.*

A lot can be said about brotherhood. We certainly hear that word bandied around in many places today. From college fraternities and inner-city gangs to our armed servicemen fighting wars huddled together in the trenches, preserving the freedoms we too often take for granted, brotherhood is a very real thing. But what does it mean? How can you describe what brotherhood really is? How did God, the author of marriage and family, *intend* brotherhood to look?

## EPHIALTES SYNDROME

In the movie *300*, King Leonidas leads three hundred of his chosen men to defend the Spartan Empire against the rampaging war machine of the Persian Army. They conquered or utterly demolished every other empire, and the one remaining (yet to yield or be wiped off the map) was Sparta. King Leonidas' meager army was going up against a military boasting millions of soldiers armed and ready to battle.

When approaching the Persian army, they notice that a lone figure has been tailing them on the cliff tops above their passageway for the last few days. It is Ephialtes, a deformed hunchback who, according to Spartan law, should have been abandoned

**EMERGE**

by his parents and left to die. Instead, his Spartan parents fled to save their only son from the fate appointed to those born with physical defects or disabilities.

Ephialtes wants to have an audience with King Leonidas. He introduces himself, *"I am Ephialtes, born of Sparta. My mother's love had us flee Sparta lest I be discarded."* Ephialtes is clothed in the crimson colors of the Spartan warrior and bears the weaponry and armor distributed to those enlisted to fight as Spartan soldiers. *"I beg you, bold king, to permit me to redeem my father's good name by serving you in combat. My father trained me to feel no fear, to make shield and spear and sword as much a part of me as my own beating heart! I will earn my father's armor, oh noble king, by joining you in the battle!"* He then proceeds to brandish his spear in a number of tactically fatal strikes, displaying perfect poise, posture, and aesthetics. King Leonidas remarks, *"Fine thrust!"* to which Ephialtes promises, *"I will kill many Persians!"*

What happens next is as essential as it is powerful; it is the definition of what encompasses brotherhood. King Leonidas approaches a prostrated, submitted Ephialtes and says, *"Raise your shield!"* Ephialtes lifts his head, looking at the king with questioning, concerned eyes.

*"Sire?"*

*"Raise your shield as high as you can!"* entreats the King. Ephialtes struggles to lift his shield. His hunched-back deformity prevents his left arm from lifting the shield very high. King Leonidas then remarks, *"Your father should have told you how our phalanx works. We fight as a single impenetrable unit; that is the source of our strength. Each Spartan protects the man to his left with his shield from thigh to neck. A single weak spot, and the phalanx shatters! From thigh to neck, Ephialtes. I am sorry, my friend, but not all of us were meant to be soldiers."*

With the sting of this rejection, Ephialtes reveals that it was not only his physique that was deformed but also his sense of honor, loyalty, and entitlement. Later in the movie, he dishonors his father's name by betraying Leonidas to the King of Persia in exchange for pleasure and vice.

The principle is powerful. The phalanx was made up of the men connecting their shields in a defense formation, protecting the life of the man to their left, creating an impenetrable unit. That was the source of their strength.

Cain, the first brother to ever exist (also the first murderer), responded with, *"Am I my brother's keeper?"* when God asked him what happened to his brother, Abel **(Genesis**

## CHAPTER FOUR: **BROTHER**

*4:9).* Cain disqualified himself from the brotherhood of man with that statement. God proceeds to banish him to wander as a fugitive. Cain protests and complains that his *punishment* is more than he can bear—no remorse, no repentance, no contriteness for his brother's murder. He *only* thought of himself. He complains even though he is reaping the harvest of the seeds he has sown!

A brother is someone who is a brother's keeper, *not* someone who is born a sibling. Brother is not a noun but a verb. It is an *action,* not a title. It is a function, not a label. You are a brother when you protect the man on your left. That means you are operating on his side. You are his strength. You function as his right eye with focus and vision during battle. You have the ability to wield his sword, to conquer. *That* is a *brother*!

## I KNEW YOU'D COME!

An old Boy Scout manual told the story of two brothers who fought side by side in France during WWI. The battle was particularly fierce that day, and the brothers lost sight of one another during the exploding artillery and perpetual gunfire. The men struggled to rejoin their unit as the gunfire ceased toward the end of the day; neither side made any real advancement. Sadly, only one of the brothers made it back to the trenches safely.

Even though he was completely exhausted from the day's battle, he ran up and down the trenches, calling for his brother. Nobody had seen him. He then ran to the medic unit, hoping his brother might be non-fatally injured. To his dismay, his brother was not among the wounded. This meant only one thing. His brother was still out there on the battlefield.

Was he already dead? Or worse yet, what if he was injured and unable to return without assistance? What if he was captured and fell into the hands of their enemy? They would most certainly not be merciful. The darkest thoughts raced through his mind, for he had heard about the cruelties of men in wartime. His love for his brother overwhelmed him. As tears began to well up in his eyes, so did a determinant courage. He approached his commanding officer and asked permission to go back into "no man's land" to find his brother.

The officer shook his head. "It's too dangerous. They call it 'no man's land' for a reason! I cannot afford to lose another soldier. If your brother is not in the trenches or among the wounded, he is most likely dead. You will have to accept that as a fact. Move on. It's war, son!" He said, but not without pity, "Your brother is probably dead, and there's no use risking your life or the life of another in my platoon just to find him dead."

## EMERGE

The brother continued to persist and begged the officer to let him try.
Finally, the officer said, "I forbid you to go out there, and that's an order! Disobey, and I will have you court-martialed!" The young soldier walked away with a nauseating knot in his stomach. He thought he could hear the moaning of someone dying on the battlefield and thought, *What if that's my brother?*

Risking everything, he lunged out of the trenches and began to dart under the dissipating fog of the gunpowder and cordite in the air. He searched desperately, looking left and right while making his way back toward enemy fire.

Sometime later, the men in the trenches could see the silhouette of one of their own carrying a fellow soldier. They called out to the officer, "Someone's returning carrying a wounded soldier, Sir. Can we help? Permission to leave the trenches, Sir?" The officer emphatically forbade them and told them to stay put. It might be a ploy by the enemy to draw them into gunfire. At that, the young man returned with his brother draped across his shoulders. As he reached the safety of the bunker, however, his brother gasped and died in his arms.

The officer, furious that his direct order had been disobeyed, shouted at the young man, "I gave you no such permission to go out there and look for your brother. You disobeyed an order, Son, you now face being court-martialed. I hope it was worth it. Your brother died anyway."

"Yes, Sir!" replied the brother respectfully. Tears welled up in his eyes once more. "His last words made it all worth it!"

The officer caustically retorted, "And what words were those, Son?"
The young man replied, "Sir when I crawled up beside him where he lay, hurt and dying, I took him in my arms. He looked up at me and smiled, then said, 'I knew you'd come, Tom. I knew you'd come.'"

## THE BOOK OF ORIGINS

In the first book of the Bible, Genesis, we discover the creation of mankind being made in the image and likeness of God, and the creation of the woman to be man's helper or help meet. From there, Genesis chapter four tells us about the first two brothers, Cain and his younger brother, Abel. Many Bible scholars believe they were twin boys, with Cain being the firstborn. The Bible says there came a day when both

# CHAPTER FOUR: **BROTHER**

Cain and Abel brought an offering to the Lord. Cain brought an offering from the fruit of the ground—for the Bible tells us Cain was a tiller of the ground, a farmer who loved the soil. Abel, however, was a shepherd, and he brought one of the firstborn lambs from his flock as his offering.

The Lord accepted Abel and his offering but did not accept Cain and his offering. Cain became distraught with God's rejection of his offering. God came to him and asked him plainly, "Cain, why are you downcast? Why has your countenance fallen? If you do what is right, will you not be accepted? Sin crouches at the door. Its desire is for you, to ensnare you, but you must rule over it!"

Instead of doing what was right, Cain chose to lure his brother into the field, where he struck him and killed him. God came down to Cain and asked him, "Cain, where is your brother Abel?"

Cain responded, "How should I know? What am I supposed to be, my brother's keeper?"

God responded, "What is this that you have done? For I hear the cry of your brother's blood calling to me from the ground, crying out!"

As Abel's older brother, Cain was absolutely meant to be his brother's keeper. First of all, he was the eldest, the firstborn. With that birth placement, he had authority, but with authority comes responsibility. As Abel was a shepherd of sheep, Cain was meant to shepherd the siblings in his family. That's the role of the firstborn son. I want you to notice the words of a murderer: *I'm not responsible for anybody else but myself.*

Envy and bitterness filled Cain's heart. Instead of repenting and bringing an acceptable offering to the Lord, Cain found it easier to lure the one who had found favor and blessing into the field and murder him. In case you're wondering why God was so discriminatory between the two offerings here, it's very simple. God knows that He is God. He doesn't have a problem knowing He is God. He knows He is worthy of all praise, all worship, and all reverence. If He allowed Cain to bring an offering that dishonored God, it wouldn't affect God so much as it would affect Cain. If God accepted an offering that Cain had compromised, He would be telling Cain that it's OK to compromise on God's laws, standards, and requirements in every area of life.

The story of Cain and Abel is a very powerful, hidden picture of the two covenants in the Bible. The old covenant is known as the law, and the new covenant is known as

# EMERGE

grace. When man sinned in Genesis chapter three, God said, "Cursed be the ground." God could not curse man because He had already blessed man in Genesis 1:28, so instead, God curses the ground for man's sake. When Cain brought his offering of the fruit of the ground, he was making an incredibly arrogant statement before God that his human effort, his works, could overcome the curse of death God put upon the ground—total hubris.

In contrast, Abel knew that no matter what work or effort he put in, he couldn't compensate for his sinful, fallen nature or the curse at work in the Earth. Something innocent had to shed its blood if he were to have any chance of being right with God. Because of this, Abel brought a lamb, the firstborn from among his flock, and God accepted this sacrifice. It has humility and reality rolled into one. It doesn't matter how hard we work at attaining perfection; right standing with a perfect God can *only* occur through grace, and grace can only come if something innocent dies to balance the scales and correct the deficit in the ledger!

Can you see the two covenants? In the old covenant, the law brings death, but this isn't because the law is evil. On the contrary, the law is perfect. It is the perfect law of God. Man is imperfect. Man is sinful. When sinful man and God's perfect law meet, God's perfect law condemns man as a lawbreaker and, therefore, deserving of death. Abel is a powerful picture of God's new covenant. Even the name Abel comes from two Hebrew roots: "A: B," which is the Hebrew word for father, and "EL," which is the Hebrew word for God. (As in Elohim and EL Shaddai) Here, we see another powerful picture hidden in the scriptures that 'AB - EL' or 'father God' would bring forth from himself an innocent lamb to be sacrificed as an acceptable offering before God Almighty to make us right with him and bring His blessing upon our lives.

We could take this one step further. Christians who are born again and have placed themselves under the blood of Christ to come into right standing with God will discover very quickly that the spirit of Cain (which is alive on Earth today) will persecute them and even threaten them with death. It *hates* the redeemed. It hates those who God has blessed. It is satanic in origin. It is the father of the "antiChrist" spirit. Do you see it? If not, give your life to Christ and begin to live out His word, laws, and commandments. As you prosper and flourish, you will find persecution and hostility even within your own household!

## YOU ARE YOUR BROTHERS KEEPER!

One of the greatest teachings in the scriptures is that man needs companionship, re-

# CHAPTER FOUR: **BROTHER**

lationship, mission, direction, fellowship, and friendship! "It's *not good* that man should be alone," shouts the Bible in Genesis chapter two. God himself made this assessment. When God said it wasn't good for man to be alone, man wasn't alone. Man had God. He walked with God in Eden, a perfect garden, which literally means "paradise in perfect beauty." Man was surrounded by an entire kingdom of animals, birds, and fish. He walked with Almighty God in the cool of the day in the garden. I believe this admission confirms He is the one true God, unlike all the other gods proclaimed in other so-called scriptures and holy writings. It was God who said it's not good that man should be alone. Through this statement, He was saying, "I am not enough!" Adam (man) needed a companion, a helper, a human touch, and connection. Only a secure God could make such a statement. The capricious and insecure gods of the Romans or Ancient Greeks would certainly *never* say such a thing! God walked with Adam, and even though Adam wasn't asking, that didn't mean our magnificent Heavenly Father wasn't discerning! *You need friends*! You need companionship in your life! You need brothers, and you need to be a brother!

In Genesis we see the powerful struggle between the first brothers that ends in the tragic death of Cain. God then comes to him and ask where his brother is, and Cain makes a statement in the negative that is meant to teach a lesson, Cain says to God, "Am I my brothers keeper?" In this God is reminding us of our call and role to relationship and care for each other.

Now, this next discovering is for believers and for anyone reading this who isn't a Bible-believing person yet. You may say I only believe in science or concrete things like archaeology. Let me show you something from the ancient Chinese language. Just as a point of reference, the entire ancient Chinese language is made up of caricatures instead of letters; each symbol has roots in the Bible's first book of Genesis, chapters 1 to 11, yet the ancient Chinese language outdates Moses, writing the book of Genesis by some 900 years. If the Bible wasn't real, how did the ancient Chinese have such impeccable knowledge of biblical events? Not just impeccable but phenomenally accurate. For example, below are the symbols for elder brother and for murderer.

## THE WORDS (DISPOSITION) OF A MURDERER!
**CAIN:**
兄 Older brother/spokesperson
兇 Cruel, ferocious, killer

# EMERGE

*In the ancient Chinese, man is depicted as a mouth with legs,* as seen in the diagram above. You'll notice in the second symbol depicting a cruel, ferocious killer; the mouth has the top removed, and instead, an X is now placed within the mouth. Do you think that this is an accident? This predates the book of Genesis by some 900 years. Kane was the firstborn son. All Eastern tradition tells us that the firstborn son is the spokesperson for the family. Cain, in the Bible, was the firstborn son. Therefore, he was the family's spokesperson. However, when he sent and murdered his brother Abel, he lost his place, was banished from the family, and was sent out and sent away. Kane, totally unrepentant, complains to God that his sentence for murdering his brother was too difficult for him to bear and that he has a tiller of the ground. He understood, sowing and reaping, and because he had murdered his brother, somebody could very easily find him and murder him. So God graciously put a mark upon Cain. Can you see it? Can you see the open box? He is no longer the voice for the family, the mouthpiece, the spokesperson. Instead, the murderer has been given a mark, or, as they say, X marks the spot!

This is in the ancient Chinese language, confirming the Bible as infallible truth, which you can put your total dependence upon and your complete trust in. You are meant to be your brother's keeper. Do not echo the words of a murderer. Instead, walk in the spirit of Christ and be your brother's keeper. Jesus said to His heavenly Father, "Of all those that You gave me, I have lost none except the one who was doomed to perdition, but of all that You have given me, I have kept them. I kept them in Your word, I gave them Your name, and they have followed me and received everlasting life." Jesus modeled what a perfect brother looks like.

## BROTHERS BY BIRTH OR BROTHERS BY CHOICE?

They say, *"You can choose your friends, but you cannot choose your family."* While that is essentially true, it is also not entirely inerrant. I have discovered I can choose to be a good brother, and I can also choose to be a brother to someone who was not born in my bloodline. We see this in David and Jonathan's relationship in the Bible. David had biological brothers who didn't fulfill their calling of brotherhood to him. Jonathan stepped into that role instead. Too often in life, while we are growing up, the conflicts, grievances, and mistakes we make in our adolescent immaturity negatively impact our siblings. Sadly, these things also often seem to trump God's best intention for brotherhood.

Some of the brothers I do life with and care about weren't born from my mother's womb. They are someone else's offspring and DNA, but they *are* my brother in

## CHAPTER FOUR: **BROTHER**

Christ because we share the same (heavenly) Father! It is my decision to be a good brother to them, to have their back, to care for and fight with and for them. I cheer and celebrate with them when they win and weep and lament when they lose. I had some friends I thought were brothers but found that they rejoiced when I lost and lamented when I was winning. These types of people are not your brothers.

## CHALLENGE

*Be* the very thing you seek to harvest. Be a brother. I have a brother in Australia. I made so many mistakes in my youth and treated the gift he was to me with indifference, taking him for granted. I didn't value who he was because I didn't see him through heaven's lens. He is one of the funniest, most brilliant, courageous men I know. He is an exceptional father, provider, husband, and worker. He climbed his way up from dysfunctional abuse and brokenness to become a prosperous, successful, extraordinary man. To this day, our distant and fractured relationship is still a deep and tender wound for me, but I am determined (through prayer and action) to repair what was lost and broken.

You can *be* a brother. You can experience what God imagined when He created brotherhood. When a man has a brother (as God designed), he is indeed the most blessed of men!

## CHAPTER FIVE
# HUSBAND

## לעב

*(BAL)*

"A happy wife, a happy life!"
- A wise man

"Leanne was born smiling—Jurgen, what have you done?"
- Holy Spirit

"A husband is a 'man in training,' and he never graduates! "
-Jurgen Matthesius
"And the Lord God said, "It is not good that man should be alone; I will make him a helper comparable to him.""
Genesis 2:18

CHAPTER FIVE: **HUSBAND**
## WHAT DOES HUSBAND MEAN?

Let's start with the etymology of the Hebrew word for husband–Bal. Bal is spelled using the three Hebrew letters Beit, Ayin, and Lamed.

ב -Beit -
- Ayin- ע
- Lamed- ל

## BEIT = HOUSE/TENT
## AYIN = EYES/SEEING/VISION
## LAMED = TEACHING/STAFF/AUTHORITY

In other words, the Hebrew word for husband is *"a visionary who sees, builds, and strengthens the house through heaven's teaching and authority."*

This definition incorporates the husband as both priest and king in the home. He is a king because he bears the burden and responsibility of building the house (name/family/legacy), and he is the priest because, just as the upper positioning of the "Lamed" letter indicates, the teaching he is supposed to bring is from heaven down into Earth.

## ARE THERE ANY "HUSBAND ROAD MAPS" TO FOLLOW?

This chapter presented challenges right away as I began to write it. I searched for *"Quotes on Husbandry,"* only to find that pretty much nothing came up! The things that did come up on the Google search engine were: *"100 nice things to say to/about your husband," "What are sweet loving words to say to your husband?"* and *"What is the best quote for a husband?"*

To which the answer was given:
*"No matter what my mood, my husband is my go-to place! Although there's nothing called a perfect marriage, everything seems so perfect because I married you! I am the most beautiful person in the whole universe, but only when seen through the eyes of my husband. The word 'soulmate' sounded meaningless until I met you."*
www.stylecraze.com/articles

Are you serious? With all the criticism from the feminists about the patriarchy and the role of the husband inside the patriarchy, there was *not one* clear and concise defi-

**EMERGE**

nition of what they were criticizing! I find it "interesting" that the world (with Google's seemingly omniscient informational reach and idolization of science, technology, and education) could *not* provide any meaningful quotes or a clear definition of what a husband is or his role!

*No wonder* so many men are struggling in this area! There's no road map. It's a man's worst nightmare. He's picked up a box from IKEA with hundreds of parts, nuts, bolts, screws, dowel pins, and glue but *no instructions!* What the heck? How is he meant to succeed? He's got to bumble his way forward and make educated guesses. The guesses are more manageable when you have a picture of what the end result is meant to look like on the front of the box. Still, sadly, with a 50%+ divorce rate, most men don't even have a good, clear picture to attempt to build toward.

Is it any wonder so many young men today are afraid to take on the commitment of becoming a husband when the world around them has absolutely no freakin' clue as to what a husband does or is supposed to look like? The most prominent models they currently have are on TV, which almost always depicts the husband as an emancipated, helpless, dim-witted fool who has no authority, weight, or wisdom and is led by the "smart" teenagers and the wise, savvy mom!

If husbandry can't be defined, how can it be explained? If it can't be explained, how can it be championed? Most men describe the term "*husband*" as a man who has lost his identity and has given up his sovereignty, becoming tamed and "*chained*" to the drudgery of household chores and duties while also being responsible for paying all the bills.

A husband is meant to please his wife, but without clearly explainable roles and definitions, how does he take on the headache of trying to figure out *what a woman wants or needs, let alone what she's thinking?* Even the greatest sages and philosophical minds of the past (like Plato, Aristotle, and Socrates) couldn't or didn't answer these questions.

> *"Women are unfinished men."*
> *- Aristotle.*

> *"Trust not a woman when she weeps,*
> *for she weeps when she wants her will!"*
> *-Socrates.*

## CHAPTER FIVE: **HUSBAND**

For what it's worth, Plato has become adopted by modern feminists as someone who attacked the hierarchical order and wealth succession of the traditional nuclear family. This is because of his critique of '*Eikos*' (a Greek word from where we get the word *Ekonomia* - Economics, literally the management of a household). Plato is seen as the indirect influence that inspired the Greeks to worship goddesses over gods. Goddesses like Diana, Venus, Aphrodite, Artemis, and the like. The reason? Following Plato's philosophies, the Greeks came to believe that women were not the weaker sex at all. This was a ruse, a deception, by the gods, for although women tended to be physically smaller and weaker than men, they were, in actual fact, the "stronger," superior sex because *they* decide whether a man gets to have sex or not!

If you want to screw up a worldview, look at it through the lens of how much sex a man gets to have! Sheesh! What happened to observing everything through the lens of *eternal, unchanging truth?* Temples were filled with temple prostitutes, exchanging sex for acts of worship, penance, and offerings. Did it liberate the Greeks? Nope. It totally disabled and emasculated them. Beginning with the men and then the entire family and society. It's proven that making men subject to their basest vices and giving themselves over to hedonistic pleasure never bodes well for that civilization. Ever!

The rise and fall of empires across the span of human history shows a familiar pattern. In a civilization's ascendency, it had morals, disciplines, chastity, and strong protection of family and family values (fidelity, honor, and submission). In its demise, however, the civilization replaces discipline, self-control, and moral virtue with revelry, drunkenness, and the pursuit of pleasure through extramarital sexual gratification and other vices. Destruction came swiftly and permanently. The ruins of these ancient empires can be toured and seen today. Sadly, the lessons of their demise are not emphatically taught on these same tours.

At its outset, the Roman Empire swore to be different, and it certainly was for hundreds of years. Marriage and family were seen as the backbone of the Roman Empire as it advanced in strength, size, and scope across the Earth. It championed qualities like self-discipline, fidelity, self-sacrifice, honor, and enterprise. Justice, law, truth, honor, and valor were exemplary virtues. Those who espoused them were elevated in position and trusted with power and influence. However, the *sinful nature* of fallen man soon corrupted the Roman ideals. Like the Greek and Medo-Persian empires before her, it fell apart and came to a dismal end when vice replaced virtue, and perversion replaced morality.

## EMERGE

When the greatest philosophers of human history, like Plato, Socrates, and Aristotle, present little or no real understanding of what it means to be a husband, what hope does plumber Bob or electrician Bill have in figuring it out? Well, the good news is there is a "textbook" or manual with all the answers. It has a wealth of treasure, information, and instruction on what it means to be a husband! If men are reluctant today and afraid to take the leap, someone must confront cultural lies with the truth! We, as the church, are the ones who must change this! But To change this dire statistic, we must first ask ourselves a couple of questions:

1. Did God not think the whole *"Husband and Wife"* thing through?
2. Has the devil been very crafty in hiding and burying God's intention and truths around *being* a husband (knowing that Hosea 4:6 says, *"My people are destroyed for a lack of knowledge!"*)

Buckle up because you're about to dive right in and discover some potent truths that will reveal God's intention for a *Husband and* what power and privilege await the man who embraces and commits himself to *being* a husband.

## YOUR WIFE IS A PRODUCT OF YOUR HUSBANDRY!

Almost all of my "WOW" moments in God came from a corrective experience. One of the most profound and memorable moments was during my first ministry assignment when I was living in South Auckland, New Zealand. My second son Ash had just been born. We had been under extreme pressure because, at the same time as the expansion of our family, we were expanding our dwelling and building a larger home. I was time-poor and financially challenged, so I agreed to hire a gentleman in our church who offered to be the *"project manager"* of our new home build. The only issue was he didn't seem to realize being the *"project manager"* meant he was responsible for *"managing the project!"* Slight oversight. In the end, we had a brand new baby and an unfinished home, and all of our savings were completely depleted.

Stress? Dear Jesus, I had never experienced such stress like this in my life. I was the father, the husband, the provider, and the visionary. And my misplaced trust in fools had put unbelievable duress on our family, my wife, our finances, and our health. I was working on my home, doing what I could do physically until about 4:30 am. I would drive back to where we were living, sleep for three hours, go to work from 9am - 5pm, then immediately leave my job and work until 4:30 am the next morning. It took a toll on everyone in my world, especially the people closest to me.

## CHAPTER FIVE: **HUSBAND**

One night, after moving into the almost completed property, my wife and I got into the biggest argument. She said, *"I didn't sign up for this. I'm done. I'm leaving!"* I yelled and pleaded, shouted and petitioned, but that only seemed to make things worse. I told her I had to get out of the house, go for a walk, clear my head, and pray. I had enough stress everywhere else in my life. I wasn't going through all this intensity and pressure to have the *same levels* of stress in the home I had just built. She just dismissively said, *"Go!"*

So I went!

As I began to pray, I talked to God, who had always been understanding with me and pretty much on my side (or at least by my side). I thought He would most certainly be able to identify with the pressure and stress I had been under. He would certainly have seen how hard I worked, how selflessly heroic I had been to survive on only three hours of sleep each night to build my wife and family this lovely new home in an upbeat neighborhood. All I could recall was my wife's "lack" of appreciation and affection. That stream of thoughts opened up another can of emotions. I began to see all the times we had argued. She had some serious issues around my leadership as a husband and the submission I expected of her as a wife. I then began to see all the flaws in her character and promptly reminded God, just in case He was unaware.

All of a sudden, God spoke to me, and the words knocked me to the ground.

He said, *"Jurgen, your wife is a product of your husbandry!"*

OUCH!

"What does that even mean?" I pondered. Then God began to show me a highlight reel of the words I had been using to describe my wife and how her behavior was lining up with those words. Words like rebellious, insubordinate, backslidden, and all the names I had called her in anger. I tried to defend my innocence and justify myself before God. I protested that I was not the one on trial here. I was only *"calling it as I see it!"* Then, a game-changer moment happened. God asked me a question, *"What did I do before I gave Adam a wife?"*

## ADAM'S FIRST LESSON

I responded immediately because the *only* book I had consistently read every year since my salvation was Genesis (yes, every year, I swore I'd read the Bible from cover

**EMERGE**

to cover, but the wheels would always come off around Leviticus)! I said, *"Oh, I know this one, God. You said, 'It's not good that man should be alone. I'll make a helper suitable for him,' and then you put him into a deep sleep, removed a rib, and made the woman!"*

God's response was swift and firm, *"Wrong!"*

Dumbfounded, I laughed internally and reminded God, the author of His book, the Bible, that I was not the one who was wrong. This was *exactly* how it played out in Genesis.

God again just said, *"Wrong!"*

So, I went back and read it to God to prove I was right. I didn't want to accuse Him of error, but with how busy He must be, He had obviously made an oversight on this one.

When I read the verses, I swear I had *never* seen this in the sequence that it plays out in scripture:

> *"And the Lord God said, "It is not good that man should be alone; I will make him a helper comparable to him." Out of the ground, the Lord God formed every beast of the field and every bird of the air and brought them to Adam to see what he would call them. And whatever Adam called each living creature, that was its name. So Adam gave names to all cattle, to the birds of the air, and to every beast of the field. But for Adam there was not found a helper comparable to him. And the Lord God caused a deep sleep to fall on Adam, and he slept; and He took one of his ribs, and closed up the flesh in its place. Then the rib which the Lord God had taken from man He made into a woman, and He brought her to the man. And Adam said: "This is now bone of my bones And flesh of my flesh; She shall be called Woman, Because she was taken out of Man."*
> *- Genesis 2:18-23*

The part that reads, *"and whatever Adam named them that became their name!"* jumped out at me and punched me in the face. In Hebrew, a name is not a name but an identity. It carries function, defines purpose, and ultimately shapes destiny! When Adam "named" the creature, he was literally determining the nature and essence of each creature and what characteristics it would develop and become. God then spoke to me, saying, *"Before I gave Adam the privilege of a spouse, I had to teach him the POWER of his mouth!"* This revelation from God so wrecked and rocked me that it left me completely flabbergasted!

## CHAPTER FIVE: **HUSBAND**

God then continued with a rebuke and said to me, *"Jurgen, I've watched and listened to you as you called her stupid, fat, dumb, rebellious (*and a list of other names that I am too embarrassed to type). *She is a product of the words you have spoken over her. I gave her to YOU, but your 'Husbandry' has produced what you now see! If you want to CHANGE the wife you have reaped, you have to begin to SOW different seeds (words)!"*

I walked home. My heart was heavy. God had given me my beautiful bride, but I had mismanaged His wonderful gift. Stewardship is the essence of the kingdom. We never graduate from stewardship. Here I was, failing with the most precious gift, my wife. Just then, I arrived at my house. It was dark outside, so Leanne couldn't see me in the yard looking into the kitchen through the window. With the lights on inside, however, I could easily see her. She was tidying up after the dinner she had cooked for me and our family. Baby bottles were drying and sterilizing for my second son, Ash. She was cleaning the kitchen, keeping it congruent with the impeccably clean and tidy house she labored so tirelessly each day to maintain and keep.

As I looked closer, I noticed the spark that used to dance so playfully in her eyes when we were first courting was gone. Her eyes instead seemed heavy, sullen, sparkless. The joy from her radiant smile and stunning personality was no longer present on her face. A heaviness replaced it. I stared for what seemed like an eternity—my heart felt like it had been stabbed.

As if I needed any more conviction or convincing, my father-in-law's voice replayed in my head: *"She was born smiling! She's always been such a joy, such a happy kid, mischievous, an entertainer... Yeah, she came out smiling, that one!"* He told me this about Leanne when he first gave me permission to court her. She was only sixteen years old and so full of life. It was *one* of the many things I found attractive about her, and it made me certain she was "the one" I wanted to spend the rest of my life with!

Then the Holy Spirit (Sent by Christ to be our Helper) chimed in, *"Jurgen, what have you done?"*

I was wrecked. Broken.

I realized *she* was not the problem. I was! I stood there and repented before God. I asked for His forgiveness for mishandling this most priceless gift and for His help to redeem the situation if possible! I walked into the house. She heard me but didn't turn around. She'd heard enough of how bad I thought she was. She didn't have anything left. I walked up behind her, touched her shoulder, and said, "I'm so sorry."

# EMERGE

As she turned around, I asked her to forgive me, promising I would be the one to change. I told her what God told me and how I had been cut to the heart. I vowed to her I would *only* be speaking life and calling her the things God had declared over her!

I'd love to tell you she immediately forgave and believed me. She didn't. I'm actually glad she didn't. It set me on a quest to prove to her I had indeed had an encounter with God and that she would *see* and experience the difference. It's always easier to say the right thing than to do it. We should always strive to let our deeds, not our words, do the talking. Actions are indeed louder than words. Much louder. I was determined that this beautiful, once always smiling girl would resurface from under the debris and rubble of my poor husbandry. It took about twenty months of *changed behavior* before Leanne really began to open up her heart to my words again. She saw I was no longer using my words to hurt, belittle, criticize, or cut her down. She began to drink from the *words of life* I was speaking over her at every possible opportunity.

Today, she longs to connect and spend time with me. She isn't content to be at the same table at the same cafe or restaurant. She longs for words. My words. I have watched these words literally cause her to exceed even the expectations and potential I had seen in her. The Bible correctly says, *"A wholesome tongue is a tree of life!"* ( ) The Bible also says a husband should wash his wife in the water of the word!

In Bible college, we would often joke that the perfect woman doesn't exist and that Proverbs 31 must be an allegory that such a woman could not possibly be a reality. God rebuked that thought and said she was indeed a reality. There is a key in that story I had never seen properly or taken any notice of. He said, *"It's down in verses 28 and 29!"* I sarcastically responded I had never made it that far down because it was too depressing reading about this perfect woman compared to the reality we have to live in! God then again commissioned me, *"READ IT!"* So I did.

> *"Her children rise up and call her blessed; Her husband also, and he praises her: 'Many daughters have done well, But you excel them all.'"*
> *Proverbs 31:28-29*

I was like, "Hang on a minute! This feels like a fairytale. Children don't '*rise up and call their momma blessed' in the real world*, anyway."

Then God showed me the secret sauce. This man had built a culture in his home:

## CHAPTER FIVE: **HUSBAND**

when Momma walks into the room, his children don't speak disrespectfully to her. Instead, they honor her and call her blessed. The *husband does this also*, because *all* leadership is done through *example*. You *lead* by example, always. This husband has set the thermostat setting in his home: "*You bless, honor, and respect your momma at all times!*" Then he goes one step further. It says there in verse 29 that he *"praises"* her!

To appraise something is to "assign value to it" (think of a house appraisal). What you appreciate and value, appreciates in value. Whatever you "appreciate" rises in value. Depreciation means the loss of value. But reread it. He doesn't just *praise* her. He says these words to her, *"Many daughters have done well, but YOU EXCEL THEM ALL!"* (Emphasis added) In other words, "There are many fine, beautiful, and extraordinary women in the world, but Sweetheart, YOU leave them all in the dust!"

No wonder she considers a field and buys it. No wonder she rises early. No wonder she has authority with the elders at the gate. No wonder her voice is one of confidence and strength—a voice that brings life. Her husband has created a greenhouse environment where she cannot help but thrive! I adopted this into my life and have championed it to our amazing pastors and leaders at Awaken church. The proof is in the pudding. Our wives are the most superb, the most extraordinary, the most beautiful, and the most capable women I know of anywhere!

## **GENESIS / ORIGINS**

The word *"husband"* comes from the Old English word "husbandry," which means house-banding—to farm the land, till, cultivate, and cause the land to be fruitful and productive, a manager, frugal, and manage the land.

*"The raising of livestock and the cultivation of crops; agriculture. "The prudent management or conservation of resources. Definition of poor husbandry: "The raising of livestock and the cultivation of crops; agriculture. "The prudent management or conservation of resources."* http://thesaurasize.com > poor+husbandry

A husband is someone who enters into a covenant with a piece of land. Through droughts, flooding rains, pestilence, and other adversities, he tills and cultivates the land to be fruitful and productive.

That is why the word *"husband"* is used for a man who marries a woman. He enters into a covenant with her. He accepts complete responsibility for her. He stays committed

**EMERGE**

through the storms, floods, droughts, and difficulties throughout life's seasons. He remains faithful and devoted to His wife with the goal of cultivating, nurturing, and developing (tilling) her so the seed he plants can cause her to flourish and be productive and fruitful.

> *"Your wife shall be like a fruitful vine In the very heart of your house, Your children like olive plants All around your table."*
> *Psalms 128:3*

The analogy is not lost because it's more than an analogy. It's a reality and truth as far as God is concerned. If a man purchases a piece of land through a contract and purchase agreement, it's because he sees something beautiful and valuable in that piece of land. He sees his future, his prosperity, and his home in that piece of land. It may have cost him everything he owned to purchase it, but he does so willingly. He is now responsible for the land. He is its chief caregiver and caretaker. He protects the land. He loves the land. The more he works the land, the more fruitful it is.

So it is with the husband and his wife.

> *"But from the beginning of the creation, God 'made them male and female.' 'For this reason a man shall leave his father and mother and be joined to his wife, and the two shall become one flesh'; so then they are no longer two, but one flesh. Therefore what God has joined together, let not man separate."*
> *Mark 10:6-9*

## THE HIDDEN TRUTHS IN GENESIS!

The book of Genesis, also known as the book of "beginnings" (Barasheit in Hebrew), is where we get the word "Genes" or "Genetics." It would make sense then to search here for clues as to God's original intention for man, His intention for woman, and the interplay of their unique relationship. The question must be asked: are there embedded clues in the creation story of Genesis we can gather to help us better understand the distinct differences between the sexes and how they complement one another? Would a lack of understanding of these truths explain the conflict many couples struggle with today?

## CHAPTER FIVE: **HUSBAND**

Let's begin in the first chapter of Genesis and see what it reveals to us:

> "Then God said, "Let Us make man in Our image, according to Our likeness; let them have dominion over the fish of the sea, over the birds of the air, and over the cattle, over all the earth and over every creeping thing that creeps on the earth." <u>So God created man in His own image; in the image of God He created him; male and female He created them. Then God blessed them, and God said to them, "Be fruitful and multiply; fill the earth and subdue it; have dominion over the fish of the sea, over the birds of the air, and over every living thing that moves on the earth."</u>
> Genesis 1:26-28

## SEX WAS GOD'S IDEA AND DESIGN.

Long before there was pornography, adult stores, or men like Sigmund Freud, Alfred Kinsey, and Hugh Hefner, sex was a thing. They didn't discover or invent sex; they monetized it for their lusts and gain.

It was God who said to man, *"Be fruitful and multiply,"* and as we have come to know, God *never* commissions or commands us to do something He hasn't equipped and empowered us to execute. If you, like most men, have struggled with looking at "naked babes" and boobies (95% of men struggle in this area, and the other 5% lie), remember this: had God done a *lousy* job in the creation of the female, we wouldn't have any temptation to overcome at all. God did *not* do a lousy job, however, and He designed the female body to perfectly complement the design of the male body. Not only that, but God designed the female form so that man is immediately drawn to and aroused by her. God's original command to be *"fruitful and multiply, filling the earth..."* was to be the most wondrous, joy-filled, pleasurable experience.

The *Devil* is a pervert. He is *not* the designer of sex or pleasure. So many times, the devil is depicted as the author and architect of sexual excitement, thrill, and fulfillment, while God is seen as the *prude in the sky* who didn't really mean for us to enjoy sex, let alone desire it. SMASH THAT LIE! *Before* the fall of man in Genesis Chapter 3, sexual pleasure existed. Sin didn't *"enhance"* it. Sin perverted it. God is the designer of sex, and just like the designer of a car, clock, or watch, the best person to go to for operating instructions is *the Designer* Himself!

# EMERGE

Need some evidence? I got some for you.

While God absolutely designed the man to enjoy sex by reaching orgasm and thus releasing his seed into the woman's womb to create life, God also designed the woman to be able to enjoy sex. When He designed her body, He made not just her womb and vagina but also the clitoris. It's the clitoris that enables the female to enjoy the pleasure of the sexual experience. Now, here's the kicker. Did you know that this most delicate part of the human female *destroys* the entire theory of evolution? How? Because the clitoris is *only* found in the human female. No ape, monkey, whale, mammal, marsupial, or any other animal has one. Only the human female. This destroys the whole "we descended from apes" theory, but more than that, it drives home a very powerful truth.

The animals mate to reproduce and promulgate the survival of their species. They do this purely by instinct. This is *not* the case with mankind. God designed sex to be more than just "mating to reproduce." He created it to serve as a way to enhance the romantic love between a husband and wife, enabling them to pleasure one another, thereby falling more deeply in love and dependent upon each other. It is the most potent and powerful of bonding tools. Human beings were designed to mate for life!

Mate for life? Where's that in the Bible?

I'm glad you asked.

Real quick, the tabernacle of God in Israel had three dimensions—the outer court, the Holy Place, and the Holy of Holies (where *only* one man, selected, consecrated, and prepared, was allowed to go). It was where God dwelt between the cherubim above the mercy seat on the Ark of the Covenant. When you court a woman, you first notice her "outer court"—her physical beauty and features. If all goes well, you get to know her holy place(s)—her heart and soul. This is where you fall in love with her story or personality. One night after church, while I was courting my beautiful Leanne, we spoke for an hour. I was so smitten. She was stunning to behold, so I thought, *"She's probably gonna have a really shallow personality because pretty girls don't need to work on their personality!"* Boy, was I wrong! She was humble, funny, kind, mischievous, bold, and loved life. I was hooked. I wanted to date her and had in mind that one day, *one day*, I would like to marry her!

This is akin to the outer court of the Tabernacle, which was available to both Jews and Gentiles alike. The inner court, the Holy Place, was reserved for the Jewish people

## CHAPTER FIVE: **HUSBAND**

only. There was one other place where *only* one man would be allowed to go from God's "chosen" people, a man who had been selected and consecrated. The "Kohenim" or High Priest would alone be allowed to enter into the "Holy of Holies." To enter here, he would have to *"enter through the veil!"* (Hebrews 10:20)

Sex is the *Act of Marriage!* Marriage is *not* a certificate. It's not a contract. It's not even an event or ritual or ceremony. These are just external expressions of an internal private truth and reality. Nobody "married" Adam and Eve, meaning no one conducted a service or performed a ceremony. There was no ceremony. When Adam took Eve to be his wife, he had sex with her. The two became *one* once again. Eve was now Adam's wife. Marriage is a *covenant!* God is a God of covenants. *All* covenants in the Bible are sealed and established with or through the shedding of blood. When Jesus established the new covenant, He had to do this through the shedding of His blood upon the cross.

What's this got to do with marriage and husbandry?

God made the animals from the ground. Male and female, He created them. When God created Eve, however, He did *not* make her from the ground as He did with Adam. Instead, He put Adam into a deep sleep and took a rib from his side, closing up the flesh. Then God formed what He took from Adam and created the woman, Eve. If animals mate and then move on, God's design was that it would *not* be so with mankind. God pulled the woman from Adam's side so there would be an incompleteness that would *only* be filled when they came together and "became one" once again!

Now, get ready. Another feature in the female reproductive part is the hymen (where we get the word hymn or hymnal). It's a piece of skin that covers the entrance of the vagina—a "veil" of skin the Bible declares is a proof of virginity!

> *"If any man takes a wife, and goes in to her, and detests her, and charges her with shameful conduct, and brings a bad name on her, and says, 'I took this woman, and when I came to her I found she was not a virgin,' then the father and mother of the young woman shall take and bring out the evidence of the young woman's virginity to the elders of the city at the gate. And the young woman's father shall say to the elders, 'I gave my daughter to this man as wife, and he detests her. Now he has charged her with shameful conduct, saying, "I found your daughter was not a virgin," and yet these are the evidences of my daughter's virginity.' And they shall spread the cloth before the elders of the city. Then the elders of that city shall take that*

**83**

# EMERGE

*man and punish him, and they shall fine him one hundred shekels of silver and give them to the father of the young woman because he has brought a bad name on a virgin of Israel. And she shall be his wife; he cannot divorce her all his days. "But if the thing is true, and evidence of virginity is not found for the young woman, then they shall bring out the young woman to the door of her father's house, and the men of her city shall stone her to death with stones, because she has done a disgraceful thing in Israel, to play the harlot in her father's house. So you shall put away the evil from among you."*
Deuteronomy 22:13-21

The evidence was the cloth placed under the bride on her wedding night. As the male Penis penetrated the Vagina, it would pierce the hymen, and blood would be shed over both his organ and hers. Thus establishing the covenant through the "*act of marriage*." Just as the high priest was the only one allowed to enter the most sacred place, the Holy of Holies, the right to enter through the veil of the woman was reserved for *one man*—the husband! He alone would be selected from among all the men in the world to be hers and hers alone. On the wedding night, when the two newlyweds have sex, as he penetrates her, he literally *enters* into the most sacred of places, where only one man, holy, separated, and chosen, is permitted to enter. The Bible says Jesus went through the veil and placed His shed blood upon the mercy seat establishing the new covenant and then sat down at the right hand of God! (Hebrews 6:19,20, Hebrews 9:12)

Neither the hymen nor the clitoris exists in any other mammal or animal because God designed sex to be the most sacred and deepest expression of love possible between a man and his wife. While the animal kingdom mates via instinct and impulse for the propagation and preservation of their species, it's *not so* among mankind. God designed *sex* between man and woman to be bookended by a "covenant" through the breaking of the hymen and mutual pleasure by the "clitoris."

Porneia is the Greek word origin of porn, and it means fornication (or sex) without or outside of covenant. Satan works so hard to defile and destroy something that God has designed to be so pure and so sacred. *Don't let* the spirit of the world hijack the truth about sexuality, virginity, and husbandry!

## THE JUMANJI PORN PULSE

In the 1995 hit Hollywood movie *Jumanji*, Robin Williams plays the character of Allan Parish, a kid who discovers a Victorian-age board game with supernatural powers.

## CHAPTER FIVE: **HUSBAND**

It promises more than just a surface-level board game experience and transports the (then-young) Allan Parish into the wild jungle of Jumanji. There, he is trapped for the next twenty-six years until the game is played again by two orphaned siblings, Judy and Peter Shepherd, who free Allan from being trapped inside the Jumanji jungle.

The movie does a fabulous job of revealing how the game has a power behind it that continually calls out to arouse curiosity. It longs for someone to come and play it so it can trap them. This is *exactly* like pornography. It has a (demonic) power behind it that has a hypnotic, pulsating, alluring drum beat, beckoning someone to come look and connect to it. Pornography wants to be found. I remember, as a ten-year-old kid, we were playing in a junkyard. We were looking for wheels, wood, steel, and other mechanical parts because we were going to make go-karts! While rummaging through the debris, we stumbled upon a bunch of discarded, high-gloss magazines featuring colored pictures of beautiful naked women. I remember the conflict. I knew what I was looking at was wrong and inappropriate, but I couldn't escape the excitement of what was forbidden. These women weren't even blushing at being photographed naked. They were smiling and looked happy to show their most private parts. It was both alluring and confusing at the same time.

That began a struggle and a battle. Like Allan Parish in *Jumanji*, I became caught up in a dangerous jungle that threatened to devour my life.

Pornography has a power, but it is not a *good* power. It is destructive. Pornography is the *number one* cause of impotence. It is demonic, and it is a *liar*! It promises sexual fulfillment but leaves you empty and alone. It promises to give but only takes instead. It robs you of virtue, power, and purity. It promises intimacy but delivers a hollow, meaningless sexual experience. It cloaks itself as something that will bring your sexual experience to new heights but only causes your experience to plummet to the lowest depths. It is the devil's deception. The devil is the great defiler. He perverts, pollutes, and destroys everything sacred God has created. *Kick* him the *hell* out of your mind, heart, marriage, and life!

### HOW DO I GET FREE FROM PORN?

Like all addictions, porn is easy to get into but difficult to leave. Like the words in the song "Hotel California," *"You can check in anytime you like, but you can never leave!"* Porn has a vice-like grip and does not willingly, easily, or readily let anyone go. BUT FREEDOM is very possible and available. The gospel has a *greater* supernatural power within it to deliver, to free, and to transform. This power is what

# EMERGE

the apostle Paul describes in the book of Romans:

> *"For I am not ashamed of the gospel of Christ, for it is the power of God to salvation for everyone who believes, for the Jew first and also for the Greek. For in it the righteousness of God is revealed from faith to faith; as it is written, "The just shall live by faith."*
> Romans 1:16-17

The Gospel releases its power from faith to faith. "Faith comes by hearing and hearing by the word of God!" (Romans 10:17) Being in church and in the Word is vital. Repentance, denouncements, breaking soul ties, casting out the demonic power operating within and behind the addiction, reprogramming the brain, prayer, fasting, and accountability are all powerful tools available to help "deliver" you and bring you to a place of total freedom! If you need to break free from the grip of pornography, this is an excellent pathway to follow:

First, you must desire freedom more than you desire the fleeting thrills that porn offers,

> *"choosing rather to suffer affliction with the people of God than to enjoy the passing pleasures of sin,"*
> Hebrews 11:25

Second, *you must see* porn as the *thief* that it is. It comes to *steal* the beauty and power of your God-ordained, fulfilling, and wonderful sexuality, replacing it with a destructive, shallow, and empty counterfeit. It *uses* your wiring against you. It comes with the most potent form and contours, but don't fall for the *lie*. It knows if it came knocking on your door dressed as it really is, you wouldn't just refuse it at the door; you'd most likely kill it on the spot as the treacherous and vile thief it is!

Third, you must break your soul ties to it. This happens in two ways:

## 1. Repent

Repentance is coming back to God, realigning yourself with Him and His word. Apologize to God and ask for His forgiveness to flow into your heart and life. Most people miss this step. *Remorse,* feeling sorry or bad for your sin, is *not* the same as *repentance*! Remorse has all the similar negative feelings and emotions that precede repentance, but its core philosophy says, "I'm never doing that again. I'm going to stop doing this. I promise I will." The problem with remorse is that it places all the power upon *you* and your human effort/strength to set you free. We can individually get ourselves addicted, but sadly, we cannot individually get ourselves free. We need outside intervention. Human beings are lawbreakers by nature. That's the point of the law coming down with Moses. It was to show us the *law* was insufficient in itself to set us free. It could *only* show us how sinful, helpless, and broken we are.

> *"Therefore submit to God. Resist the devil, and he will flee from you."*
> *James 4:7*

Repentance is re-submitting to God. It then allows God's power and authority to flow through you so you *can* resist the devil and have him *flee* from you! Authority flows through our lives from submission. A U.S. Embassy has all the authority of the U.S. government, even though it exists on foreign soil. Why? Because it is *under* Authority. When we sin, we come out from under God's authority. Repentance is re-submitting and re-aligning our lives to come back under God's authority!

## 2. Renounce

Once you have repented and come back to alignment with God's word, His cleansing power can flow into your life.

> *"If we confess our sins, He is faithful and just to forgive us our sins and to cleanse us from all unrighteousness."*
> *I John 1:9 NKJV*

Sadly, just because *you* have gotten right with God doesn't mean the devil "honors" that precious moment by packing his bags and leaving. He is the architect of dishonor and *must* be *evicted* and driven out. We do this by renouncing the sins and breaking the soul ties attached to them! It's as powerful as it is simple and methodical!

> *"Father, I renounce lusting after pornography in my heart, and in the name of Jesus I break all soul ties that I have formed with _____(name of pornstar). I command it to be broken and to depart from my life in the name of JESUS!"*

We have deliverance available in our Awaken churches and a wonderful recovery

# EMERGE

program equipped to help you in this part of the process!
After you renounce the sin and break the soul ties, destroy access to any remnants of the porn that, just like Jumanji, seek to be found and beckon you to come and play. Destroy them! This is a great start. Freedom is your portion in God!

> *"For it is for FREEDOM that you have been set free!"*
> *Galatians 5:1*

Get into recovery and recover all that the devil has stolen from you!

## OPPOSITES

Adam was created in the wilderness and then placed in the garden. He loves the rugged. He is at home in the wilderness. He has an affinity for the 'wild.' He is tough. He can handle the rough and tumble of this world.

Eve was created in the Garden—the Garden of Eden. It was the Garden of Paradise. Eden means paradise. She likes order. She likes beauty. She likes pretty things. She likes perfumed smells, exotic colors, adventure, fragrances, animals, order, function, clean things. A husband will give his wife a house, but she will give back to him a *home*! Its a magic our wives have. A husband will give his wife groceries; she will convert those groceries into a nutritious and delicious dinner. A husband will give his wife a seed; she will convert that seed into a child. No wonder the Bible says,

> *"Husbands, love your wives, just as Christ also loved the church and gave Himself for her, that He might sanctify and cleanse her with the washing of water by the word"*
> *Ephesians 5:25-26 NKJV*

After the fall of man, God declared that the woman's rebellion and sin would immediately interrupt and affect God's divine order, specifically in her body. She would bring forth children through difficulty and pain. She would have thirteen periods a year, where she would bleed and be unclean for a week each time. Thirteen is the number of rebellions in the Bible. A woman has a cycle. Every month, her body "resets" itself. What does that mean? It means if you told her she was beautiful last month and took her on a date and bought her flowers… that was *last* month!
Do you mean I have to do this every month?
Yep!

## CHAPTER FIVE: **HUSBAND**

For the rest of my life?
Nope.

Only for as long as you want a thriving, happy, and wonderful marriage!

## SUBMISSION ISSUES

Many years ago, in the very early days of our church, I had a young marine ask if we could have coffee. Because of our deep appreciation and love for all those who pull on the uniform (Marine, Army, Navy, Air Force, Coast Guard, Police, Firefighters, etc) who fight for the freedoms we all too often take for granted, I said an emphatic, "Yes! I'd love to!" The church was much smaller back then and in only one location, so it was much easier to coordinate a coffee.

At coffee, this young man said, "Could I ask you for a favor?"

I said, "Sure, what is it?"

He then proceeded to tell me how his wife had left him because he had gotten carried away with the boys a few too many times and had been caught in infidelity. He told me, *"Pastor, I want you to tell her what the Bible says about 'submission' and tell her that she needs to forgive me and come back to me!"*

I immediately went, "Whoa! Hang on there a minute!"

It became clear that his wife was no longer listening to or, in his words, "submitting" to his headship as a husband. He decided to go up the metaphorical authority ladder to the pastor and ask if he would tell her to submit.

As you can imagine, when I began to explain that the only reason he was speaking with me, requesting my intervention, was because he had forfeited his authority through his neglect and betrayal of his marriage vows. He did not want to hear it. He told me he'd find another church where a pastor would believe and enforce what the Bible says! So sad. To this day, I don't know how it went or whether he found a pastor willing to do that for him. Whether she forgave and received him back or they are now separated. All I know is I would never subjugate a woman to a perversion of what the Bible speaks of when it says that wives ought to submit to their husbands!

89

**EMERGE**

> *"Wives, submit to your own husbands, as to the Lord."*
> *Ephesians 5:22*

*Submission* means "to come under"—(sub) a mission. The Bible says women ought to *"submit to their own husbands as to the LORD!"* It's amazing how every man who asked me to help them get their wives to submit didn't want to "behave or act" like The LORD! God has a vision for our lives. His leadership over us is *always* for our benefit, not our harm or demise. He is always faithful. He is gracious, kind, and loving. In other words, He's easy to submit to!

I tell husbands and men everywhere that IF you want your wife to be in SubMission, ask yourself, *"Do I have a MISSION my wife would like to come under?"* In over three decades of marriage, I cannot remember the last time I had to challenge my wife about submission. She knows I have a mission that champions her. One where she sits prominently with her future, looking bright and brilliant. One where she is loved, cherished, esteemed, prosperous, honored, and celebrated. In fact, she has fought alongside me, even picking up the sword and shield and fighting the enemy several times when I was spent and had nothing left in the tank! If you have a "mission" where your bride can see her future, betterment, and development, you will *never* have an issue with submission!

## ISN'T GOD MISOGYNISTIC?

The Bible says the husband is the *head* of the wife (Ephesians 5:23), but what does that mean? Well, it doesn't somehow sanction a dictatorship. Far from it! It does mean the husband, as the head, bears the burden of responsibility for the house, the bills being paid, the well-being and prosperity of the family, and so on. Authority and responsibility are two sides of the same coin. You cannot have one without the other. If you have all the responsibility but no authority, you are an abused slave. If you have all the authority and no responsibility, you are a tyrant. Jesus has been given *"all authority, in heaven and on earth!"* (Matthew 28:18) because Jesus *"Took total responsibility for our sins and transgressions making atonement between heaven and earth, by his suffering and death upon the cross!"*

This concept means that when there's a conflict or disagreement, the *"responsibility bearer"* has the final say because responsibility and authority are two sides of the same coin. The husband is the burden bearer, and the husband is also the burden reliever in the home. When we lived in New Zealand as newlyweds, we had no money. We also had our first two sons born there—with babies came needs. Needs for a bigger

## CHAPTER FIVE: **HUSBAND**

home—food, diapers, cribs, blankets, and post-natal health care. Our church was in an impoverished area, and we never had surplus funds. We literally scratched a living for seven years from hand to mouth. God, however, was with us and promised to provide for us if we stepped out in faith. We bought a miracle home there, against all odds, and then we sold it for a tidy profit to build a beautiful home in a lovely estate.

Both ventures required incredible risk and contained an unbelievable amount of stress. My wife did not want to move forward on several occasions. The stress, pressure, and risk were too great for her. This is where I learned that I *must* let her express her fears, concerns, and thoughts. I *must* let her ask every question (*no* matter how annoying they seemed at the time) and then reassure her I was trusting God. She *saw* that I alone *bore* the burden and the responsibility to look after our family and advance our prosperity. Each and every time, afraid and still somewhat fearful, she would *trust* me and support my decision. Because I bore the responsibility, she realized the authority that must go with it.

## **WISE MEN LISTEN TO AND LEAD THEIR WIVES!**

Many years ago, I read the story of a man who lived in one of the Canadian provinces and was a runner. Weather reports often warn of impending storms and blizzards and instruct the citizenry to remain safe indoors instead of venturing outside. The runner was determined to go for a quick 7-mile run. These warnings often turned out insignificant, passing by as quickly as they arose. He set out. At about mile three, the clouds and fog descended so rapidly that the light snow turned into a blinding blizzard. The temperature plummeted. Visibility all but vanished. The runner decided to try and wait out the storm, doing his best to furrow into a small hill covered in trees, hoping the storm would cease quickly. Instead, the weather worsened. Minutes turned into hours. He was now covered in the falling snow and had to continually try to dig himself out. He was shivering, his clothing inadequate for survival as the darkness of night crept in.

He tried to get up and run, but the almost zero visibility meant he was running blind. As he prayed and begged God to help him, he fell over an embankment and tumbled down into the base of a tree, stopping with a thud. He resigned himself to succumb to the elements, giving in to the inevitable. He would die here. As he lay there, he could hear the whimpering of what sounded like a small dog also caught in the severe elements. Though he couldn't see, he could hear and began to crawl towards the whim-

# EMERGE

pering cries. Finding the terrified, trembling puppy, he drew it close to him, burying it into his chest, and thought to himself, *I'm doomed, but maybe I can save this little guy.*

All night, he worked to keep his newfound companion alive. The next day, rescue workers searching for missing folks who had gone out into the storm found the man and the small dog covered in snow. Both were very much alive and had survived. The rescue workers said that if the man had not worked so hard to save the dog's life, both would have perished. The energy and effort he selflessly put into saving the puppy saved his life!

I tell that story to say I had no idea that *learning* how to *love* my bride, how to be selfless instead of selfish, and how to honor, value, cherish, and look after my bride would actually *save my life!* Most men think marriage is about free sex. That thinking is doomed to a failing relationship because any great transaction's essence is mutual blessing and benefit. If you go into marriage "to get" what you believe you're owed, it's doomed. But, if you go into marriage with the mindset of, "I will be a blessing. I will give. I will make her wishes and dreams come true," you will find a euphoria and bliss that the (self-centered, my rights) world doesn't know!

This attitude disarms selfishness, which is the *cancer* that destroys relationships everywhere, every time!

Learning to love your wife is the greatest challenge that brings the greatest reward and joy! I say "learning" because *men* do *not* understand how to love their wives. They have to learn it. Each wife is different. She will teach you if you let her. She will show you what she loves and what she dislikes. She is a mystery. She is *not* a problem to be solved but a mystery to be pursued. If you think you have figured her out, you have failed. God made her a mystery to keep you in the pursuit and in the hunt. Because men are hunters by nature, we think, "Because she wears my ring on her finger now, the hunt is over. I won the prize. I conquered the mountain." Actually, she didn't marry *you*! She married the *ideal* you set for her when you were courting. Men make promises to women. Women don't marry the man so much as they marry the promise!

## HOW YOU GOT HER IS HOW YOU KEEP HER!

She fell in love with the man who courted her, took her on dates, and told her she was the most beautiful woman of all the women in the land. She married a guy who loved to listen to her and was interested in her stories, life, and dreams. Heck, he was even interested (or at least pretended to be) in the mundane dramas at her work and how

## CHAPTER FIVE: **HUSBAND**

"Susie dyed her hair an obnoxious burgundy, and it is so not her color!"

For a man, this is hard to take. *"You mean I gotta keep this up?"* Yep! But guess what? You will come to see, know, and experience the mysteries hidden by God within her. These treasures do not belong to her lovers or paramours—*only* to her *husband*!

I've been married to my Leanne for thirty-one years; we married when she was seventeen. I am more in love with her today than when we first fell in love. Because of the "let her teach you how to love her" paradigm, I feel like I am only beginning to scratch the surface of the incredible gifts, gold, and treasures God has hidden within her.

*"He who finds a wife finds what is good and receives favor from the Lord."*
*Proverbs 18:22 NIV*

Be a husband. It's the most challenging terrain you will ever encounter in this life, but it brings the greatest reward you could never accomplish as a single man.

*"Marriage is the closest you will get to heaven or hell while you are on this earth!"*
*- Dr Edwin Louis Cole*

## WHEN A MAN LOVES A WOMAN!

In the three-plus decades I have been in ministry, I have discovered that many people who struggle within their marriages do so because they overcomplicate things or have never been taught the *kingdom keys* and truths that lead to quick and easy resolution. It's like they are disoriented and lost in a forest. There is no *exit sign* indicating the way out and no compass pointing true north. Let me show you something simple yet powerful and profound.

Marriage is not a contract or a certificate. It is a covenant, but let me simplify it further. Marriage is not just exchanging vows at an altar before God, family, friends, and loved ones. It's literally... (Ready for it?)

## AN EXCHANGE OF HEARTS!

What does that mean? It means that in marriage, you give your heart, and the care of it, to your spouse. She likewise entrusts you with the same. *You* made a vow and a

## EMERGE

covenant before God to love, care for, and become responsible for another human as though they are you yourself. Selfishness is the cancer and antithesis of this. My responsibility as Leanne's husband is to steward the gift she entrusted to me on our wedding day, namely her heart. What does she love? My job is to make sure she gets that in abundance. What does she dislike? My job is to ensure I seek to eliminate and weed this out every chance I get. What brings her joy? Delight? Happiness? These things have *now become* both my assignment and my responsibility.

When you go into marriage, you *exchange hearts*. She placed hers in your hands, and you placed yours in hers. This understanding changes the entire game. How are you doing on a stewardship level with the most precious gift another human can entrust into your care? Instead of dwelling upon what your spouse *isn't* doing for you, focus instead on being the *best steward* of your spouse's heart. It is the *antidote* to selfishness. It is *the key* to marital bliss!!!

> *"When a man loves a woman*
> *Can't keep his mind on anything else*
> *He'd trade the world*
> *For the good thing he's found*
> *If she is bad, he can't see it*
> *She can do no wrong*
> *And turn his back on his best friend*
> *If he puts her down*
> *When a man loves a woman*
> *Spend his very last dime*
> *And trying to hold on to what he needs*
> *He'd give up all his comforts*
> *And sleep out in the rain*
> *If she said that's the way, it ought to be*
> *When a man loves a woman..."*
> Lewis, Calvin Houston / Wright, Andrew James

There is something so wonderful about a man loving a woman. In theory, it should come innately. Maybe in times past, it did. However, with all the dysfunction and brokenness in the world today, it seems to only come through a man allowing his bride to "teach" him how to love her. The reward of *loving her* right has few, if any, comparisons.

## CHAPTER FIVE: **HUSBAND**
# CHALLENGE

Go to God! Dive into His word. Find and plant yourself into a *life-giving* church! The world tries desperately to make men into "players," treating sex with a woman like it is a sport or recreational activity without ever discovering the mysterious depths and beauty that exist in the devoted, loving pursuit of *one woman* for a lifetime. If their way worked, they wouldn't have to go from one woman to the next and the next and the... you get the idea.

Don't settle for the empty, fleeting, shallow lie of a self-centered, consumer-oriented worldview around sex, love, and relationships. Go with God. Chase the mountain-top experience of marriage by pursuing His utmost for your life! Yes, it is the higher and more challenging road. It may even be "the road less traveled," but it is a magnificent highway that leads to life, fulfillment, and satisfaction! Become God's blueprint *husband*, and then get yourself ready to experience *heaven's best* right here on Earth!

## CHAPTER SIX
# FRIEND

## רבח

*(HEB)*

*"Real friends are those who, when you've made a fool of yourself, don't feel that you've done a permanent job."*
*- Erwin T Randall*

*"A man who has friends must himself be friendly, But there is a friend who sticks closer than a brother."*
*Proverbs 18:24*

*"A friend loves at all times, And a brother is born for adversity."*
*Proverbs 17:17*

*"He who walks with the wise will be wise, but a companion of fools will be destroyed!"*
*Proverbs 13:20*

## CHAPTER SIX: **FRIEND**
# TRUE WEALTH

I have concluded that true wealth is *not* measured by the number of zeros you have after the dollar sign in your bank account, nor is it measured by the number of toys or possessions you own. True wealth is measured in friendships—the number of real "friends" you have. I intentionally put quotation marks around "friends" because many people *think* they know what a friend is but don't. In my three-plus decades of ministry, my work has been predominantly with people. I've had to learn to navigate the intricacies and nuances of difficult relationships, challenging personalities, egos, narcissists, and betrayers, as well as the many conflicts associated with interpersonal networks, navigating relational equities, and setting healthy boundaries to protect what is most sacred to me. I have learned a thing or two.

Firstly, I have learned that *too many* people, and sadly even many pastors and leaders I know, do *not* have a healthy comprehension of genuine friendship. They too easily confuse associates and acquaintances as friends.

A friend *loves* and cares for you at their expense, requiring nothing in return. The connection and relationship are their own reward. Many pastors believe they have "friends," but these relationships are predicated upon a mutual financial transaction where pulpits are shared, honorariums are given, and books are promoted and sold. The basis of the relationship is financial equity. This is *not* a friendship. No matter how "*friendly*" or sentimentally gushy they are with their words and endearments, they will be gone if the relationship *costs* them.

A true friend stands with you; come *hell* or high water. This is the defining, quantifying line. This is the litmus test. This is the demarcation of the real friend from the acquaintance who benefits from you equitably or financially.

Jesus powerfully annunciates this in the gospel of Luke chapter 16,

> *"And I say to you, make friends for yourselves by unrighteous mammon, that when you fail, they may receive you into an everlasting home."*

Jesus teaches us that friendships are the highest use of money (mammon). He didn't say the highest use of friendships is money. Jesus makes it clear when it comes to *friendships;* you *must* understand that it is to *cost* you financially, *not* benefit you per se. Now, that doesn't mean my friends cannot give me sound financial advice or counsel

**EMERGE**

around financial matters. It means they are my friends, irrespective of any financial losses or gains.

Secondly, a "friend" in the biblical, God-ordained sense is someone who loves you for you. Their affection is *not* tied to a benefit or transaction. The reward is the relationship with you. The test for me is, *"Can I be the real me around them, or do I have to put up a front, a pretense, an altered persona?"* A friend is one whom you can be real and honest with, knowing they love you on both your best days and your worst days. We have all been burned by the people we *believed* were our friends, but as soon as it cost them something to be in our corner, they ran for the hills or went zero dark thirty!

If you can only count two or three people in your world who fit this description, *you* are already a rich man. Many people go their entire lives without building any real friendships. They too often find themselves alone, wounded from betrayals, and bitter from disappointments of those who promised to be there but defected in the heat of battle. Many build monuments and financial empires and see women as sexual conquests in a veiled and feeble attempt to numb themselves from the inner ache of having no friends.

"How do I get *real* friends then?" you may ask. Before this chapter closes, I will show you the most powerful, magnetic way to draw *real friends* into your world so your life is rich, powerful, and meaningful.
But first, let's look at the biblical definition of a friend.

## WHAT IS THE BIBLES DEFINITION OF A FRIEND?

What title does Jesus bestow upon His faithful disciples after they served Him for three years through all kinds of storms, highs, lows, rebukes, challenges, miracles, and moments? Jesus gathers them together and then pronounces,

> *"No longer do I call you servants, for a servant does not know what his master is doing; but I have called you friends, for all things that I heard from My Father I have made known to you."*
> *John 15:15*

Jesus doesn't declare that after three years of serving, *"y'all are now champions."* He doesn't declare they are entrepreneurs, CEOs, lion-chasing warriors, innovators, or masters. He pronounces upon them the highest of values. He says, "You are now *friends*!"

## CHAPTER SIX: **FRIEND**

It has often been said, *"Life moves at the speed of relationships!"* Better still, the direction and velocity of your life are determined by the relationships and friendships you keep. Another saying worth quoting is, *"Show me your friends, and I'll tell you your future!"* In other words, your life, the quality of it, your future, and even your destiny are predicated upon this powerful principle of "The *friends* you keep!"

Looking back over my life, I have realized that I made my worst decisions when hanging with a not-so-good circle. I began to make better choices when I started to hang out with better friends. In thirty-plus years of ministry, we have seen that completely freeing someone from addiction to drugs, alcohol, or other vices requires more than just completing rehab, going cold turkey to rid the craving, and getting dependency from their human system. Total freedom only comes when the person *changes their friends!* I have seen people beat an addiction to a substance and dependency *only* to fall straight back into it when they returned to the *same friends* they had while struggling. Sadly, I have also witnessed deadly consequences for those who couldn't change their friendships to align with where they were meant to go.

*"As Iron sharpens Iron, so too does a man sharpen the countenance of his friend!"*
*- Proverbs 27:17*

### YOU'VE GOT A FRIEND

*"When you're down and troubled*
*And you need some lovin' care*
*And nothin', nothin' is goin' right*
*Close your eyes and think of me*
*And soon I will be there*
*To brighten up even your darkest night*
*You just call out my name*
*And you know, wherever I am*
*I'll come runnin'*
*To see you again*
*Winter, spring, summer or fall*
*All you have to do is call*
*And I'll be there*
*You've got a friend"*

*- Carole King, Sony Music*

## EMERGE

The hit children's animated movie *Toy Story*, had a theme song that went like this:

> "You've got a friend in me
> You've got a friend in me
> When the road looks rough ahead
> And you're miles and miles
> From your nice warm bed
> You just remember what your old pal said
> Boy, you've got a friend in me
> Yeah, you've got a friend in me
> You've got a friend in me
> You've got a friend in me
> You got troubles, I've got 'em too
> There isn't anything I wouldn't do for you
> We stick together and see it through
> 'Cause you've got a friend in me
> You've got a friend in me
> Some other folks might be
> A little bit smarter than I am
> Bigger and stronger too
> Maybe
> But none of them will ever love you
> The way I do
> It's me and you, boy
> And as the years go by
> Our friendship will never die
> You're gonna see it's our destiny
> You've got a friend in me
> You've got a friend in me
> You've got a friend in me"

- Randy Newman - Disney Company Music

An entire generation saw the need for friendship and the power that lies within it. My kids grew up on this movie. It had a lasting and indelible impact on their values, especially around friendships. In the movie, Woody is jealous of Buzz Lightyear stealing the affection of Andy, their child owner. He thought Andy would surely replace

## CHAPTER SIX: **FRIEND**

"boring, old" Woody for the Space Ranger, Buzz Lightyear. In the end, they all came together, forgave one another, and deepened their bonds of friendship. It was a powerful movie, underscoring the power and fragility of friendships.

## WE ALL NEED FRIENDS, WHY AREN'T WE BETTER AT IT?

Life without friends is like money without purpose, love without a spouse or family, and sight without vision. *Friendship* takes our lives out of the ports and safe harbors of monotony and into the open seas of laughter, celebration, vision, adventure, and purpose. It is *more* than a clever play on words. *Friendship* is the transport mechanism instituted by God to carry you further than you could ever possibly go by yourself. As the old adage goes (and is worth repeating), *"Show me your friends, and I'll tell you your future!"*

*Friendship* is designed to be a carrier for your life—much like an actual ship. What kind of "ship" is it? At times, it is a cargo ship carrying all kinds of goods from exotic and distant lands. At other times, it is a cruise liner, where you find yourself laughing and celebrating so much you lose track of time and surroundings. At other times, it's a battleship. When you're under attack, you know you have the firepower to protect yourself and win the battle.

*Bear: What happened to you?*
*Matt Johnson: I got into a fight, caused a wreck, and my friends left me.*
*Bear: That's no way for friends to act!*
*Matt Johnson: I was wrong!*
*Bear: So what? That's when you need a friend. When you're right, you don't need anything!*
- the movie *Big Wednesday*

At other times, friendship is a "mercy ship," bringing medical relief when we are infirm and fighting disease or illnesses. The wealthiest person in the world is not the one who has the most money. It is the person who has the greatest friendships. Friendship is so powerful that the Bible teaches that it has a multiplying effect. It says, *"One shall set flight to a thousand, and two to ten thousand!"*

And the book of Ecclesiastes says,

*"Two are better than one, Because they have a good reward for their labor. For if they fall, one will lift up his companion. But woe to him who is alone when he falls, For he has no one to help him up. Again, if two lie down to-*

## EMERGE

*gether, they will keep warm; But how can one be warm alone? Though one may be overpowered by another, two can withstand him. And a threefold cord is not quickly broken."*
*Ecclesiastes 4:9-12*

## TOLKIEN CAPTURED A GLIMPSE

One of my favorite scenes from *The Lord of the Rings* trilogy is when Samwise Gamgee decides to re-ascend the mountain he has just descended after being falsely accused, maligned, and mistreated by his childhood friend, Mr. Frodo! Frodo, who carries the one ring to rule all rings, carries an even greater burden—the daily battle to resist the ring's persistent calls and tempting offers of power and global domination. Frodo's judgment at this time is as fractured as he is emotionally frazzled. He's barely able to sleep, is under constant attack from Sauron's armies, is exhausted from the journey to Mordor, and has limited food and water supplies. To top it all off, he's led by Mr. Shmeagal, a deeply troubled guide with a broken soul. Under all this stressful duress, Frodo accuses the one closest to him, Samwise, of acting improperly.

It's a scene that plays out all too often in our very own lives. We reserve the harshest criticism and judgments for those closest to us. Perhaps it's because we think our friends will be the most likely to have grace and forgive us, or perhaps we subconsciously believe we have enough collateral deposited in our relational bank account to afford such a large withdrawal. I don't know exactly, but I do know that, as human beings, we seem to be harshest with those closest to us.

It's not long after Samwise Gamgee's banishment from accompanying Mr. Frodo that the true nature of Mr. Shmeagal emerges. He wants the ring and has made a pact with Shelob, a giant tarantula-like spider who lives in the mountainous caves and craves the sweet meat-flesh of a Hobbit promised her by Shmeagal. In the movie, Shelob climbs stealthily along the cave's ceiling, avoiding detection by Mr. Frodo until it's too late. In one seemingly fatal blow, her poisonous fang pierces Mr. Frodo's abdomen, paralyzing him. She coils him in her spinning web to be deliciously eaten later. At that time, Samwise Gamgee arrives at the crevasse where Shelob stands over her prize. Sam, in an act of Herculean heroism, pulls out his "orc fighting" sword and battles the giant spider. Against all odds, he wounds her so potently she shrieks back into her cave recess.

Sam's heroism shows the true nature of what it means to be a *friend*.

## CHAPTER SIX: FRIEND

*"A friend loves at all times..."*

Sam was Frodo's friend, despite Frodo's poor judgment and emotional outbursts toward Sam. Judas Iscariot made a deal with the Roman soldiers and the religious priests, saying, *"The one whom I kiss, that's Jesus!"* Jesus was in the garden of Gethsemane with the disciples when Judas approached Him with an affectionate greeting (*"Rabbi"* meaning teacher) and then kissed Jesus on the cheek with a feigned act of endearment. Jesus looks into Judas' eyes and asks, *"Judas, do you betray the Son of Man with a kiss? Friend, do what you have come to do!"*

Judas was *not* behaving like a friend.

Yet Jesus never stopped being a friend to Judas. True friendship is a quality of the heart and character of the person being the friend. It's not based on circumstantial convenience or the beneficiary's performance. True friendship endures the severest of "winter seasons" in relationships. Can you continue to love, believe in, and forgive someone who has wounded you, misunderstood you, or mislabeled you? Sam is the quintessential definition of a true friend! May the God of Heaven bring you at least one Sam in your lifetime. You will reach and fulfill your divine purpose much easier when you have a Sam as your friend. I pray you don't just receive a "Sam" in your life; I pray you will *be* a "Sam" to someone in your life!

Back to the movie. No sooner has Sam defeated Shelob than he discovers fierce warrior Orcs have stolen Frodo's body, believing they would serve their master, Sauron, faithfully by bringing him the ring directly from Frodo, the ring bearer. Sam then takes on the garrison of Orcs twice his size by himself, defeating them in a slaughter of biblical proportions. He cuts open the webbing, entombing his friend, unsure whether Frodo is alive or dead. As Frodo opens his eyes, love and remorse fill his heart. He cries, *"Oh, Sam, it's you! I'm so sorry, Sam; I shouldn't have doubted you. I'm so sorry! But the ring... I've lost the ring... the Orcs have taken it. They are bringing it to Sauron. I've failed..."* Just then, Sam puts his hand into his pocket. When he retrieves his hand, he opens it to reveal the ring. He then hands it back to Frodo, saying, *"Oh, Mr. Frodo, I may not be able to carry the ring, but I can certainly carry you!"*

This is real, true *friendship* as defined by the scriptures. Sadly, this friendship is almost non-existent in the world. Satan knows that men with this kind of friendship reach the fires of Mordor to destroy the one ring that rules all rings, fulfilling their mission and God-given purpose for their lives! Satan perverts and distorts this kind of friendship with homosexuality or the accusation that this kind of friendship is "gay" or weak. The pervasiveness of our "faithless and perverse" generation has rendered this type of friendship almost extinction.

## DAVID AND JONATHAN

*"Now when he had finished speaking to Saul, the soul of Jonathan was knit to the soul of David, and Jonathan loved him as his own soul."*
*I Samuel 18:1*

The scripture above says, "Jonathan loved David as his own soul." Later, after Jonathan's tragic death, David reflects on his friendship with Jonathan and declares that this friendship surpassed the love of women.

*"I am distressed for you, my brother Jonathan; You have been very pleasant to me; Your love to me was wonderful, Surpassing the love of women."*
*II Samuel 1:26*

The homosexual community has long tried to manipulate and hijack this story to justify their own perversion and sin. David's reflection on his relationship with Jonathan, surpassing that of women, was the exact opposite of sexual, which was pretty much the depth of David's relationship with his wives. They bore David his sons, his heirs, and his posterity. Jonathan, on the other hand, was a fellow warrior. As David's armor-bearer, he often went into battle with David and saved David's life on more than one occasion.

David confided in Jonathan. There was an immense amount of pressure and stress around David's life. He carried the anointing to sit on the throne possessed by another man, who was neither excited nor willing for David's God-ordained purpose to come to pass. David had to flee for refuge to the region of En Gedi and dwell in the caves of Adullum. Meanwhile, Saul (who was Jonathan's father) regularly dispatched up to three thousand assassins to eliminate the life of the "would-be" successor to his throne. David had done nothing wrong and had to live like a fugitive in a foreign and harsh land.

However, there was one friend who assured him repeatedly that God's will would be done—Johnathan. Jonathan would often speak with David about the future, declar-

## CHAPTER SIX: **FRIEND**

ing to David that not only would he most certainly be King of Israel but that Johnathan would be beside him as his first servant, loyal friend, and chief armor bearer.

David had many wives.

David did *not* have many friends like Jonathan. In fact, after Jonathan's death at the hands of the Philistines, David never had another friendship like the one he had with Jonathan. Jonathan was the muse for J R R Tolkien's Sam Wise Gamgee! When Sam declared that *he couldn't carry the ring, but he could certainly carry Frodo*, it was based upon the fact that Jonathan knew the throne of Israel was *not* his burden to carry, and Jonathan knew he could "carry" David to fulfill the God destiny for his life.

*"To the pure, all things are pure, but to the perverted, all things become perverted!"*

Don't let the spirit of perversion in this world *rob* you from being a Sam (or Jonathan) or keep you from having one in your life. To say that David had a homosexual relationship with Jonathan would be to say that David was wicked before the LORD because God had emphatically condemned homosexuality as an abomination in the Old Testament.

> *"If a man lies with a male as he lies with a woman, both of them have committed an abomination. They shall surely be put to death. Their blood shall be upon them."*
> *Leviticus 20:13*

The Bible declares that David was a man after God's own heart. After David's sexual sin with Bathsheba in his palace bedroom, God brings David's sin from the secret place into the light, exposing this egregious sin and forcing David to have to publicly deal with it. God is Holy. If David had committed an abomination, don't believe for one minute that God would have overlooked it or justified it with the satanic mantra *"love is love!"* God cannot and does not bless perversion. If He did, He wouldn't be HOLY!

GOD is LOVE. Not "love" is love.

> *"Love suffers long and is kind; love does not envy; love does not parade itself, is not puffed up; does not behave rudely, <u>does not seek its own, is not provoked, thinks no evil; does not rejoice in iniquity, but rejoices in the truth;</u>"*
> *I Corinthians 13:4-6*

**EMERGE**

God is love. God thinks no evil. God does not rejoice in iniquity (think Pride marches) but rejoices in the *truth*!

## FAITHFUL ARE THE WOUNDS OF A FRIEND

*"The wounds of a friend are faithful, but the kisses of an enemy are deceitful!"*

To experience the true heights and depths of *friendship*, you must create room for wounding. As the Bible says, *"Faithful are the wounds of a friend!"* After Jonathan's tragic departure, David longed to replace Jonathan's role and presence in his life. He drew comfort from men who heard the word of the LORD—prophetic, insightful, God-sensitive men. David was the King of Israel. There was nobody higher than him in all the land of Israel, *yet* David surrounded himself and his throne with men who heard from God—men like Nathaniel the prophet who brought a stinging rebuke to David when he sinned with Bathsheba and had her husband, one of David's most loyal and mightiest warriors, murdered to cover his sin.

*"Then the Lord sent Nathan to David. And he came to him, and said to him: "There were two men in one city, one rich and the other poor. The rich man had exceedingly many flocks and herds. But the poor man had nothing, except one little ewe lamb which he had bought and nourished; and it grew up together with him and with his children. It ate of his own food and drank from his own cup and lay in his bosom; and it was like a daughter to him. And a traveler came to the rich man, who refused to take from his own flock and from his own herd to prepare one for the wayfaring man who had come to him; but he took the poor man's lamb and prepared it for the man who had come to him." So David's anger was greatly aroused against the man, and he said to Nathan, "As the Lord lives, the man who has done this shall surely die! And he shall restore fourfold for the lamb, because he did this thing and because he had no pity." Then Nathan said to David, "You are the man! Thus says the Lord God of Israel: 'I anointed you king over Israel, and I delivered you from the hand of Saul. I gave you your master's house and your master's wives into your keeping, and gave you the house of Israel and Judah. And if that had been too little, I also would have given you much more! Why have you despised the commandment*

## CHAPTER SIX: **FRIEND**

*of the Lord, to do evil in His sight? You have killed Uriah the Hittite with the sword; you have taken his wife to be your wife, and have killed him with the sword of the people of Ammon. Now therefore, the sword shall never depart from your house, because you have despised Me, and have taken the wife of Uriah the Hittite to be your wife.' Thus says the Lord: 'Behold, I will raise up adversity against you from your own house; and I will take your wives before your eyes and give them to your neighbor, and he shall lie with your wives in the sight of this sun. For you did it secretly, but I will do this thing before all Israel, before the sun.'" So David said to Nathan, "I have sinned against the Lord." And Nathan said to David, "The Lord also has put away your sin; you shall not die. However, because by this deed you have given great occasion to the enemies of the Lord to blaspheme, the child also who is born to you shall surely die." Then Nathan departed to his house. And the Lord struck the child that Uriah's wife bore to David, and it became ill."*
*II Samuel 12:1-15*

David received a word from a man he could have so easily executed. How dare he accuse the king of wrongdoing? How easily David could have set up a corrupt dictatorship, as we see throughout history and today. But NO! David feared the God who elevated him from the forgotten sheepfolds and exalted him to the heights of fame and honor. This forgotten, rejected shepherd boy became the slayer of the Giant Champion of Gath, Goliath, and was crowned King not only of his tribe, Judah but also over all the other eleven tribes of Israel. David knew his proclivities and surrounded himself and his throne with men who heard from God, who could speak into his life and even have the liberty to bring a rebuke without fear of losing their heads. Every other kingdom of this world, in contrast, is filled with people who are sycophants, receiving rewards by pretending the "emperor's new clothes" are splendid so they can keep their lives, privileges, and positions. No, not David. He set it up so men who heard from God could speak a rebuke into his life!

*"Let the righteous strike me; It shall be a kindness. And let him rebuke me; It shall be as excellent oil; Let my head not refuse it."*
*Psalm 141:5 NKJV*

## EMERGE
# LESSON FROM THE LION KING

The hit animated Disney movie The Lion King follows the journey of a young lion cub named Simba from cub to king. The journey is a perilous one. Conspiracy, murder, treason, deception, lies, and wickedness all gather against Mufassa's young, naively optimistic son, who, against all odds, eventually becomes king over the pride lands.

*None* of this would have been possible without the intervention of a certain "priestly" baboon named Rafiki!

"Rafiki" is Swahili for *"friend."*

Rafiki is the friend who carries a stick. With this stick, he knocks some sense into Simba, who is the captain of the greatest pity party of his life, keeping him from his potential and destiny! Simba, upon hearing from Rafiki that *"Mufassa is not dead. No, he lives. Come, I show you!"* follows the gallivanting, speedy, little baboon on a chase under tree boughs, over creeks, and through rugged terrain to finally arrive at a river brook. Upon arrival, Rafiki tells Simba, *"Look, der e is. Der e is!"* Simba gazes over the embankment into the brook, where he sees what appears to be Mufassa staring back at him. His eyes grow big, and tears begin to well when, all of a sudden, the water shimmers, and Simba realizes it's *not* Mufassa. It's just his own reflection.

Simba lifts his voice in angry lament, *"You said you'd never leave me. You said you'd always be here for me!"* The clouds begin to swirl above Simba's head, and his Heavenly Father speaks, *"Simba, you are my son, but you've forgotten who you are. You are my son. Remember... remember who you are!"* It's at this moment that *everything* changes! Simba is awoken out of his identity crisis and out of his despair and shame. The chains of the burden of guilt around his father's death that he had been carrying since his childhood snapped like twigs under the feet of stampeding elephants. It was like he was "born again!" Courage and justice pulsated through his being, and he knew what he needed to do—face his evil uncle Scar, drive out and banish the hyenas from the pride land, and restore order to the kingdom—which he does in heroic fashion. (It's a must-watch. I don't want to spoil it further if you haven't seen it yet!)

Rafiki, as his name means, really is a true *friend*!
He is there at Simba's birth and dedication.
He is there as Simba grows into a young cub.
He never gave up on the promises of God concerning Simba's life and destiny.

## CHAPTER SIX: **FRIEND**

He was a prophetic seer. He saw that Mufassa's seed was *not* wiped out. He knew a glimmer of hope remained in the midst of the hopelessness and despair from Scar's subversion of Mufassa's throne into that of an illegitimate and corrupt government.

It was Rafiki's challenge to Simba that the pain of the past did not remove him from the obligation of fulfilling his divine assignment or excuse him as he sabotaged his future, which got Simba to move past his pain into his destiny. Rafiki takes his stick and hits Simba over the head.

*"Ouch! What did you do that for?"* bemoaned Simba.

*"It does not matter. It's in De Past!"* Rafiki brilliantly retorted, *"De past can't hurt you!"* he added.

*"It sure feels like it!"* responded Simba, still rubbing his head from the blow of the stick.

The point landed.

How long would Simba allow the pain of his past to rob him of his divine destiny and powerful future? How long would he remain a victim of things he could not change but were still keeping him paralyzed from creating a different future?

We all need a Rafiki in our lives—a friend with a stick who's not afraid to use it, not because they are given to violence, but because they see something greater inside us that we are sabotaging and omitting.
Do you have a Rafiki in your life?

Rafiki sees the father in the son and the son in the father. *This* is what makes him such a powerful *friend* in the story.

> *"At that day you will know that I am in My Father, and you are in Me, and I am in you."*
> *- John 14:20*

Rafikis cause us to make better choices, to face the pain of our past, and to live without excuses and beyond regrets. They champion what God has placed inside of us and call it out of us. Rafiki is the friend of your potential, your destiny, and your greatness!

## EMERGE

If you don't *have* a Rafiki, then *be* a Rafiki. You cannot reap what you don't sow. If you *sow* Rafiki, you will reap one! It's a law of the universe that cannot be broken! In Eastern mysticism, they call it "karma." Down under, they say, *"What goes around comes around!"* The Bible beats them all by thousands of years, calling it the law of *"Sowing and Reaping!"*

## HOW DO I GET REAL FRIENDS?

Ah, now we arrive at the question driving this chapter. How do I attract or cultivate friends like the ones described in this chapter? It's very simple. The Bible teaches a *powerful* law/principle that is *in motion* (in play perpetually) in the universe. It's the Law of Reciprocity. Some call it *"sowing and reaping,"* in Eastern mysticisms, they call it Karma; in the West, we have a crude saying, *"What goes around comes around!"* The Bible says this:

> *"While the earth remains, Seedtime and harvest, Cold and heat, Winter and summer, And day and night Shall not cease."*

> *"Do not be deceived, God is not mocked; for whatever a man sows, that he will also reap."*

Did you see that? Do you know what this means? It means that *whatever* you want in life, you must first *become* that yourself! If you want a real and true friend, you must first become a real and true friend. A man *cannot* reap what he has not sown. You cannot expect a harvest from a field you have not sown into. Imagine driving through the countryside and stopping at a roadside diner for lunch. You notice some big, old Ford F100 pickup trucks in the parking lot. As you sit at the counter, the gentleman next to you starts to complain that his fields have not produced any crops. In a moment of compassion, you ask, "What kind of seed did you sow?" The farmer then looks at you and, with a puzzled expression, replies, *"Seed? I didn't sow any seed?"*

You cannot reap what you haven't sown! *Become* the very thing you want to reap. I know men who are "believing" for a wife. They even have precise and detailed checklists they call "faith goals!" However, the Bible says, *"he who finds a wife finds a good thing..."* Notice it doesn't say he who finds a smoking hot babe or a girlfriend. It says "*he who finds a wife,*" meaning that *you* must already be operating as a "husband!" If you *want* real *friends*, you must *first* become a real friend.

## CHAPTER SIX: **FRIEND**
## COMRADES, CONSTITUENTS, AND CONFIDANTS.

People in our lives fit into three categories: Comrades, Constituents, and Confidants.

A comrade is someone who stands against what you're against. They are in the trenches with you because of an alignment of vision, mission, and objective. They feel like they are your friends, but they are not. They are "with you" so long as you are on a mission and on their side. Should you depart from the mission or question sides, they will be gone quicker than a bride's nightie on her wedding night!

A constituent is someone who is *for* what you are for. They work alongside you and attend your BBQs, dinners, and lunch meetings. They may even vacation with you. Their alignment is also missional and assignment-based. They are with you because it's good for them. It's advantageous to them. They are *not* bad people. They are not wrong or shallow; they are just not your friends. Don't beat yourself up if you confuse them as being your friends. It is very easy to believe they are, but they are not. Should they no longer benefit from the alignment, you will feel immediate distance. They may even continue to be friendly to you, but they are not a friend. They were always just a constituent.

A confidant is with you for *you*! They deeply care about *you*. They are for you, even at their own expense. They fight you to pick up the check when you go out to eat or go for coffee. These are the people who refuel you. They recharge you. They don't drain you emotionally, financially, or spiritually. These are your real friends; if you have one of these confidants, you're a blessed man. If you have a few of them, you're wealthy! A confidant will take the things you share and divulge with them to the grave. They are there for you, whether it be your darkest secrets, innermost struggles, or personal regrets and transgressions. They provide safety. They create cover and provide a refuge for you to be real. You don't have to perform, and you don't have to pay them for executing the duties of a therapist because they are a confidant. They are your friend.

Incidentally, the word for "therapist" comes from the Greek word "*Therapeuo*," which literally means *"one who walks alongside of."* It also means *"to heal, to cure, to relieve."*

We live in an age where a lot of people *require* therapists because they *lack* "Therapeuo"—one who walks alongside them, healing, relieving, and helping them.

Ask God to "make" you a friend. Don't just ask Him to "give" you one.

**EMERGE**

# "GIVE ME" VS. "MAKE ME"

*"A man who has friends must himself be friendly,
but there is a friend who sticks closer than a brother!"*
*- Proverbs 18:24*

One of the most powerful principles in the Bible is found in the book of Luke in the story of the prodigal son. The story tells of a father who has two sons. The younger of the two decides he doesn't want to be part of the family anymore, but he wants the inheritance (of being in the family) due to him at that moment. The younger son petitions his father, "*Give me* the inheritance that is due to me, *now*!"

The father, representing God, was benevolent and gave the younger son his inheritance early.
The son goes off on a Vegas-style spring break lifestyle—partying it up with all his newfound wealth and the friends who are attracted to other people paying for their good time and indulgences. *But,* when you carry a spirit of "GIVE ME," you are a consumer, not a contributor. Your world will shrink, getting smaller and smaller. In the story, the money runs out, and so too do his friends. He ends up getting a job feeding swine. Jesus, telling this story to a Jewish audience, was both provocative and emotionally charged. Pig feeding was anathema to a Jewish person. Pigs represented the heathen, the Gentiles, and the ungodly nations around them.

"GIVE ME" has this younger son starving and feeding that which is unclean in his life, always hungry for more but never satisfied. This is the *destiny* of all who carry a "GIVE ME" spirit.

Everything changes when the younger son comes to his senses and realizes that in his father's house, even the servants have bread enough to spare, and here he is, perishing with hunger. He says, "I know what I will do. I will return to my father's house and I will say to him, *'Father, I am no longer worthy to be your son, please MAKE ME like one of your hired servants!' (Luke 15:19)* At this precise moment, everything shifts in this young man's life. His world *increases.* What was squandered, lost, and wasted is now restored.

I say all this to say to you that coveting in the Bible is a "GIVE ME" spirit. Humility in the Bible is a "MAKE ME" spirit. God gives grace to the humble but resists the

## CHAPTER SIX: **FRIEND**

proud! (James 4:6-7) Right now, you may be tempted to say "GIVE ME" a Rafiki, a Jonathan, a Samwise Gamgee, but if you will change your prayer to "God, *make me,*" what you long for will come to you! Your life will enlarge.

> *"God is NOT mocked, whatever a man sows that he shall also reap!"*
> *-Galatians 6:7*

Here's an Aesop fable that describes this law.

### The Ant and The Dove
Once, an ant was drinking water at the bank of a river. Suddenly, a huge wave laughed at him, and he fell into the water. The tiny ant could not swim against the strong current and reach the shore. A dove saw a tree near the riverbank and saw the ant struggling in the water. The dove plucked a leaf from the tree, flew over to where the ant was, and threw the leaf into the water. The ant climbed onto the leaf and floated safely to the riverbank. Shortly afterward, a bird catcher came to catch birds at the river. He laid out a net and started spreading twigs and grains on the net. The ant watched the bird catcher and understood his intentions. He crawled up to the bird catcher and stung him on the foot. The bird-catcher cried out loudly in pain. The dove heard his cry and flew away to safety.

## ONE OF MY FAVORITE STORIES OF WHAT A FRIEND IS!

### Beethoven's Gift
A story is told about Beethoven, a man not known for social grace. Because of his deafness, he found conversation difficult and humiliating. When he heard of the death of a friend's son, Beethoven hurried to the house, overcome with grief. He had no words of comfort to offer. But he saw a piano in the room. For the next half hour, he played the piano, pouring out his emotions in the most eloquent way he could. When he finished playing, he left. The friend later remarked that no one else's visit had meant so much.
*- Philip Yancey*

A story that absolutely haunts me is the one I'm about to present. *Nothing* ruins a friendship faster than self-centeredness, greed, and covetousness. As you read this story below, allow the Holy Spirit to do a deep dive heart check to see if any of these qualities are in you. If they are, give Him permission to root them out!

# EMERGE
## The Window

Two seriously ill men shared the same room in a hospital. The room housed only the two of them and had only one window. One of the men, as part of his treatment, was allowed to sit up in bed for an hour in the afternoon (something to do with draining the liquid from his lungs). His bed was next to the window. The other man had to spend all his time flat on his back.

Every afternoon, when the man looked out the window, he would pass the time by describing what he could see outside. He described ducks and swans in a lake in which little children would come to throw bread and sail model boats. Young lovers walked hand in hand beneath the trees, and there were flowers, stretches of grass, and games of softball. And at the back, behind the fringe of trees, was a fine view of the city skyline. The man on his back would listen to the other man describe all of this, enjoying every minute. He heard how a child nearly fell into the lake and how beautiful the girls were in their summer dresses. His friend's descriptions eventually made him feel he could almost see what was happening outside.

Then, one fine afternoon, the thought struck him: Why should the man next to the window have all the pleasure of seeing what was happening? Why shouldn't he get the chance? While he felt ashamed, the more he thought of it, the worse he wanted to change places with his friend. He'd do anything! One night, the chance came. He was woken up by the coughing and spluttering sound of the man next to the window drowning in the liquid in his lungs. Try as he might, the man near the window could not reach the button that would rouse the nurses. Rather than do anything, the other man just watched, pretending he was asleep and could not hear his gargled pleas for help—even when the sound of breathing stopped. In the morning, the nurses found the man dead and quietly took his body away. Shortly afterward, the man asked if he could be switched to the bed next to the window. So they moved him, tucked him in, and made him comfortable. The minute they left, he laboriously propped himself up on one elbow painfully and looked out the window.

It faced a blank brick wall.

*Author Unknown,*
*Submitted by Ronald Dahlsten and Harriette Lindsey*

DON'T BE THAT FRIEND!

# CHAPTER SEVEN
# KING

## דלמ

MELECH

*"A male ruler of a nation or state usually called a kingdom; male sovereign, limited or absolute; monarch."*
*- Webster's New World Dictionary.*

*"A male monarch of a major territorial unit especially: one whose position is hereditary and who rules for life."*
*- Merriam Webster's dictionary.*

*"Power makes you a monarch, and all the fancy robes in the world will not do the job without it!"*
*- Laurell K Hamilton*

**EMERGE**

> *"I am indeed a king, for I know how to rule myself!"*
> *- Pietro Aretino*

> *"In the kingdom of the blind, the one-eyed man is king."*
> *- Desiderius Erasmus*

> *"There is no king who has not had a slave among his ancestors, and no slave who has not had a king among his."*
> *- Helen Keller*

> *"He who reigns within himself and rules passions, desires, and fears is more than a king."*
> *- John Milton*

## WHAT DOES IT MEAN TO BE A KING?

> *"And it came to pass in those days that there was no king in the land..."*
> *- Judges 19:1*

Kings are hereditary. Their authority comes down from their father. They are not elected democratically. They are a king because they were born into a royal family! *You*, as a born-again believer, are now born into a royal family. You are a son of the King. God anointed and appointed you to *operate* in authority, *govern* a territory, and *rule* a jurisdiction.

What does it mean for a man to be a King? What does it entail? Few monarchies remain in the world today, so it's difficult to point to examples and healthy sources. Many of the few remaining kings are powerless figureheads, stripped of any real authority. They are more of an ornament or decoration than a display of a *monarch* operating in full power!

Given all that, you might ask, "So why even write this chapter?"

We have all heard the term, "*A man is the king of his castle!*" In his home, however small it may be, he is indeed the king. It is the place where "*his authority*" is final, and thereby, he enjoys at least a glimpse of what it means to be a monarch! A king is a man who reigns and rules over a kingdom, a region, or a territory. It is the place where his rule is final, where there is no authority above his (except God, from whom all authority is derived).

# CHAPTER SEVEN: KING

God made man sovereign.

It's a controversial statement, I know. That's why it has its own line. The most powerful will in the universe is *yours*, not God's. Why? Because God ordained it so that *your will* can shut down His will in your life. That was the price God was willing to pay for you and me to have *free will*. We don't worship God as pre-programmed automatons. We have to freely, willingly choose Him. We have to choose to *love* Him and choose to serve Him. God respects and honors the authority structure He has set in place. God will never *force* His will upon you (He does have some wonderful powers of persuasion though, just ask Jonah). You have to accept His will. In fact, a better way to say it would be that God has ordained that His will can *only* be done in your life when it becomes *your* will! We see this modeled so well in the scriptures by our Savior: *"Not my will, but thy will be done!"* says Jesus, the son of God, in the Garden of Gethsemane.

For God's will to find its home in your life, you must *choose* to make *His will your will*! That's how incredible God is. *You* have been given self-autonomy and sovereignty over your decisions and choices in this life. In fact, to be honest, your life is a direct product of your choices! God does *not* stop the consequences of our bad decisions. He gave us the Torah, (The first five books of the Bible which contain The Law, and the Ten Commandments) so that we can *"Choose this day whom we will serve, blessing or cursing, life or death!"*

> *"But as for me and my house, we will serve the LORD!"*
> *- Joshua 24:15*

The question isn't *"Am I a King?"* The question is, *"What Kind of a King am I?"* The Bible teaches that there is a day called Judgement Day. It's a day when we have to give an account of how we lived on Earth. How can there be a judgment day if we are not self-autonomous? If we had no free will and *only* did what we were pre-programmed to do, how could a righteous judge render any judgment? That's like feeding your child gummy bears while they sleep and then punishing them when they wake up for eating the gummy bears. That is wicked. That is unjust. God is *not* unjust!
With *all* authority comes the incredible weight of responsibility.

It's like young Simba in the movie *The Lion King* when he discovers there's a lot more to being king than unbridled privilege, fun, and perks. Simba is sitting with his father, Mufasa, overlooking all of the pride lands from Pride Rock. Mufasa explains to Simba, a very young lion cub, that one day, the sun will indeed set on his time as king, but that same sun will

## EMERGE

rise on Simba's time and season. His father tells Simba that he would govern everything he sees, but it would require great care and extreme responsibility, to which a puzzled Simba inquires, *"But I thought a King can do whatever he wants?"* His father, the king, responds, *"Oh, there's more to being king than just getting your way all of the time!"* An immature Simba responds optimistically, *"There's more??"* Immaturity *loves* the privileges and perks of being a king, but maturity recognizes that *"with great power comes great responsibility!"* (To quote Peter Parker's uncle in the Spider-Man movie!) Many men lust, covet, and desire the *power* and privilege that come with absolute authority (think of every corrupt politician in the world), but you cannot make a coin one-sided. The two sides of being king are authority *and* responsibility!

## THE SWORD OF DAMOCLES

*Cicero, A Roman Philosopher, and Proconsul, wrote the famed "Sword of Damocles" dating back to his 45 B.C. book "Tusculan Disputations." Cicero's story centers on Dionysius II, a tyrannical king who once ruled over the Sicilian city of 'Syracuse' during the fourth and fifth centuries B.C. Though rich and powerful, Dionysius was supremely unhappy. His iron-fisted rule had made him many enemies, and he was daily tormented by fears of assassination—so much so that he slept in a bedchamber surrounded by a moat and only trusted his daughters to shave his beard with a razor.*

*As Cicero tells it, the king's dissatisfaction came to a head one day after a court flatterer named Damocles showered him with compliments and remarked how blissful his life must be. "Since this life delights you," an annoyed Dionysius replied, "do you wish to taste it for yourself and make a trial of my good fortune?" When Damocles enthusiastically agreed, Dionysius seated him on a golden couch and ordered a host of beautiful servants to wait on him. He was treated to succulent cuts of meat and lavished with scented perfumes and ointments. Damocles couldn't believe his luck, but just as he was starting to enjoy the life of a king, he noticed that Dionysius had also hung a razor-sharp sword from the ceiling. It was positioned over Damocles' head, suspended only by a single strand of horsehair. From then on, the courtier's fear for his life made it impossible for him to savor the opulence of the feast or enjoy the servants. After casting several nervous glances at the blade dangling above him, he asked to be excused, saying he no longer wished to be so fortunate.* https://www.history.com/news/what-was-the-sword-of-damocles

## HEAVY IS THE HEAD THAT WEARS THE CROWN

Marcus Tullius Cicero (a Roman statesman, philosopher, scholar, lawyer, and member of the Roman Pro-Consul) used the tale of Dionysius and Damocles to present the idea that "leadership" and authority are not to be viewed through the lens of "privilege, power, and perks" alone. Leadership comes with a price. The "sword of

## CHAPTER SEVEN: KING

Damocles" story has become associated with sobriety around the fleeting reality of leadership perks in the face of daily, persistent pressure!

Likewise, the saying "hanging by a thread" has become the cautionary catchphrase of impending fragility and uncertainty in life and leadership! In 1961, during the Cold War, President John F. Kennedy gave a speech before the United Nations in which he said, *"Every man, woman, and child lives under a nuclear sword of Damocles, hanging by the slenderest of threads, capable of being cut at any moment by accident or miscalculation or by madness."*

One of the great Netflix series my wife and I enjoyed watching was *The Crown*, winner of the Golden Globe Award for *best* television series. It follows the story of Queen Elizabeth II, the monarch of Great Britain who reigned for seventy years (from February 1952 until her death in September 2022). Queen Elizabeth II wore the crown that ruled over thirty-two sovereign states in her lifetime and governed fifteen realms as the head of state. Beyond the palaces, thrones, crown jewels, wealth, and prestige, *The Crown* brilliantly captures the saying, *"Heavy is the head that weareth the crown!"*

From the personal anguish, pain, and loss of a life lived the way you want to live it, Elizabeth must prepare for a life that requires selfless service in all seasons. From family crises to personal betrayals, sibling rivalry, economic chaos in the nation, and war, Elizabeth must provide her citizenry solace, comfort, and strength. Heavy indeed is the head that wears the crown.

## THE GREATEST ACT OF A KING

If I am a king, and kings are remembered, measured, and valued by their acts and deeds, the question must be asked: *"What is the greatest act a king can perform on the Earth?"* We know kings take territory. They rule over regions. They protect and provide for all their subjects. They conquer defeat and drive out evil whenever it threatens the peace and welfare of the kingdom, but is there still another act that kings can perform?

The answer is a resounding *"yes,"* and it is wonderfully revealed in one of my favorite Christmas carols:

### WE THREE KINGS

*We three kings of Orient are;*
*bearing gifts we traverse afar;*

# EMERGE

*field and fountain, moor and mountain,*
*following yonder star.*

*O star of wonder, star of light,*
*star with royal beauty bright,*
*westward leading, still proceeding,*
*guide us to thy perfect light.*

*Born a King on Bethlehem's plain,*
*gold I bring to crown him again,*
*King forever, ceasing never,*
*over us all to reign.*

*Frankincense to offer have I;*
*incense owns a Deity nigh;*
*prayer and praising, voices raising,*
*worshiping God on high.*

*Myrrh is mine; its bitter perfume*
*breathes a life of gathering gloom;*
*sorrowing, sighing, bleeding, dying,*
*sealed in the stone-cold tomb.*

*Glorious now behold him arise;*
*King and God and sacrifice:*
*Alleluia, Alleluia,*
*sounds through the earth and skies.*

The *greatest* act of the kings of the earth is this: *to crown God as King over their kingdom and lives!*

In this most magnificent hymn, each of the three kings has traveled an immense distance, possibly spanning several hundred miles. Their pilgrimage took many years to sojourn. Each brings a priceless treasure they prepared as a gift. It's a sacred, dedicated, and intentional offering to be presented in recognition and honor of the King of Heaven and Earth. The gift is as prophetic as it is costly, meaningful, and powerful.

## CHAPTER SEVEN: **KING**

The first king brings *gold*—the earth's most precious and costly metal. The things of greatest value in the earth exist solely to *crown* the LORD God as King over our lives! This king brings his very *best*! That's the *first* act and test of all living on earth. Do you honor Him above all else and with your very best? Many a "religious" person would say, "I Honor God 'above' everything else," but this is often just a cheap excuse for poverty and laziness. Honoring Him with the *best* of the earth has *always* been a statute and command of God to His people.

*"And the Lord spoke to Aaron: "Here, I Myself have also given you charge of My heave offerings, all the holy gifts of the children of Israel; I have given them as a portion to you and your sons, as an ordinance forever. "All the best of the oil, all the best of the new wine and the grain, their first fruits which they offer to the Lord, I have given them to you."*
*Numbers 18:8, 12*

The best of the earth was brought to God and given to Him as an offering. (*God then gave these offerings to His priests, highlighting His priority that those who bear His burdens and hear His words are of the utmost value to Him*)

The second King brings gifts of *frankincense*. Frankincense is an antiseptic, perfuming oil that can eliminate bacteria and viruses. For millennia, its sweet fragrance was used in the Holy of Holies to bring the worship and the prayers of the saints before the *Most High!* The second king in this magnificent hymn is saying that the most beautiful fragrance of our devotion belongs to the LORD. He alone is worthy of all our worship. He alone is worthy of all our praise! What you worship will determine your strength. There is no higher or greater God than the Almighty. When you worship Him, His strength flows into your life and manifests in courage and valor.

*"He who kneels before God can STAND before any man. The fear of God always displaces the fear of man!"*
*- Steven Lawson*

The third king brings forth *myrrh*. Myrrh is an expensive spice and perfume used to anoint and embalm the dead. This king recognized that Jesus Christ, the King of Kings, the one born to be the King of the Jews, would have to suffer and die so we might live. He didn't just acknowledge and benefit from this fact. This king brought one of the most costly burial and anointing spices to worship and declare his im-

**EMERGE**

mense gratitude for the King of the Universe, who would die to redeem even the lowliest of His subjects. What a God!

The *wisest* of kings (as these men are commonly referred to as "the wise men") honor God above all else with their very best. They worship Him and serve Him alone. They recognize that this God loves them so much that He willingly *suffered and died* so they can live. Rather than trying to *work or earn* their way into heaven, they put their complete *trust and devotion* into the sacrificial death the King of Kings paid upon the cross!

## KINGS RULE OVER KINGDOMS

*"It is the King's office to protect and settle the true interpretation of the Law of God within his Dominions."*
*- James I, King of England.*

The word "kingdom" is derived from two words. The first obviously is "king," and the second is "dominion!"

Dominion is where we get the word "dominate." It means that it is an area where the king has total, final, and complete rule or domination.

The story of the Bible is one of jeopardy. It is one of conspiracy. The Bible, unlike any other religious literature, outlays the *truth* that there is a despot who operates through stealth (occult means "hidden or covered") and seeks to undermine, subvert, and overthrow all legitimate authority to execute his anti-God agenda.

To rule over a kingdom, one must acknowledge the forces seeking to overthrow, subvert, pull down, and destroy the rule of the legitimate king.

Jesus said it this way when He was teaching His disciples about spiritual warfare and casting out demons:

*"But if I cast out demons with the finger of God, surely the kingdom of God has come upon you. When a strong man, fully armed, guards his own palace, his goods are in peace. But when a stronger than he comes upon him and overcomes him, he takes from him all his armor in which he trusted,*

# CHAPTER SEVEN: KING

*and divides his spoils."*
*Luke 11:20-22*

In other words, Satan seeks to find strongholds and access points of entry in order to get into your home to steal, kill, and destroy. He *wants* to cause devastation and pain. It's his mission. You *must* become proficient in defending your kingdom from all enemies, foreign and domestic. You must protect what is entrusted to you to steward—specifically your marriage, family, wealth, and God's purpose/mission/assignment for your life. Praying isn't begging. Prayer is not for those who have exhausted all other options. Prayer is not weakness. Prayer is *powerful*. Prayer is the *first* go-to, long before throwing money at your problem or trying to solve things in your own strength. Did you know the devil trembles when even the weakest Christian prays? Why? Because the God to whom the Christian is praying absolutely *terrifies* him.

The Apostle Paul gives the following instructions:

> *"Put on the whole armor of God, that you may be able to stand against the wiles of the devil. For we do not wrestle against flesh and blood, but against principalities, against powers, against the rulers of the darkness of this age, against spiritual hosts of wickedness in the heavenly places. Therefore take up the whole armor of God, that you may be able to withstand in the evil day, and having done all, to stand. Stand therefore, having girded your waist with truth, having put on the breastplate of righteousness, and having shod your feet with the preparation of the gospel of peace; above all, taking the shield of faith with which you will be able to quench all the fiery darts of the wicked one. And take the helmet of salvation, and the sword of the Spirit, which is the word of God; praying always with all prayer and supplication in the Spirit, being watchful to this end with all perseverance and supplication for all the saints—"*
> *Ephesians 6:11-18*

*You* are at *war* with a spirit who hates you and plots to destroy you. However, in Christ, you have been given authority *over* this foe. Two thousand years ago, Jesus Christ defeated the devil. The reason he runs rampant today isn't because he wasn't defeated; it's because (sadly) he largely goes uncontested!

> *"... For this purpose the Son of God was manifested, that He might destroy the works of the devil."*

**EMERGE**

*I John 3:8b*

Jesus didn't *just* come to die for our sins. He didn't *only* come to Earth to make atonement before God, the Creator of the worlds. He also came to *destroy* the works of the devil. Why? *Because that's what kings do!* They defend their kingdoms. They defeat wickedness wherever they see it!

## KINGS WIPE OUT EVIL WHENEVER AND WHEREVER THEY SEE IT!

*"A wise king sifts out the wicked, And brings the threshing wheel over them."*
Proverbs 20:26

Despite the bumper stickers that say otherwise. You cannot "coexist" with evil because it will *not* peaceably coexist with you. It cannot. It's the very nature of evil to be that which can never be trusted. Evil seeks to usurp, overthrow, undermine, devour, and destroy all of God's blessings and gifts to you. Evil does *not* possess any virtue whatsoever. That's why it is called evil. It doesn't care about what is right, just, or fair. In fact, it delights in the exact opposite. Evil is behind all injustice, murder, child abuse, and exploitation. The *level* at which you tolerate evil will be the level at which your house will be ruined. Have a ZERO tolerance policy toward evil, and you will thrive and prosper.

## KINGS GO TO WAR AGAINST OTHER KINGS

Much of the Bible is about battles, territorial skirmishes, oppression, injustice, freedom, and triumph over evil—whether it's from Israel being delivered from four hundred years of bondage and slavery in Egypt to the continual battles they fought against enemies such as the Philistines, Amalekites, Midianites, Moabites, Ammonites, Rephites, Canaanites, and so on. We love the story of David defeating the giant Philistine champion named Goliath in a battle where the future king of Israel is unprotected, outmatched, and outarmed.

Why do we battle? Why must we learn spiritual warfare?

Because *"how we get something is how we keep it!"* Whether it's six-pack abs, fitness, a wife, or wealth, God knows that the warfare required to *take* a territory will be the warfare

CHAPTER SEVEN: **KING**

required to *keep* that territory!

> *"Now these are the nations which the Lord left, that He might test Israel by them, that is, all who had not known any of the wars in Canaan (this was only so that the generations of the children of Israel might be taught to know war, at least those who had not formerly known it), namely, five Lords of the Philistines, all the Canaanites, the Sidonians, and the Hivites who dwelt in Mount Lebanon, from Mount Baal Hermon to the entrance of Hamath. And they were left, that He might test Israel by them, to know whether they would obey the commandments of the Lord, which He had commanded their fathers by the hand of Moses."*
> *Judges 3:1-4*

God intentionally left enemy combatants in the land so a new generation, who had inherited the blessings and wealth from previous generations, might also learn the art of warfare. It was necessary for them to keep and preserve those very blessings. They weren't the first, either. Abraham, whom many religious teachers like to paint as a nomadic herdsman, was an expert in warfare. To rescue his nephew, who was taken captive in battle, he had to fight five kings and their armies. He doesn't hesitate from the battle, but rather, he arms up and takes them down!

> *"And it came to pass in the days of Amraphel king of Shinar, Arioch king of Ellasar, Chedorlaomer king of Elam, and Tidal king of nations, that they made war with Bera king of Sodom, Birsha king of Gomorrah, Shinab king of Admah, Shemeber king of Zeboiim, and the king of Bela (that is, Zoar). All these joined together in the Valley of Siddim (that is, the Salt Sea). Twelve years they served Chedorlaomer, and in the thirteenth year they rebelled. In the fourteenth year Chedorlaomer and the kings that were with him came and attacked the Rephaim in Ashteroth Karnaim, the Zuzim in Ham, the Emim in Shaveh Kiriathaim, and the Horites in their mountain of Seir, as far as El Paran, which is by the wilderness."*

These kings are on a conquest tour. The Rephaim, Zuzim, Emim, and Horites were all giant races—the genetic mutations of the fallen angelic hosts seeking to eradicate the *imago Dei* (Image of God) from the Earth by producing hybrids (originally called the Nephilim). The kingdoms of Sodom and Gomorrah are in their way. Because of their gross and obscene sexual perversions, they are also seen as infected with the influence of these rebellious fallen angels. Sadly, Lot, Abraham's nephew, is caught up in the middle of this conflict because he has chosen to live in Sodom.

## EMERGE

*And the king of Sodom, the king of Gomorrah, the king of Admah, the king of Zeboiim, and the king of Bela (that is, Zoar) went out and joined together in battle in the Valley of Siddim against Chedorlaomer king of Elam, Tidal king of nations, Amraphel king of Shinar, and Arioch king of Ellasar—four kings against five. Now the Valley of Siddim was full of asphalt pits; and the kings of Sodom and Gomorrah fled; some fell there, and the remainder fled to the mountains. Then they took all the goods of Sodom and Gomorrah, and all their provisions, and went their way. They also took Lot, Abram's brother's son who dwelt in Sodom, and his goods, and departed.*

The lesson here is that sexual perversion and vice weakens a man. It doesn't strengthen a man. Samson LOST his strength, vision, and vitality when he chose to longingly lay in the lap of Delilah, whose name means *'Lustful!'* You were created by a moral and upright God. His laws strengthen both men and nations. When we depart from His laws, we are in danger of becoming 'De-moralized!' The dictionary defines the word Demoralized as without meaning, purpose, hope, or strength. The Bible says that when a woman who had suffered from bleeding for 12 years came behind Jesus in a crowd and touched him, Jesus swung around immediately and asked, *"Who touched me?"* When the disciples tried to explain the difficulty they were having in keeping the crowds at bay, Jesus said, *"No, somebody touched me because I felt VIRTUE flow out of me!"* The woman was instantly healed by the power of God. Notice how Jesus equates POWER with Virtue!

Let's keep reading...

*Then one who had escaped came and told Abram the Hebrew, for he dwelt by the terebinth trees of Mamre the Amorite, brother of Eshcol and brother of Aner; and they were allies with Abram. Now when Abram heard that his brother was taken captive, he armed his three hundred and eighteen trained servants who were born in his own house, and went in pursuit as far as Dan. He divided his forces against them by night, and he and his servants attacked them and pursued them as far as Hobah, which is north of Damascus. So he brought back all the goods, and also brought back his brother Lot and his goods, as well as the women and the people. And the king of Sodom went out to meet him at the Valley of Shaveh (that is, the King's Valley), after his return from the defeat of Chedorlaomer and the kings who were with him. Then Melchizedek king of Salem brought out bread and wine; he was the priest of God Most High. And he blessed him and said: "Blessed be Abram of God Most High, Possessor of heaven and earth; And blessed be God Most High, Who has delivered your enemies into your hand." And he gave him a tithe of all. Now the king of Sodom said to Abram, "Give me the persons, and take the goods for yourself." But Abram said to the king of Sodom, "I have raised my hand to the Lord,*

# CHAPTER SEVEN: KING

*God Most High, the Possessor of heaven and earth, that I will take nothing, from a thread to a sandal strap, and that I will not take anything that is yours, lest you should say, 'I have made Abram rich'— except only what the young men have eaten, and the portion of the men who went with me: Aner, Eshcol, and Mamre; let them take their portion."* **Genesis 14:1-24**

Abraham went out and opened a can of whoop on these kings. In this life, there are still kings you will need to war against. They are any "ruling authority" or "power" that seeks to rob what is most precious to you, bringing you into captivity and enslaving you in bondage! The WEF (World Economic Forum) is one cluster of kings trying to take you captive by 2030. They promise that by the year 2030:

*"You will own nothing and be very happy!"*
*- Klaus Schwab WEF Davos.*

These are kings. We call them billionaires and globalist elites. They use illegitimate (unelected) authority to force this agenda upon mankind in order to dispense their dystopian vision upon the world. These people are immoral reprobates. They are Luciferic. They hate God and rebel against Him, seeking to extinguish His laws and His word from the Earth. You didn't ask for this war, but here it is anyway. One of their key voices is that of the sociopathic Microsoft founder, Bill Gates, who wants to drastically reduce the world's population to below one billion people through the implementation of forced vaccinations, which will sterilize men and women while eliminating the "unwanted" from the gene pool.

*"The ransom of a man's life is his wealth!"*
*Proverbs 13:8*

*"The Rich rules over the poor and the borrower is servant to the lender!"*
*Proverbs 22:7*

The *laws* of God are in operation perpetually. They are never switched off or annulled. The reprobates doing the devil's work at the World Economic Forum seek to overthrow society and subjugate *you (*and mankind) to their demonic dystopia, which is deeply entrenched in the *lie* that the world is "overpopulated!" Nothing could be further from the truth. They know if you have *no wealth,* you have *no ransom* for your life. That's why they seek to take away your wealth. They seek to "depose" kings and make themselves the *kings* of slaves, deciding who gets to live and who doesn't.

# EMERGE

They also know that the rich rule over the poor. If they can make you poor, they rule over you, giving them the power to decide your fate, value, and destiny. Trust me. You do not want these godless perverts and reprobates to have any decision whatsoever in measuring your worth, value, and existence.

> *"In the land of the blind, the one eyed man is king!"*
> *- Erasmus*

Don't give away your vision, or the devious one-eyed man will rule over you! When Joshua conquered the promised land, he had to defeat and depose thirty-one kings.

> *"And these are the kings of the country which Joshua and the children of Israel conquered on this side of the Jordan, on the west, from Baal Gad in the Valley of Lebanon as far as Mount Halak and the ascent to Seir, which Joshua gave to the tribes of Israel as a possession according to their divisions, in the mountain country, in the lowlands, in the Jordan plain, in the slopes, in the wilderness, and in the South—the Hittites, the Amorites, the Canaanites, the Perizzites, the Hivites, and the Jebusites: the king of Jericho, one; the king of Ai, which is beside Bethel, one; the king of Jerusalem, one; the king of Hebron, one; the king of Jarmuth, one; the king of Lachish, one; the king of Eglon, one; the king of Gezer, one; the king of Debir, one; the king of Geder, one; the king of Hormah, one; the king of Arad, one; the king of Libnah, one; the king of Adullam, one; the king of Makkedah, one; the king of Bethel, one; the king of Tappuah, one; the king of Hepher, one; the king of Aphek, one; the king of Lasharon, one; the king of Madon, one; the king of Hazor, one; the king of Shimron Meron, one; the king of Achshaph, one; the king of Taanach, one; the king of Megiddo, one; the king of Kedesh, one; the king of Jokneam in Carmel, one; the king of Dor in the heights of Dor, one; the king of the people of Gilgal, one; the king of Tirzah, one—all the kings, thirty-one."*

There are approximately thirty days per month. This means that each day, you are in a battle with a king who seeks to overwhelm and overthrow you! God's kings enjoy the victory! Do *not* let the kings of this world triumph over you and take His blessings from you!

> *"Through God we will do valiantly, For it is He who shall tread down our enemies."*

## CHAPTER SEVEN: KING

God gives victory to His kings. The kings who remain devoted to Him become undefeatable in battle!

*"Gilead is mine, and Manasseh, too. Ephraim, my helmet, will produce my warriors, and Judah, my scepter, will produce my kings."*

Judah produces God's kings. What does Judah mean? It means *"Praise!"* The most fruitful tribe in all the land of Israel was Judah. The strongest of all the tribes was Judah. The people group that has been the most viciously and vehemently attacked, persecuted, and singled out for genocide is the Jewish people—the people from Judah. Satan wants to *eliminate* praise (Judah) from the Earth because it produces Heaven's kings—*praise precedes breakthrough*. When Paul and Silas praised God in the midnight hour while in prison, God broke through with an earthquake that opened every door and caused every chain and shackle to fall supernaturally off their wrists and ankles. Average men will praise God *after* He delivers performs miracles, but Kings know that praise precedes breakthrough!

*"It's better to die on your feet than to live on your knees!"*
*- Emiliano Zapata*

*"You will not need to fight in this battle. Position yourselves, stand still and see the salvation of the Lord, who is with you, O Judah and Jerusalem!' Do not fear or be dismayed; tomorrow go out against them, for the Lord is with you." So they rose early in the morning and went out into the Wilderness of Tekoa; and as they went out, Jehoshaphat stood and said, "Hear me, O Judah and you inhabitants of Jerusalem: Believe in the Lord your God, and you shall be established; believe His prophets, and you shall prosper." And when he had consulted with the people, he appointed those who should sing to the Lord, and who should praise the beauty of holiness, as they went out before the army and were saying: "Praise the Lord, For His mercy endures forever."* <u>Now when they began to sing and to praise, the Lord set ambushes against the people of Ammon, Moab, and Mount Seir, who had come against Judah; and they were defeated."</u>

When they *began* to sing and praise, the LORD set ambushes. Heaven's kings are the product of a life of praise. Praise precedes all breakthroughs. Praise is the weapon of

## EMERGE

the mighty kings who have walked the earth. The nine-foot, nine inches tall champion from Gath named Goliath *fell* at the hands of a youth who loved to *praise* the LORD His God and who went on to become king! If you're facing a Goliath right now, it's probably a "praise test!" Start praising God in your battle. Start thanking Him for the victory coming your way!

## CHALLENGE

As an EMERGE man, you *know* you are a son of the MOST HIGH GOD. You carry His *Imago Dei (*His image) on the Earth. He is the King of Kings. You have been commissioned to have dominion over the earth. Live like a king. Conquer. Take territory. Govern with Righteousness and Justice. Drive out evil and wickedness and bring Glory to the KING of KINGS. If you do this, you will live a life that echoes in eternity, carrying the words *"Well done thou good and faithful servant"* to infinity and beyond. Give Him the glory and the praise that is due His holy name! Amen!

# CHAPTER EIGHT
# PRIEST

## כהן

### Kohen / Kohenim
*Atonement Justice Just virtue in the earth*

*"O wretched man that I am! Who will deliver me from this body of death?"*
Romans 7:24

*"And the priest shall offer the burnt offering and the grain offering on the altar. So the priest shall make atonement for him, and he shall be clean."*
Leviticus 14:20

**EMERGE**

## WHAT BURIES MEN

Few things are more devastating to a man than guilt, shame, regret, and failure. These are the things that bury a man. Suicide among men is three times higher than among women. When men struggle, societies struggle. When men struggle, families languish, and strength diminishes in the household. When men fail, they often fail devastatingly and sometimes permanently. Men are wired by their Creator to perform and produce. When they fail, are laid off, made redundant, or are told they are not needed anymore, a sense of hopelessness often descends upon them, like several tons of dirt burying them, making it hard to rise again.

It is the nature of all progress to include failure. We actually fail forward. When you first tried to walk, you fell and, therefore, failed, but that's how you learned. That's how you develop your sense of balance and the skill to put one foot in front of the other to walk and then run! Thomas Edison, the inventor of the lightbulb, was once asked what it felt like to fail a thousand times. He responded, *"Oh, I didn't fail a thousand times. It was just that the invention of the lightbulb happened to be a one-thousand-and-one-step process!"*

Resilience is the ability to keep getting up when you fall or fail! Sadly, many men don't know how to get back up or feel buried by the weight of the guilt, shame, and gravitas of their failure. Many turn to drugs and alcohol, and sadly, some resort to something more fatalistic, like suicide. This is *why* God set up a priesthood, and by priesthood, I don't mean old men dressed in long black gowns. The priesthood comprises men who know how to make atonement for themselves, their loved ones, and their families.

*"Three things never come back - Time, Word and opportunity! Therefore, do not waste time, choose your words carefully, and don't miss your opportunities!"*
*- Confucius.*

*"To err is human, to forgive is divine!"*
*- Alexander Pope.*

*"There are a thousand lessons in defeat but only one in victory!"*
*- Lao Tzu*

While it is absolutely human to err, we can not just move on or pretend it didn't happen. We also cannot just sweep our mistakes and regrets under the rug. Hiding these things eventually becomes a tripping hazard and a stumbling block. God set up

## CHAPTER EIGHT: **PRIEST**

atonement for our sins. Jesus Christ is the atoner. He is the high priest, and He is also the sacrifice, the innocent lamb slain to redeem our lives.

> *"If we confess our sins, He is faithful and just to forgive us our sins and to cleanse us from all unrighteousness."*
> *I John 1:9*

The *"priest"* function required of a man is a very simple one. The priests in the Old Testament had to first bring sacrifices to atone for their own sins. Then, they could atone for the people. It's the same at home. As the head of the household, the man is the spiritual climate setter of the home. He needs atonement, and he must bring atonement. We don't need judgment when we fail, but mercy. Judgment is reserved for those who *reject* all mercy. Judgment has been set by God for the final day, known as Judgement Day. Up until that time, mercy and atonement were available to all. As a man, husband, and father, your job is *not* to bring judgment and condemnation when your spouse or children err and fail. Be quick to atone, cleanse, and bring mercy and deliverance!

Set an atonement climate in your home. Just like a thermostat can be dialed up or down to set the temperature of the home, in the same way, the father is the one who sets the spiritual climate of the house. He is the "values" setter and the determiner of the spiritual climate of the home. Sometimes, wives feel they must step up when it appears the man is abdicating his role in this area. It doesn't have to be that way. It is *not* hard to be a priest in the home. When men discover what it is to be a priest, it's the *most potent* force for household health and vitality. When Mom and Dad operate in *unity*, the devil is defeated and cast out!

The *values* of hard work, worship, gratitude, thankfulness, respect, and honor are all values that every *priest* is responsible for. They are what the *man* of the house sets, either by *design* or by *default*! Your kids are watching you. They are listening to you! One of the most sobering things in life is that our children are like sponges, soaking everything in. The frustration for many fathers is that their kids don't *"do what I say."* Your kids will always do what *you do* over what you say! *You set the bar. You set the example. You set the thermostat.*

Worshippers become warriors in the Bible. David was a worshipper and became one of the most powerful warriors in history. Moses was a worshipper and went down in history as one of the most powerful deliverers and destroyers of enemies that came against him and God's people. Abraham was a worshipper and defeated five kings

**EMERGE**

and their armies in battle with the three hundred and eighteen men he raised in his house. Time restricts me from talking about Joshua, Gideon, Caleb, and others who were mighty warriors because they were devoted worshippers. Set your children up to flourish. Set the atmosphere in your home to one that worships God and is devoted to His house and His word!

- **Worshipper (place in warrior)**
- **Trauma**
- **Guilt reliever**
- **Kingdom Culture setter in the home**

## LAW, JUSTICE, PUNISHMENT, ATONEMENT.

The ancient Romans had no such punishment as "life in prison." Many historians today marvel at the society the Roman Empire created, with a population (at its height) of over thirty-five million people. The Roman Empire lasted over five hundred years (from 27 BC to 476 AD) and had no police force. The people were expected to police themselves. Rome had a strong, regimented, disciplined military that policed for the emperor, the senate, and the proconsul. This is where the word militia comes from.

The Roman Empire authored cruel and brutal punishments, believing dissuasion was the best way to reduce crime. As followers of Jesus Christ, we know crucifixion was one of these capital punishments. Thieves, robbers, murderers, insurrectionists, and anyone unlucky enough to be deemed an enemy of Rome or Caesar would often be sentenced to Crucifixion, which would take place on the busiest roads in and out of Rome.

The saying "all roads lead to Rome" was not an exaggeration. All roads led to what was believed to be the center for commerce, trade, wisdom, and culture. These roads were littered with criminals being crucified, groaning, and crying out in agony. The goal was for this horrific display to deter any would-be thief, robber, or other criminals. It was a statement that Roman justice would be swift, merciless, brutal, and final!

One of the capital punishments invented by the Roman Empire was that of *Poena Cullei* (meaning Penalty of the Sack). Under Roman law, this capital punishment was imposed on a subject found guilty of patricide. The punishment consisted of being sewn up in a leather sack with various live animals, including a dog, a snake, a monkey, a chicken, or a rooster, and then being thrown in the water to drown. In early ancient

## CHAPTER EIGHT: **PRIEST**

Rome, the family was considered the basic cell of society. It was a vast institution containing the members of the family and included even adopted servants. All authority lay in the patriarch, the father. To kill one's father was considered to be a capital crime, punishable by this type of death, because, in Rome, this was seen literally as "striking at the authority" of the Emperor himself.

Another one of the cruel punishments invented by the Romans was the penalty for murder. The murderer would be tied to the dead corpse of the one that he had killed. He would have to carry upon his back the burden of the life which he had taken. The corpse would succumb to rigor mortis and decay. Being attached directly to his body, the stench alone would have been overwhelming, but even worse would be the physiological impact of a dead, decomposing corpse directly infecting the cells, skin, and flesh of the guilty murderer. His penalty was to carry the corpse for the rest of his life, which was now dramatically cut short by the decomposing burden. Again, this was to not only punish the perpetrator but also dissuade other would-be murderers to rethink their choices.

> *When the apostle Paul wrote to the Roman church, he asked, "Who will deliver me from this body of death?" The Roman church knew exactly the context in which he was speaking. "I find then a law, that evil is present with me, the one who wills to do good. For I delight in the law of God according to the inward man. But I see another law in my members, warring against the law of my mind, and bringing me into captivity to the law of sin which is in my members. O wretched man that I am! Who will deliver me from this body of death?"*
> *Romans 7:21-24 NKJV*

Who will "deliver him from this body of death?" We know the answer! It is Jesus Christ, our High Priest and Atoner. He is the one who delivers us from the decomposing corpse of guilt, shame, and condemnation brought upon us by our sins and transgressions. Guilt buries many a man. Shame is a decomposing corpse that slowly eats away at your soul until nothing is left but the death of your dreams, purpose, self-esteem, confidence, and morale. Jesus Christ died on the cross to *pay* for your freedom from these things. You are *not* meant to carry guilt, shame, and condemnation. They are literally "bodies of death." Today, let Jesus Christ the Deliverer free you from all shame, all guilt, and all condemnation brought on by the "dead works" of our past sins and violations of God's law. Your punishment has been *paid in full*! Like a credit card that has had its balance paid, "no need to send payment" sits upon your account from heaven.

**EMERGE**

## YOU ARE A PRIEST

When my first grandson Joel-Ashley was born, we were ushered into the delivery room about 30 minutes after he came into the world. I'll never forget the first moment I laid eyes upon the son of my son! This precious little life, lying on the chest of his beautiful but exhausted mother. My eyes welled with tears, overcome by a flood of emotion and joy. The moment will be forever stamped upon my mind and heart as a picture of God's exceeding goodness and loving kindness toward my life. It was just so wonderful.

However, as we drew near, we could hear little Joel-Ashley whimpering, which is not unusual for a newborn coming to grips with his new, unfamiliar environment outside the womb. His mother, Aubrey, then began to tell us of the ordeal surrounding his arrival into the world. It immediately became clear that the birth had been neither easy nor straightforward but rather quite dramatic. As baby Joel was crowning, the doctors became alarmed that Joel-Ashley's and Aubrey's heart rates had dropped. An air of panic had swept the delivery room as nurses and doctors rushed to implement "emergency" birth procedures to get the baby out and preserve the mother's life. Now, it made sense. This was the trauma I was discerning behind my little grandson's whimpering cry as he lay there, continuing to cry on his mother's chest.

The Holy Spirit reminded me that as Joel-Ashley's grandfather, I am both king and priest. As the patriarch in this picture, I had the authority to command the spirit of trauma to leave him. In an instant, the Holy Spirit showed me that this spirit is not the spirit we would want Joel-Ashley to view the world and his life through. The disposition of trauma or fear is a broken lens that would have a devastatingly negative impact on his judgment, especially when it concerned doing new things, taking risks, or stepping out in faith, all of which are essential building blocks to success in this life.

So I stepped forward and placed my hand upon his precious little head and then gently but authoritatively commanded the spirit of trauma to depart. I asked for the peace of the person of the Holy Spirit to come and fill him in its place! Within seconds, the crying went from helpless whimpering to a usual, strong little cry. Within thirty seconds, he wasn't crying at all as a magnificent peace came over him and filled the room.

This is what operating in the role of a "Priest" looks like, and it is a power that God has given every man over his posterity. We are called and anointed to be both king

## CHAPTER EIGHT: **PRIEST**

and priest and to bring our children and their children into the fullness of all God has promised.

As the head of the house, every man is responsible for being both king and priest! To be the priest means *you* have been given by God the authority to minister Christ's redemptive work upon the cross into your family. Everywhere you see generational curses, transgression, guilt, shame, addiction, struggle, and disease, *you* take the blood of Christ and bring atonement.

Human beings were not created to carry guilt, shame, and condemnation. We were made to carry the presence of God—joy, love, Heaven's power, and purpose. Our sins, however, weigh us down badly. The writer of the book of Hebrews tells us in Hebrews chapter 12, *"Let us cast off the weight and the sin, which so easily entangles us."* Jesus Christ was crucified, so this body of death might be removed from you, with all of its burdens and the foul stench of all your wrongdoings. All of your sins are now forgiven! They've been washed away. You have been totally cleansed by Christ's innocent blood shed upon that cross. It is like they never happened. The Bible says you have been justified. "Justified" simply translates to "Just as if I'd" never sinned!

Everybody needs a priest—someone to minister to us when we are burdened by our past mistakes and failures and when we feel overwhelmed by our shortcomings and struggles. That's why you need to belong to a church and why you need to be submitted to good leadership. This chapter, however, is not just about what you and I need in our lives from others. It is also about the fact that both you and I are called to be priests. You may say, "How can I be a priest? I am not perfect! I'm far from it!" The good news is you don't have to be perfect to operate as a priest in your home. Aaron, the priest of Israel, wasn't perfect, nor were his sons. God made amends for that by requiring them to sacrifice bulls and rams for their own sins before they tended to the sins and transgressions of the nation Israel. There is, however, a perfect priest, Jesus Christ. He is described in the Bible as "the high priest," and He commissions you and me to operate under His priestly atoning perfection with His full authority.

*"And when He had called His twelve disciples to Him, He gave them power over unclean spirits, to cast them out, and to heal all kinds of sickness and all kinds of disease. And as you go, preach, saying, 'The kingdom of heaven is at hand.' Heal the sick, cleanse the lepers, raise the dead, cast out demons. Freely you have received, freely give."*
*Matthew 10:1, 7-8 NKJV*

EMERGE
# THE PRIEST STANDS BETWEEN THE LIVING AND THE DEAD!

One of my favorite Bible stories is the rebellion of the Israelite leaders against Moses and Aaron (and, in turn, God himself). God alone selected these men to lead His people, *not* because they were perfect (no man is) but because they were devoted and willing. Judgment from God breaks out on the rebels, and what Moses does at this time is mind-blowing, brilliant, and simply fascinating;

> *"On the next day all the congregation of the children of Israel complained against Moses and Aaron, saying, "You have killed the people of the Lord." Now it happened, when the congregation had gathered against Moses and Aaron, that they turned toward the tabernacle of meeting; and suddenly the cloud covered it, and the glory of the Lord appeared. Then Moses and Aaron came before the tabernacle of meeting. And the Lord spoke to Moses, saying, "Get away from among this congregation, that I may consume them in a moment." And they fell on their faces. So Moses said to Aaron, "Take a censer and put fire in it from the altar, put incense on it, and take it quickly to the congregation and make atonement for them; for wrath has gone out from the Lord. The plague has begun." Then Aaron took it as Moses commanded, and ran into the midst of the assembly; and already the plague had begun among the people. So he put in the incense and made atonement for the people. And he stood between the dead and the living; so the plague was stopped. Now those who died in the plague were fourteen thousand seven hundred, besides those who died in the Korah incident. So Aaron returned to Moses at the door of the tabernacle of meeting, for the plague had stopped."*
> Numbers 16:41-50 NKJV

What is the role of the priest? To stop the plague, atone for iniquity, stay the hand of the angel of death, drive out the demonic, and enforce Christ's victory over Satan in every sphere of your life.

## THE POWER OF COMMUNION

I remember many years ago when I lived in New Zealand. I was a youth pastor, but I would often get invited to go and speak at youth camps and conferences. We just

## CHAPTER EIGHT: **PRIEST**

had our second son, Ash. He was an almost ten-pound baby, larger than life and boisterous. However, being born in May in Auckland, New Zealand, in 1997, we had an incredibly severe winter. It was freezing most of the time. Auckland is wet and continuously rainy. While I was away preaching and ministering at a youth camp, we had an incredible move of God with hundreds of young people pouring forward on the altar to dedicate or re-dedicate their lives to Jesus Christ.

During that time, I received a phone call from my wife saying that Ash had to be rushed to the hospital because he stopped breathing. The doctors thought he had asthma, but his entire lungs were blocked. My wife was unbelievably stressed and tearful because she had a brand new baby who had almost died while her husband was not present to be with and support her. I remember reiterating to my wife, "Well, Honey, this is just confirmation that I'm in the middle of the will of God, that I'm doing what I meant to be doing. The devil must be terrified. He must be so mad." I took it like a bitch. I was doing God's work, and all these people were getting saved. No wonder the devil was attacking my family. That night, as I was praying for my son and wife, God clearly spoke to me. He said, "Why are you putting up with this? Why are you tolerating this?" I told God, "I thought I had to! I thought this was confirmation that I'm hitting the devil where it hurts." At that point, God spoke to me about the blood of Jesus, reminding me of the story of the Passover. The Book of Exodus tells of the "pass over." God didn't just deliver His people from Egypt. On their final night in Egypt, God told every Israelite household to slaughter a lamb and put its blood on the lentils of the doorpost to their dwellings. God told the Israelites that the destroyer would be coming over the land of Egypt to strike the firstborn in every single house. The destroyer, however, would pass over any house bearing the blood of the lamb.

God told me I didn't need to allow the destroyer to come into my home and ransack my wife, children, and finances while I was away. The blood of the perfect Lamb, Jesus Christ, is more than powerful enough to stave and ward off the devil. I called my wife back and said, "Baby, go and get some grape juice and some bread. We're going to do communion right now over our son." I told her what the Lord had just spoken to me. As I shared with her, joy began to resurge in her voice. Instead of tears caused by pain, anguish, and hopelessness, she now cried tears of joy. We took communion together, and within hours, our son started breathing on his own and was released from the hospital. From that time forward, Leanne and I take communion in our home whenever we have felt the attack of the enemy. You, as a priest in your home, have been given authority by Jesus Christ himself to atone for sin and to ward off the attacks of the destroyer.

## EMERGE

How often are you taking communion in your home? Whenever you perceive that the destroyer is having a field day (whether that's sickness, disease, financial attack, or in another area of your life), take some bread and wine and begin to administer the blood of Jesus Christ. Take communion and then take authority over the evil one. Command him to pass over and leave your dwelling. Let him know he is not permitted. Remember that this is where the blood of the Lamb is present. The destroyer must pass over. He cannot enter. He must depart immediately. He cannot touch. He cannot harm. He cannot have what is under the blood of the lamb.

*"And looking at Jesus as He walked, he said, "Behold the Lamb of God!""*
*- John The Baptist. Jordan River circa AD27.*
*John 1:36 NKJV*

*"For the Lord will pass through to strike the Egyptians; and when He sees the blood on the lintel and on the two doorposts, the Lord will pass over the door and not allow the destroyer to come into your houses to strike you."*
*Exodus 12:23 NKJV*

## I'M NOT EMOTIONAL LIKE MY WIFE...

Over the thirty-plus years of being a pastor, I have heard many interesting and many stupid things confessed to me, as you can well imagine. I remember one of those occasions vividly. It was from an astute businessman trying to excuse his lackluster heart for the things of God and the church. He tried to tell me that the reason he didn't pray, lift his hands, or engage in worship was because he was not "emotional" like his wife!

I told him, "Your wife isn't being 'emotional,' Sir. She's being spiritual! We don't lift our hands and sing worship songs because we are emotional. We do it because we are spiritual. You, sir, are a spiritual being, but you are not engaging your spirit. Instead, you are neglecting your spirituality. You must take authority and lead your home in prayer, devotion, and communion. *You* are the priest and the atoner of iniquity in your home."

This man would complain about his wife not respecting his leadership and then turn around and not *lead* his home!

# CHAPTER EIGHT: **PRIEST**

In the movie *Braveheart*, William Wallace is finally captured by the British army and Longshanks, the king. They are going to publicly execute him by disemboweling him in the center of Marketplace Square. The princess and daughter-in-law of Longshanks' heir to the throne has fallen in love with William Wallace. She comes to him the night before his execution, bringing a narcotic to numb the pain he is about to endure. As she leaves his cell, he spits out the anesthetic. The next scene shows him kneeling, looking up at a small window high on the wall as the sun dawns on his last day on Earth. He begins to pray, "My Father, give me the strength to do what I have to do!"

Every time I watch this scene, it moves me to tears because I see courage. I see devotion. I see a man willing to pay the highest sacrifice for what he believes in and stands for. It inspires me to want to be that courageous for my God, my faith, and my convictions. Prayer is not weakness. Prayer is where a man draws supernatural strength. The priest in the home is a man of prayer. The priest is the gatekeeper of supernatural power in the home. The priest is both the possessor and the pastor of supernatural power to those in his home. You are a priest. You access heavenly power and authority. If you lead, your family will both respect and follow you.

## BUT HOW CAN I MAKE A DIFFERENCE?

There's a story about an old man taking his daily walk along the beach. One particular morning, the sun was just beginning to rise. It was summer, and again, it was forecasted to be another scorching, hot day. As he walked along, he spotted a young boy in the distance crouched over by the water, scooping something up from the sand and throwing it into the sea. The tide was already a long way out. The beach was normally empty at this early time of the day, so the old man stopped to watch the young boy for a while.

He noticed the young boy kept shuffling further down the beach, repeating the same action—stopping, scooping, throwing, and moving. Finally, the old man had to see what the boy was up to. He walked toward the boy. As he approached, he yelled out, "What are you doing there, *boy?*"

"I'm saving the starfish that are stranded," replied the boy, "If they stay on the beach while the sun comes up, they will dry out or die, so I'm throwing them back into the ocean so they can live!"

## EMERGE

The old man was silent for a few seconds, surveying the beach. As he looked up and down, he was struck by the fact that literally thousands upon thousands of these starfish had been washed up in the high tide. With the draining low tide, they could not make it back to the water and would all very soon perish as the scorching hot sun rose that day.

*"Young man,"* he said, *"On this spread of the beach alone, there must be more than ten thousand stranded starfish. Around the next corner, there'll be thousands more. This goes on for miles and miles. I've done this walk every day for the last ten years. It's always the same. I hate to say it, but you'll never make a difference!"*

The boy looked at the old man, paused momentarily as if to ponder his words, then looked down and stooped once again to pick up a starfish by the old man's feet. With grit and determination on his face, he flung it into the ocean with all his might. He then turned to look the old man in the eyes and said with a steely conviction, *"I just made a difference to that one!"*

You may feel overwhelmed by the problems plaguing your life, household, family, finances, and world, but we can learn much from this magnificent story. Begin where you are. Don't let the paralysis of analysis overwhelm you into apathy, lethargy, or procrastination. Start somewhere today. What is your starfish? What is within your reach that may require a little stooping down (humbling yourself) and bringing life where death was setting in?

## MEN'S PRAYER

*One* of the secret sauces of our church is our *men's* prayer meetings at 5:30 AM. Close to a thousand men gather weekly across all our campuses to cry out to God for their nation, state, city, wives, families, and personal worlds. Men gather and confess their struggles with pornography, infidelity, insecurity, weakness, sin, and other issues with one another. They then minister and pray for one another. It is *pure* power!

There is nothing like it. *You* need to belong to a men's prayer group like this. Priests pray, and priests minister, even to one another.

## CHALLENGE

God's priests stand between the living and the dead. Life is in their wake. Wherever

## CHAPTER EIGHT: **PRIEST**

they go, sins are atoned for. Demons are driven out. Chains of addiction lie shattered in pieces on the ground. Prison cells are emptied, and the wicked flee even while no one pursues! You are called to carry a priestly mantle on the Earth. God has anointed you to bring atonement into the areas where men have struggled with the chains of sin, shame, guilt, condemnation, and hopelessness. Christ is our High Priest. Point men to Him. He alone holds the keys of death and hell. He has victory over the devil and fallen angels. He shed His blood to deliver all mankind from the power of darkness, death, and eternal damnation. He is with you. GO!

*"And Jesus came and spoke to them, saying, "All authority has been given to Me in heaven and on earth. Go therefore and make disciples of all the nations, baptizing them in the name of the Father and of the Son and of the Holy Spirit, teaching them to observe all things that I have commanded you; and lo, I am with you always, even to the end of the age." Amen."*

EMERGE

## CHAPTER NINE
# WARRIOR

# מחול

### (LOCHEM)

**Hebrew:**
"fighter, warrior, combatant, soldier, crusader, brave servicemen, cavalryman."

"The LORD is a man of WAR! The LORD is His name!"
- Exodus 15:3

"Courage above all things is the first and finest quality of the warrior!"
- Carl Von Clausewitz, Prussian Army General

"Weakness is strong. I must be stronger!"
- Jocko Willink, Seal Team 3

"A Warrior with a cause is the MOST dangerous soldier of them all!"
- Michael Scott, The Office

"Come back with your shield, or on it!"
- Spartan Wife

"PEACE IS NOT THE absence of conflict, but the presence of Justice!"
- movie AirForce One

## CHAPTER NINE: WARRIOR
# THE WARRIOR VACUUM

Throughout the Trump administration of 2016 -2020, we were subjected to an endless barrage of media hit pieces citing *"walls are racist"* and *"walls don't work!"* This was snapped up by the gullible, the woke, and those moved by emotion over reason and logic. The *same* media hit pieces then told the impressionable public with relentless messaging that *gun possession* and the 2nd Amendment are dangerous to public safety, endanger children, and groups like the NRA are terrorist organizations. Again, these were more smear jobs to attack President Trump, his connection to the NRA, and his defense of the 2nd Amendment. Two quick things that you need to know before you keep reading:

1. There has *never* been a mass shooting by a *member* of the NRA. Not one!

2. All school shootings and mass shootings have *one* common denominator. They take place in *"Gun Free Zones!"*

On a recent trip to Israel, we had the pleasure of visiting an anti-terrorism defense training center known as Caliber 3. The facility trains warriors. It makes *no apologies* for that fact. Israel contains seven million Jews surrounded by over a billion Muslims whose governments chant daily that they seek to wipe Israel off the map. Colonel Gat, who commands twenty thousand troops, explained that Israeli armed forces, like the IDF and Mossad, literally foil terror plots daily. One of the warriors we met asked me a question. He said, *"Do you know why Israel wins all its wars?"* I thought for a moment about their superior training, discipline, devotion to their nation, and God... but before I could answer, he answered his own question, *"Because we have to. If we lose, we will no longer exist!"* The saying is true, *"If the Muslim nations surrounding Israel laid down their weapons, there would be PEACE in the Middle East, but if Israel laid down her weapons, she would no longer exist!"*

We were told of a warrior who died in an ambush. He divided his forces based on intelligence that Hezbollah were tunneling under Israel's border to fill it with explosives. At around 3 am, he received an urgent call from his sniper, who noticed through the telescopic lens of his weapon that about two dozen young children were walking in a group toward the border. This set off a warning immediately in both the captain and the sniper, as children are in bed asleep at that time, not wandering around outside near national borders. Upon closer inspection, they saw there were indeed terrorists behind the children using them as human shields. They know that Israel will

145

**EMERGE**

not fire upon them when women and children are present because of their virtue in warfare. If Israel placed their women and children before their soldiers, the Muslims wouldn't think twice before opening fire. They do *not* share the same value for human life or virtue. You may be thinking, "*How can you say that? That's racist. That's politically incorrect!*" However, these are the terrorists who enter crowded shopping centers, theaters, and sporting arenas to detonate themselves, killing innocent civilians as they strike *fear* into the hearts of the ones they deem to be "*the enemies of Allah!*" The Israeli soldiers could not take the shot, not because they couldn't see the target, but because their protocol forbade them. The terrorists, knowing this, had set an ambush. An undetected sniper, located to the west of the children and terrorists, shot two bullets through the captain's head, killing him instantly. They *used* Israel's virtue against itself. That is *evil*, my friend.

Because *evil* exists, we must protect our loved ones, all that is dear to us, and God. That is what this chapter is all about!

## THE WARRIOR

The word *warrior* is used almost flippantly in our world today, usually describing a multiplicity of disciplines other than that of someone proficient in or enlisted in warfare. Today, we see it thrown about to describe the elite fighters in the world of boxing, mixed martial arts, and various other combat sports. It is even used to describe folks who push themselves beyond the pain barrier in CrossFit, tough mudder endurance runs, and Ninja Warrior obstacle courses.

Today, being referred to as a warrior is a compliment to those who press through pain barriers and obstacles that usually cause men to quit, give up, or throw in the towel. I have watched boxing matches where the contestant who lost was referred to as a *warrior* because they picked themselves up off the canvas after being knocked down multiple times. Though cut, bruised, and bleeding, they kept fighting back, refusing to quit.

It's obvious that a *warrior* has to do as much with heart as it does with someone who battles to defend his nation. I dedicate this chapter to outlining the heart of a warrior because if you allow God's Spirit to develop a warrior's heart within you, everything else will develop and flourish around it. A warrior never quits. A warrior fights to the end. A warrior never gives up and devotes himself to a cause greater than himself.

*You* are called to be a *warrior!*

# CHAPTER NINE: **WARRIOR**
## **GOD'S WARRIOR**

The Bible is a book that emphatically reveals to us the reality that life in this beautiful but fallen world is not a bed of roses. While the finalists in beauty pageants may *wish* for "World Peace," the reality is that peace is not slipping us by because there aren't enough people desiring it. Peace is not achieved through simply wishing or desiring it. Peace is not a universal reality simply because of the presence of evil in the world. The Bible alone teaches this as its default worldview position. The Bible is filled with stories of war, conflict, oppression, tyrannical agendas, cruelty, and conspiracy to overthrow God's righteous authority on Earth. Until *evil* is defeated, conflict, wars, and times of distress are the world's default position.

Search the world and human history over, and you will see that wherever there is strife, war, and conflict, there is a tyrant, a corrupt and illegitimate regime, or a dictator. Hitler, Mussolini, Idi Amin, The Taliban, ISIS, cartels, and warlords are all men possessed by evil spirits with one intention: to subjugate, dominate, and enslave other men. The old adage is true:

> *"The only thing necessary for the triumph of evil is for good men to do nothing."*
> *- Edmund Burke*

I believe the *main reason* masculine strength is vilified and labeled as *"toxic"* is because the evil one knows if men take their place as *God's warriors*, he has no chance of accomplishing his wicked agenda. Man is God's vice-regent on Earth. He is the one to whom God gave both the authority and the command to *exercise dominion* and *subdue!* God never intended for us to dominate or subjugate other men. That's a perversion of this commandment (Genesis 1:28). Its sole intention was directed at the presence of *evil* in the world—the serpent, Lucifer, banished from heaven and cast onto the Earth. When Jesus taught the disciples to pray, he admonished them to pray, *"Our father who art in heaven, Hallowed be thy name, thy Kingdom come, thy Will be done on earth as it is in heaven!"* (Matthew 6:9-10)

Our assignment is to *war* against everything that blocks or obstructs the Earth from looking like and reflecting heaven! See this powerful verse in Revelation:

> *"And war broke out in heaven: Michael and his angels fought with the dragon; and the dragon and his angels fought, but they did not prevail, nor was a place found for them in heaven any longer. So the great dragon was cast out, that serpent of old, called the Devil and Satan, who deceives*

# EMERGE

*the whole world; he was cast to the earth, and his angels were cast out with him. Then I heard a loud voice saying in heaven, "Now salvation, and strength, and the kingdom of our God, and the power of His Christ have come, for the accuser of our brethren, who accused them before our God day and night, has been cast down. And they overcame him by the blood of the Lamb and by the word of their testimony, and they did not love their lives to the death. Therefore rejoice, O heavens, and you who dwell in them! Woe to the inhabitants of the earth and the sea! For the devil has come down to you, having great wrath, because he knows that he has a short time.""*
*Revelation 12:7-12 NKJV*

According to Jesus' words, our assignment is to *drive* the devil out wherever we see him! If we are to do God's will *"on earth as it is in heaven,"* then we must acknowledge that God's will was for Satan to be cast out of Heaven, and now Heaven has peace. The Earth has woe, misery, wars, strife, and conflict because he (satan) has been cast down to Earth, and he's furious because he knows he only has a short time!

## THE UNQUALIFIED WARRIOR

"What if I am not qualified to be a warrior?"

This is the number one question men wrestle with internally. We rightfully look at insufficient strength, training, ability, prowess, and a litany of other legitimate issues that can, on the surface, disqualify us. However, in the 20th century, our world went through two world wars. In both of these wars, men as young as sixteen years old *faked* their ages and enlisted to go off to war to fight against *evil*. Many of them never returned home. They certainly didn't have all the right qualifications.

There is a great saying worth quoting here;
*"God never calls the qualified. He qualifies the called!"*

God makes it a habit to call His warriors from the people who feel most disqualified. David was a shepherd boy with *zero* man-to-man combat experience, yet he destroyed the undefeated Champion of Gath, Goliath! Moses was an eighty-year-old shepherd who grew up a secondary prince in Egypt's lush palaces, and yet he destroyed every army that opposed him in battle. Then there's Gideon:

*"And the Angel of the Lord appeared to him, and said to him, "The Lord*

## CHAPTER NINE: **WARRIOR**

*is with you, you mighty man of valor!" Gideon said to Him, "O my Lord, if the Lord is with us, why then has all this happened to us? And where are all His miracles which our fathers told us about, saying, 'Did not the Lord bring us up from Egypt?' But now the Lord has forsaken us and delivered us into the hands of the Midianites." Then the Lord turned to him and said, "Go in this might of yours, and you shall save Israel from the hand of the Midianites. Have I not sent you?" So he said to Him, "O my Lord, how can I save Israel? Indeed my clan is the weakest in Manasseh, and I am the least in my father's house." And the Lord said to him, "Surely I will be with you, and you shall defeat the Midianites as one man.""*

*Judges 6:12-16 NKJV*

Gideon, whose name means *"warrior"* or *"one who cuts in pieces,"* is hiding in a wine press, threshing wheat to keep from starving. For his entire life, he has known only one thing—the oppression and cruelty of the Midianite people. Every year, the Midianites would come with their vast hordes of warriors as Israel was about to reap and enjoy their harvest. The Bible says they would come in as innumerous as the locusts and leave absolutely *no sustenance* for Israel. For Gideon, this was the way it had always been. The response from Israel's leadership was to build dens, caves, and strongholds in the mountains to try to hide from their enemies. Nobody was fighting back or resisting. Maybe some had tried? *"Resistance is futile"* was the mantra of the Israelite people.

*"Then the children of Israel did evil in the sight of the Lord. So the Lord delivered them into the hand of Midian for seven years, and the hand of Midian prevailed against Israel. Because of the Midianites,* <u>the children of Israel made for themselves the dens, the caves, and the strongholds which are in the mountains</u>. *So it was, whenever Israel had sown, Midianites would come up; also Amalekites and the people of the East would come up against them. Then* <u>they would encamp against them and destroy the produce of the earth as far as Gaza, and leave no sustenance for Israel, neither sheep nor ox nor donkey</u>. *For they would come up with their livestock and their tents, coming in as numerous as locusts; both they and their camels were without number; and* <u>they would enter the land to destroy it. So Israel was greatly impoverished because of the Midianites, and the children of Israel cried out to the Lord.</u>*"*

*Judges 6:1-6 NKJV*

Then God shows up, and *everything* changes! God *sees* a mighty warrior and deliverer within Gideon because God sees us through the Spirit of truth. He sees us as we

**149**

## EMERGE

can be. He sees our potential, our very best! However, Gideon sees himself through the lens of the "wine press." He views himself as weak, cowardly, deficient, and small. Gideon and God have two different angles they are seeing this situation through. Which one is correct? Sadly, the answer is *both*, or at least both *can* become Gideon's reality. "How does that work?" you might ask. It's rarely preached that Gideon would become whichever word he *chooses to believe*. A man *cannot* rise higher than *how he sees himself!* When the disciples asked Jesus in the Gospel of John 6:28, *"What must we do to work the works of God?"* Jesus responds:

> *"'This is the work of God, that you <u>believe</u> in Him whom He sent.'"*
> *John 6:29 NKJV*

We believe our way into the kingdom. We believe our way forward in life. The first attack we read of in scripture is the serpent in the garden attacking the word of God. *"Has God really said? Pfff.. God knows the day you eat of what He's forbidden, you'll be just like him! You can't trust anything He says... I've known him a lot longer than you..."* (My liberal paraphrase of Genesis 3:2)

## PRIMARY WARFARE

> *Take the helmet of salvation and the sword of the Spirit, which is the word of God.*
> *Ephesians 6:17 NIV*

Interestingly, the final piece of protective armor for the warrior is the helmet. Ephesians lists this as the last item before the warrior picks up his sword and shield and enters the battle arena. It's not a coincidence. This is the most significant and vulnerable area for the warrior. Remember, David took down the giant with a *headshot!* Likewise, you and I can be easily taken down by the relentless enemy with his headshot. Your life moves in the direction of your belief. Your life will rise and fall upon the thoughts you think.

> *"I don't know HOW I am going to win. I just KNOW I'm not going to lose!"*
> *- Gohkam Saki, Mixed Martial Arts*

Your first and *primary* battle (meaning, if you don't get this one right, everything else will rest on a poor foundation of shifting sands) is in your head— what you believe.

# CHAPTER NINE: **WARRIOR**

Gideon stands at a crossroads. He can either believe his genuine reality and life experience—that of being oppressed, too weak, and insignificant in the face of such injustice—or he can believe the word from Heaven, which says, *"He is a mighty man of valor, and the LORD is with him, and he will defeat the entire Midianite army as though they were one man!"* (Judges 6:12-16)

Does he believe his history, his life experience thus far, and the words of other men, or does he believe what Heaven has declared? This is the first and most crucial battle for every man of God. This is the defining battle for the warrior of God. Win this one, and the devil knows he is toast! It's always harder to believe *Heaven's word* because negative words and thoughts already have an *"amen"* through your life experiences, emotions, memories, and circumstances.

On the other hand, Heaven's word is calling you *up* into a place you have never been to before. You don't have previous experience to reference, making it easy for you. You have to bring your own amen in faith. That's why reading the Bible is so powerful. You will find your amen in the dealings of God with other men in history who were just like you and I!

Amen to what God has said, despite how you feel and your current circumstances yelling at you! Go *up* into a place you have never been before and become what you *cannot* become on your own!

> *"Putting on the helmet of salvation..."*
> *-Ephesians 6:17*

Gideon does believe God and becomes the warrior who not only defeats the Midianites but also tears down the idols of Baal and Asherah in his father's house. When the men of the town see their beloved idol has been desecrated and destroyed by Gideon, they demand his execution. Gideon's father intercedes for his son, saying, *"If Baal really is a god, then let him plead his own case!"* (Judges 6:31) After this incident, Gideon was no longer called Gideon. He became "JerubBaal," meaning "Let the devil plead" or "Contender of Baal."

Like Gideon, there's a warrior in each man even though we face a world that tries to control and weaken men. This song illustrates that tension.

*"I promised you, Dad, not to do the things you've done*
*I walk away from trouble when I can*
*Now, please don't think I'm weak, I didn't turn the other cheek*

**EMERGE**

*And Papa, I sure hope you understand
Sometimes you gotta fight when you're a man."*

*Everyone considered him the coward of the county.*
- Kenny Rogers

## WHY DO WE NEED MEN TO BE WARRIORS?

There are two main reasons we need men to be warriors today:

1. *Evil*

This world contains a very real "resident evil!" It's the evil that traffics children, placing them into the hands of wicked and perverted men. It's an evil that enters a schoolyard and shoots innocent children that pose no threat. It's an evil that destroys all that is beautiful, pure, holy, and sacred. It *must* be opposed. It *must* be withstood. Evil does not rest. It is *never* at peace. It is insidious. It is nasty. It is cruel. Evil has a source, and it's *the devil*. The Bible has many names for him. One of them is "The Cruel One!" (Proverbs 5:9). He is the spirit of *wickedness and* the master over the *evil spirits that torment, afflict, steal, kill, and destroy.*

The spirit operating behind the "toxic masculinity" movement is a satanic spirit. It seeks to weaken households and society by pacifying men and eradicating the heart of a warrior within them so it can do as it wishes unimpeded to cause desolation and destruction.

2. *The Defenseless*

We are in desperate need of warrior men because a great number of people are defenseless against this rise of evil in our time. The devil attacks our children in the womb through abortion and now also post-birth through radical infanticide laws. Add to that the pedophilic LGBTQ "Drag Queen" assault on the innocence of our children and gender reassignment, which is just another term for mutilating and sterilizing our kids. It's been left up to the women to fight for our children while the men sat back and let them. It's time for *men* to stand up and push back!

Throughout antiquity, men have gone to war to defend those who cannot protect themselves. Men became warriors or, at the very least, *took on* the role of a warrior to

## CHAPTER NINE: **WARRIOR**

defend the women and children of their village or tribe. Those who cannot speak up, get up, or stand up for themselves require someone to stand up and fight for them. This is a biblical pattern spawning both the old and the new testaments, and it is in desperate need of revival again in our times today! If you believe God or Jesus was a pacifist, then you are biblically ignorant.

> *"Blessed be the Lord my Rock, Who trains my hands for war, And my fingers for battle— My lovingkindness and my fortress, My high tower and my deliverer, My shield and the One in whom I take refuge, Who subdues my people under me."*
> *Psalms 144:1-2 NKJV*

Whether it's a sixteen-year-old shepherd boy walking into a valley to face an undefeated giant warrior, Gideon forging the original "300" warriors who took on and defeated an army one hundred times larger, or the Black Robe Regiment that fought the British and won America's independence and freedom, the evidence is insurmountable. Men are called to be warriors, and we need them more than ever today!

## **THE LEAST LIKELY WARRIOR**

I was twelve when I started high school at Dapto High School in NSW, Australia. I distinctly remember feeling excitement and nausea at the "bigness" of this next chapter of my life. I would be there with thousands of students, many of whom I had never met. It was quite daunting, but those feelings were soon alleviated by seeing the number of pretty girls all attending this large school. I remember thinking that it would be inevitable that I would get to meet them, talk to them, and maybe at some point date someone who could turn out to be my one true love! I mean, who knows? Anything is possible, right? Or so I thought.

Five major public primary schools fed students into this high school, creating a micro cosmopolitan metropolis of cultures, colors, ethnicities, and backgrounds. Everything was different, bigger, and unfamiliar. I felt lost and nervous trying to find my way to places like the science department, home economics, and the woodwork/metalwork buildings.

When the bell rang, indicating it was lunchtime that first day, I made my way up to the canteen (as we called it down under.) There were a dozen windows to line up in front of, each serving delicious food. You were spoiled with choice. Each window

## EMERGE

specialized in a different type of food and beverage. I had heard about how good the meat pies and sausage rolls were in this school and soon found out that this was served from window four. Upon finding the correct window, I lined up about thirty people back, but my anticipation for a "meat pie with sauce" made the case that the wait was totally going to be worth it!

After about fifteen minutes, I progressed closer to the window, and there were probably about ten people from the front of the line. My tummy was growling with hunger pains as much as my mouth was watering, anticipating the *meat pie* with sauce (ketchup). I watched people leaving the window, their faces dancing with delight as they walked past me carrying their bountiful pastries, licking their lips, ready to devour their fare. Suddenly, three *men* walked right up and cut in line in front of me. They weren't *men* yet, but they certainly appeared so—facial hair, muscular physiques, at least six inches (or more) taller than me in size. I remember thinking they seemed to be as big as my dad. Two of them were even bigger. I politely announced, *"Hey, you're cutting in line. I've been waiting for the last fifteen minutes!"* Thinking they may have just been in conversation and hadn't realized their error. They looked at me and laughed.

*"What are you going to do about it?"* one of them gestured, poking his finger into my chest.

*"I'm gonna... I'm gonna tell the teacher on playground duty..."* I snapped back threateningly.

*"Bwahahaha!"* they laughed. *"I tell ya what, how about we meet you after school today, and we will let you know what we think of snitches!?"* I learned that day that not only do bullies exist, but in my prepubescent feeble state, there was very little I could do about it. I was a skinny kid and a late bloomer.

## Peace through Strength

It was 1980, and roller skating was a massive fad that swept across Australia. Roller Rinks (as they were called) popped up everywhere. It was not only great exercise, but it was a wonderful place to hang out with friends. A DJ played all the latest top hits, and there were cute girls to ask to join you in the "couples skate" that always closed out the end of the skating session.

Lights would be lowered, romantic songs like "Endless Love" would play, the disco ball would spin, and the mood was set, creating the most colorful and romantic environment I had ever seen. My friends and I would spend the first hour or so *"checking*

## CHAPTER NINE: **WARRIOR**

*out the chicks*" (sizing the prettiest girls), and then we would fight over who would ask the prettiest one to the couple skate. The truth was, we were all too chicken. In the end, we were "more talk" than action!

One week, while skating and singing along to one of my favorite songs, I noticed quite a cute girl who would repeatedly brush right up to me, smile with a stunning smile, her beautiful, big, bright brown eyes lighting up her face as though to give me permission to befriend her and end the "stranger" status. Then she'd skate off, only to look back at me with that same beautiful, magical smile. Before I could process my thoughts or develop an appropriate response, Stefan Mueller, an 8th grader, skated up to me and interruptingly blurted out, *"Have you heard of the Dugans?"*

I spluttered at the radical shift of thoughts racing through my head and responded, *"Err... Yes, aren't they that crazy gang from the projects who fight with nunchucks, baseball bats, chains, and knives?"* Stefan stared at me with a serious look on his face, telling me I wasn't going to like what came next.

*"Yep, that's the one. Anyway, they are after you!"* He stated almost nonchalantly. *"What?? What did I do?"* I protested.

*"You see that girl there?"* He pointed at the cute girl who kept skating past me and smiling.

*"Yes."*

*"Well, she was dating the leader of the Dugans, and she broke up with him today. She told him that she was done with him and just wanted someone who would love her and whom she would like to be with. Someone like you and not a gang leader like him! He's raging mad. Anyway,"* he went on, *"They are going to wait for you outside at the end of skating, where he is going to beat the living sh\*t out of you!"*

*"Hang on!"* I again protested, *"I've done nothing to encourage this; I don't even know her name... I've never even spoken to her... in fact, I'm not sure I'm even interested!"* I stated emphatically.

To which he responded, *"It doesn't matter. She pointed you out, and now they're going to take you out!"*

What the HECK?

## EMERGE

I had done absolutely nothing to solicit this current threat. Yet here I was about to get a beating from a gang with a reputation for putting people they didn't like into hospital. Not long after this, they pulled their car over, got out with their baseball bats, and beat and bloodied their target unconscious, leaving him brain-damaged with severely injured motor neuron skills. Later, they discovered that their identities had been mixed up and that he was "not" their intended target. But the damage was done, and it was permanent. Bullies do bad things to good people, whether they are warranted or not.

Thank God for the head of security that day. He saw the gang amassing outside the glass exit doors. I had favor with him. I played soccer with his younger brother and had always been a good friend to him. He was also a black belt in karate and was most revered by the gang members, having hospitalized a few of them in an altercation a few months earlier as they tried to jump him and his girlfriend. He walked me out to my mother's car, where my mother waited, totally oblivious to all that was happening. As we passed by the leader of the gang, he rose up and gestured he was going to make an advance toward me. My security friend stepped toward him, flexing and gesturing a posture that said, *"You want some of this?"* I watched as this gang leader totally backed down, and all the other members who had followed his lead now retreated, lowering their bats and chains and hiding their nunchucks.

I learned that day that *"peace"* can *only* be secured through strength!

## HOW TO BEAT A BULL!

I still hadn't come to grips with the roller skating incident when one of the guys from the high school football team decided he also didn't like me because his girlfriend commented that she thought I was cute. He was a couple of years older than me, an athlete, and sported the muscles and manliness that comes from a post puberty boost of testosterone. On the other hand, I was still a skinny, barely ninety-five-pound, thirteen-year-old. I had to run around in the shower just to get wet, waiting (almost pleading) for my testicles to drop and to hopefully develop some "manly" strength so I could shed my Sunday school choir boy persona. As you can imagine, once again, I was an "easy target," and this guy and his friends would make sure to let me know by punching me as they passed by me on the way to classes. I would dread walking down the corridors. Whenever I ran into them, they would punch me in the face or stomach for no reason other than they were bigger than me and didn't like me.

One of my friends received similar treatment for about a week, but he had an older brother who, upon finding out, threatened these guys. They promptly backed off and

## CHAPTER NINE: **WARRIOR**

gave him a reprieve from these hallway beatings. I, on the other hand, had no "older brother." Nobody defended me. What was I to do?

At that time, the movie *Rocky* came out. It's about a boxer from the streets of Philadelphia who, against all odds, becomes the heavyweight champion of the world. The hit song "Eye of the Tiger" provided the soundtrack to the most inspirational workout preparation scenes for Rocky Balboa's fight! That was it! I decided I wanted to take up boxing and learn to defend myself. I didn't know how to go about it, as there was no Google search, internet, or "Alexa" to ask, *"Where's the nearest boxing academy?"* Well, as luck would have it (bad luck, not good), one week later, there was the Dapto Show, a massive carnival with rides and attractions. Everyone was going. Dapto, the town where I grew up, was a lower socioeconomic town and had a lot of youths from broken homes. As the adage goes, "Hurting people Hurt people!"

I remember being in line with my friends to ride *The Tornado*. *This ride* spun you around at high speeds, ensuring a 99% chance you would either throw up after the ride (or perhaps even during) or, at the very least, be cognitively and physically impaired, requiring months of chiropractic care. All of a sudden, it felt like my eyeball burst in its socket, as what seemed like a cricket ball hit me right in the cheekbone below my eye. I turned to see what it was, and a deranged guy was swinging his next punch toward my face. I did my best to duck and weave, receiving countless blows to the top of my head, my arms, and any other body part that was protecting my face. Then, all of a sudden, he stopped and said, *"Wellsy?"*
I responded that *no*, I wasn't this *"Wellsy"* character he was looking for. To which he stated, *"Oh Sh\*t, sorry, I thought you were somebody else!"* I went home with a black eye, bruised ribs, and absolutely no self-esteem whatsoever. The guy was again bigger and older than I was, and even though he caught me off guard, I would not have chosen to fight with him had I had the choice.

This was all I needed to find a boxing academy, where I would learn to defend myself against my discovery that the world is a place where the strong not only "rule over" the weak but oppress them at every turn. I joined the North Wollongong Police Boys Boxing Gym. Three to four nights a week, I would train and learn the skill and art of boxing. I have never been as fit as I was back then. I remember coming out of the surf, and one of my friends commented: *"Wow, muscles!?!"* I had not even noticed my entire physique had developed.

## EMERGE

The training was brutal. To begin, we would have to run five miles. Then we would do eight rounds of three minutes on the heavy bag, eight on the light bag, and four rounds on the speedball, followed by six hundred sit-ups/crunches. The trainer would drop a fifteen-pound medicine ball on our stomachs (to resemble being punched) as we finished the last hundred. Then, it was one hundred push-ups, and upon completion of those exercises, we would enter the ring and "spar" with the other boxers. You learned pretty quickly that if you lowered your right hand whenever you threw a jab, your opponent would left-hook you right in the jaw!

Brutal as it was, I absolutely fell in love with boxing and developed a passion and respect for it as an art form rather than a pugilistic sport. It was more like "high combat chess by super fit athletes" than thuggery and violence. When the bell rang, for the next three minutes, you would try to exploit a weakness in your opponent and knock his *ss onto the canvas, but afterward, you would hug, shake hands, and buy each other a drink. I had no idea the bonding, the affirmation of "you got what it takes to be a man," and the mutual respect boxing would bring. What I never received from my absent, self-absorbed, partying, carousing father, I received from my "opponents" (who became my friends) in the ring.

After my third amateur fight and win, I developed more than skill and muscle. I now had confidence in my "masculinity" that should have been instilled by my father but was instead instilled here in the sweaty, un-air-conditioned Police Boys Club. In my third fight, I had just turned sixteen, and my opponent was a twenty-four-year-old mechanic. To say I was nervous and even scared before the fight was an understatement. My trainer told me, however, that I was one of the best counterpunchers he had seen, that I had impeccable hand speed, and I could easily beat this guy. At the bell, he came out so aggressively, like he wanted to knock me out in the first ten seconds. I remember bobbing, weaving, and throwing straight jabs to keep him at bay. Then I started counterpunching everything he was throwing, landing at will, and rocking him several times. At the end of the fight, he came straight over to my corner and said, *"Wow, you've got incredible hand speed and power. I had to muster everything I had not to go down and stay on my feet!"* We hugged, exchanged pleasantries, and had the most profound respect for one another afterward.

With this newfound confidence, I was in my sophomore year, and "Shane," the bully, was a senior. I remember seeing him walk toward me in the hallway (we say corridor in Australia). He spotted me, and I knew he was sizing me up for another punch. This

## CHAPTER NINE: **WARRIOR**

time, I wasn't about to just receive it. As he approached, I saw him clench his fist and raise it, ready to throw. This time, I anticipated the punch. I remember thinking then, "How could I have let these pathetic punches of such poor technique land on me?" I easily slipped the punch, clenched my left fist, and from my waist, came up with a left hook that landed on his jaw and knocked him onto the floor. I then stood over him and, in an "alpha gorilla" like gesture, said to him, *"You ever even look at me wrong, and I'll knock you into tomorrow!"* Adrenaline was coursing through my body as people began to cheer. The bully was knocked down, and man, did it feel good!

If this is what the spirit of the world calls "Toxic Masculinity," count me in. I'll take more of it!

> *"Weak men, create bad times. Bad times create strong men. Strong men create good times. Good times create weak men!"*
> *- Way of the warrior*

## BE A WARRIOR

Is it possible to describe "biblical masculinity" without referring to the quality of manhood, known as "warrior?" Please note a warrior is very different from a warmonger. In fact, it's because of "warmongers" (bullies) that we need to discover and develop the warrior within us! The Holy Spirit of God will develop the warrior within you *if* you let Him!

> *"They shall be like mighty men, Who tread down their enemies In the mire of the streets in the battle. They shall fight because the Lord is with them, And the riders on horses shall be put to shame."*
> *Zechariah 10:5 NKJV*

When King Saul was suffering from a tormenting and troubling evil spirit, relief was sought for him from among the tribes of Israel. A search went out for someone who could minister to the king and relieve him from the tormenting and vexing spirit that robbed his sleep, stole his peace, and ensured that he executed his leadership tasks and responsibilities under a fog of fatigue, distress, and weariness.

They discovered a young man and brought him before the king. This young man was no other than David, the son of Jesse the Bethlehemite and Israel's future king! In the book of 1 Samuel 16:18, the servants highlight the following attributes of the one

## EMERGE

who can stand before the king, minister to him effectively, and relieve the distress and torment of this devil spirit.

> *"Then one of the servants answered and said, "Look, I have seen a son of Jesse the Bethlehemite, who is skillful in playing, a mighty man of valor, a man of war, prudent in speech, and a handsome person; and the Lord is with him."*
> *I Samuel 16:18 NKJV*

Two of the six attributes described here for David's qualification are:

*Mighty man of Valor*

*A man of WAR*

The servant didn't say things like, *"He's kind, tolerant, loving, gracious, and merciful."* These are all wonderful traits, but a mighty man of valor and a man of war are centerpieces in his leadership bio. Why? Because *evil* exists in the world. Warfare, valor, courage, and bravery are required. Bullies *must* be stood up to. Evil *must* be overcome by good. Peace through strength is the *only* peace that lasts. When the strength is gone, the peace will depart. Evil always seeks to overthrow, exert its will, enslave, rob, and steal.

> *"The Thief comes only to steal, kill and destroy, but I have come that you may have life and have it more abundantly!"*
> *- John 10:10*

Nowhere does the Bible teach that we are to coexist with evil. All through the scriptures, we are implored to overthrow, defeat, subdue, overcome, conquer, and vanquish it! This is what Jesus did. Sadly, many pastors, preachers, and leaders have departed from the truth about God. They prefer a woke, pacifist Jesus, who spent his days with the down and out, the homeless, and the hopeless, who just loved everybody and judged nobody. It sounds nice, but this is a farce at best and a grave heresy. If you ask these folks, "Why did Jesus come to Earth?" They will say, *"To die for our sins!"* And while this is correct, it is only *part* of why Jesus came.

1 John 3:8 Tells us that Jesus came to do more than just deal with sin:

> *"He who sins is of the devil, for the devil has sinned from the beginning.*

# CHAPTER NINE: **WARRIOR**

*For this purpose the Son of God was manifested, that He might destroy the works of the devil."*
*I John 3:8 NKJV*

Jesus came to destroy the works of the devil!

During His time here on earth, Jesus healed the sick, raised the dead, cleansed lepers, defeated demonic powers, and broke curses everywhere He went! He came as a warrior. He operated in warfare. He came to tear down the kingdom of darkness and replace it with the kingdom of light. He came to overthrow and defeat the evil one. He "cast out" demons because they wouldn't (and still won't) leave arbitrarily. They are not law-abiding. They are not kind, considerate, or compassionate. They *only* depart when they are *cast out* (literally thrown out).

*"But if I cast out demons with the finger of God, surely the kingdom of God has come upon you. When a strong man, fully armed, guards his own palace, his goods are in peace. But when a stronger than he comes upon him and overcomes him, he takes from him all his armor in which he trusted, and divides his spoils."*
*Luke 11:20-22 NKJV*

As a man, you are made in the image and the likeness of God. The Bible says in Exodus 15:3, "*The LORD is a man of WAR. The LORD is His name!*" As an image and likeness bearer of the Almighty, *you* are walking in your fullness when you walk in a warrior mindset.

Sun Tzu (the great Chinese military strategist, philosopher, general, and writer) authored a magnificent piece of literature, *The Art of War*, which has become somewhat of a respected voice in the arena of warfare and winning, even as the generations have moved toward a more of a "woke," pacifist mentality. He is often quoted by motivational speakers, football coaches, military commanders, etc. He has many fine quotes on not just warfare but also winning. Here are a few of my favorites:

*"He will win who knows when to fight and when not to fight!"*
*- Sun Tzu*

*"In war then, let your objective be VICTORY, not lengthy campaigns!"*
*- Sun Tzu*

# EMERGE

Steve Bannon of the War Room and former adviser to the 45th President of the United States says:

*"There is no substitute for VICTORY!"*

A warrior doesn't fight for fighting sake. He is not a warmonger or a bully. He fights to protect what is his, what God has allotted to him. God help the man who tries to take it from him. His wife, his family, his home, his freedoms—none of these things are taken for granted by the man of war. Freedom isn't free. It *never* has been, and it never will be. The warrior knows that. Somebody fought to ensure the freedoms you enjoy today are afforded you. Tyranny always seeks to take these freedoms from you. If you are to pass these freedoms on, you have no choice but to *war* for them.

I am sad when I look at the current state of America. When will men realize that *"HOW you get something is how you KEEP it?"* America fought a *war* of independence from a tyrannical king. Still, we have a generation that has become intoxicated by pleasure and carousing. They've lost their hunger for justice, truth, righteousness, and freedom. We have a generation that willingly trades freedom for pleasure. Never in our history have we had so many people addicted to substances, devices, pleasures, and the possession of "things." The enemy is crafty. As Sun Tzu so aptly put it:

*"Hence, fighting and conquering in all your battles is not supreme excellence; supreme excellence consists in breaking the enemy's resistance without fighting!"*

This quote shows how the enemy of human souls has already gained the upper hand. We have the most feminized generation of men in history. Low sperm counts and dropping testosterone rates plague this generation[1], which largely catalogs being a warrior under the label of "toxic masculinity!"

## COURAGE

One of the greatest prerequisites to being a warrior is that of courage. Courage has been called the virtue upon which all other virtues hang. Without courage, the other virtues fail. Courage stands up to and defeats bullies. Courage finds a young man standing alone before a tank in Tiananmen Square. Courage caused a teenage shepherd boy to bring down an undefeated giant named Goliath. It is courage that God necessitates for Joshua, the successor of Moses, to possess if he is to not only enter the promised land but also dispossess the nations currently occupying the promised territories of God!

## CHAPTER NINE: WARRIOR

*"Be strong and of good courage, for to this people you shall divide as an inheritance the land which I swore to their fathers to give them. Only be strong and very courageous, that you may observe to do according to all the law which Moses My servant commanded you; do not turn from it to the right hand or to the left, that you may prosper wherever you go. This Book of the Law shall not depart from your mouth, but you shall meditate in it day and night, that you may observe to do according to all that is written in it. For then you will make your way prosperous, and then you will have good success. Have I not commanded you? Be strong and of good courage; do not be afraid, nor be dismayed, for the Lord your God is with you wherever you go."*
Joshua 1:6-9 NKJV

*"Courage is contagious. When a brave man takes a stand, the spines of others are often stiffened!"*
- Billy Graham

*"Freedom is never more than one generation away from extinction. We didn't pass it to our children in the bloodstream. It must be fought for, protected, and handed on for them to do the same!"*
- Ronald Reagan

## EVERY MAN HAS BATTLES

One of the truest statements I have ever heard is, *"Life's not fair!"*

I think it's the first truth we discover in our childhood years. Any father will have seen their child with the glum, cat's bum face, arms folded, followed by an exasperated blurting of the statement, *"That's not fair!"* Whether it's allowance portions, curfews, or a younger sibling being allowed not to eat certain vegetables that the older sibling had to finish before being allowed to leave the table... life isn't fair.

We hear this saying again and again. Perhaps God is not working overtime to try and make life "fair" for every individual. Perhaps He has something greater in mind and much higher value than our comfort. Perhaps the fact that life is unfair brings the warrior out in us.

**EMERGE**

# HERO DEVELOPMENT

*"You were born to be a HERO to someone. Life will find its highest purpose and meaning when you find out who that someone is!"*

What creates heroes? That question reminds me of the first responders in New York City on 9/11 when deranged terrorists attacked the Twin Towers. While people were fleeing the collapsing disaster, first responders ran directly into the chaos and danger. Many ran in and, sadly, never made it out. They died trying to save as many lives as they could. Many of these men had wives and children waiting at home. They all had something to keep living for, yet willingly gave their lives that day!

*"For greater love has no man than this that he lay down his life for his friends!"*
*- John 16:3*

Is there a school that teaches heroism? Is there a training course? An online forum one can participate in and graduate from? Are some people born heroes while others are born victims? How do we even define what a hero is? Could there be heroes who would never have EMERGED had it not been for the stark, negative, and unfair circumstances of their day? There seems to be a common denominator throughout history and folklore concerning the emergence of heroes. It is always accompanied by villainous tyrants and bullies who must be stopped. It seems like every hero has a nemesis, an arch-rival. Superman has Lex Luthor. Batman has the Joker, the Riddler, and the Penguin. We know of King David because of a Giant bully named Goliath. It was the Philistine dominance and subjugation of Israel that gave birth to the hero Samson!

The Jedi are heroes because of the evils of Emperor Palpatine and his dark side cavorting with Sith Lords. Frodo and Samwise Gamgee are heroes because the evil Sauron seeks to plunge the world into eternal darkness with the one ring that rules all rings. History truly holds freedom fighters like William Wallace in high esteem, in the most heroic of proportions, because of the tyranny and oppression they suffered and overcame.

I suggest you *never* pray for God to make your life "fair!" Do not ask for an easy life. Instead, ask that the unfairness of life gives birth to the hero buried inside you! All stories, movies, and legends involving heroism and bravery include a nemesis, an oppressor, cruelty, or unfair times. *You* have the power to choose to be a victim or a hero! It's that simple. It's a choice. Simply deciding that "victim" is *not* an option will set you on the path to the heroic!

The man who grew up in a home with a father who was overcome by alcoholism and

## CHAPTER NINE: **WARRIOR**

who chooses never to drink is a hero. The man who experienced the devastation of his father's infidelities that led to divorce, pain, and heartache and who chooses to stay married come hell or high water is a *hero*!

The Holy Spirit is a *"hero-producing"* spirit. Every time He falls upon someone, heroism follows. In my life, He (the Holy Spirit) has required me to "be" for others what I didn't have myself. Growing up, my father never told me, *"I'm proud of you!"* or *"I love you, son!"* Instead, my childhood was filled with berating and belittling words. I was continually reminded of what a disappointment I was. I loved and played competitive soccer as a youth. My dad almost never came to watch my games. If he did have to be there, it was because there was a transportation deficit, and the coach had to specifically ask him to drive and help out. He would sit in the car. I would hear all the other fathers cheering on their sons. I would often make a tackle, score a goal, or be the assist that set up a goal and immediately search the faces of the parents cheering on the sidelines for my father's face. Just for a smile, a nod... approval. Sadly, it never happened.

When I got saved at eighteen years of age, God began a massive healing venture into the brokenness of my heart. That's what He does. He *"heals the brokenhearted"* (Luke 4:18). Over the years, God has required me to be for my children and for others what had never been to me. This is what heroes do. They don't wait to be rescued. They rescue. They don't wait to be delivered. They deliver others. They don't withhold because it was withheld from them. They give. They sow. They sacrifice.

## OUR GREATEST ENEMY IS OUR 'INNER' ME!

*"It is not the mountain we conquer but ourselves."*
- Edmund Hillary

*"There is little that can withstand a man who can conquer himself."*
- King Louis XIV

The *first* and *last* of all battles is the one we face within ourselves. The biggest enemy who can do the most damage in my life is not the devil on the outside but my selfish, sinful "inner me!" You will read many quotes saying that the greatest warrior is the one who can or has conquered himself. Alexander the Great, who had conquered the known world by the time he was just twenty-five years old, remarked in his later years, *"I have conquered nations and kingdoms, as have many others before me. However, I have yet to meet a man who has conquered himself!"*

## EMERGE

When I first read that quote, I was most discouraged. I thought to myself, *"If a man as disciplined, focused, and as great as Alexander the Great can't conquer himself, what chance do I have?"* I had tried to conquer my lusts, my selfish desires, and my iniquities (sins that are generational, passed down from father and mother), and I had failed *every time!* I thought doing so was an impossibility. To a large degree, this is true, and that's why the Lion of Judah had to become the innocent *lamb* to take away the world's sins.

However, I have found that you and I can totally conquer ourselves in every area of our lives that is out of alignment with God's word, purpose, and will for us. It's not through greater discipline. Although discipline does play a part, discipline alone won't suffice. When you war against yourself, you will always lose!

"What does that mean?"

I'm glad you asked.

It means you will *always* end up choosing what *you* prefer over what is right and honoring to God. That's why He passed down the Ten Commandments to us. These are ten inclinations and dispositions of your heart and its desires that choose against the perfect law of God. The keeping of God's perfect law isn't difficult. It's impossible. How, then, do you and I conquer ourselves? It can only be accomplished one way. Discipleship. You and I need someone to help us when we get stuck and to challenge us when we choose poorly, selfishly, or incorrectly. Someone who loves you and is committed to your betterment and to seeing God's best manifest in your life.

This requires you to allow someone to deal with the dirt, debris, and destructive thoughts and patterns of your inner world. Who do I trust? It can't be someone who *only* sees the dirt. Any jackass can point out our faults, failings, and weaknesses. *Only trust* someone who *sees* the *gold* in you and sees the dirt as an impediment to you realizing the power, purpose, and potential lying untapped and undeveloped beneath it!

How does a man conquer himself? By recognizing that by himself, he is *unable* to do this. God determined from the beginning that it was *not good* for man to be alone and that he needed someone to help him. The day you open your life to someone who loves you, sees the gold in you, is *not afraid* to point out the dirt in you, and then works *with* you to help you shift it—that's the day you will begin to conquer yourself in every area, bringing it into subjection to the King of Kings, the Creator of the universe.

# CHAPTER NINE: WARRIOR
## CLOSING INSPIRATIONAL WARRIOR QUOTES

*"Every great warrior must learn to endure and overcome the adversities of life."*
*– Lailah Gifty Akita, Author of Think Great, Be Great*

*"The warrior fights with courage, not with anger."*
*– Ashanti Proverb*

*"Tomorrow's victory is today's practice."*
*– Chris Bradford, Black Belt MMA*

*"Your mind is a battlefield, be its commander, not its soldier."*
*- Unknown*

*"Protecting yourself is self-defense. Protecting others is warriorship."*
*– Bodhi Sanders, Author, 6 time MMA Champion*

*"God doesn't give the hardest battles to his toughest soldiers, he creates the toughest soldiers through life's hardest battles"*
*– Warrior Saying*

*Some must be warriors, that others may live in peace."*
*– Mercedes Lackey, Author*

*"It is better to die on your feet than to live on your knees."*
*– Emiliano Zapata, Mexican Revolutionary*

*"Being a warrior is not about the act of fighting. It's about being so prepared to face a challenge and believing so strongly in the cause you are fighting for that you refuse to quit."*
*– Michael J. Asken, Phycohlogist*

*"Fear doesn't go away. The warrior and the artist live by the same code of necessity, which dictates that the battle must be fought anew every day."*
*– Steven Pressfield, Author*

*"Weakness is strong. I must be stronger."*
*– Jocko Willink, Seal Team 3*

# EMERGE

# CHAPTER TEN
# PRODUCER
(WORKER/STEWARD)

## ורצי

### *QUOTES*

*"Efficiency is doing things right. Effectiveness is doing the right things."*
**Peter Drucker,** *management consultant*

*"Work gives you meaning and purpose, and life is empty without it."*
Stephen Hawking, English theoretical physicist, cosmologist, and author
*"Productivity is being able to do things that you were never able to do before."*
– Franz Kafka, Novelist from Progue

*"When a man is unemployed, it devastates the man. Suicides during the Great Depression among men who were unemployed or made redundant were massive!"*
- The Boy Crisis.

*"Then God blessed them, and God said to them, "Be fruitful and multiply; fill the earth and subdue it; have dominion over the fish of the sea, over the birds of the air, and over every living thing that moves on the earth."*
*Genesis 1:28*

EMERGE

# A PRODUCER

Men come alive when they produce, win, and conquer. Everything God created had seed within itself to "reproduce after its own kind!" (Genesis 1:29) As a *male*, you are a "seed bearer." You are, therefore, "hardwired" to reproduce. You have the innate ability to produce a great marriage, a family, a business, and a stream (or better yet, streams) of income. You're designed to produce joy in those closest to you and trustworthiness in those who employ or deploy you. Your life is always producing. The question isn't, "Am I producing?" The question is, "What am I producing?"

Just as the ground "produces" thorns, thistles, weeds, and poisonous plants because of God's curse in Genesis 3:17, when we operate outside of God's word and Spirit, we don't produce thorns and snares instead of life and peace. You may have produced addiction, dysfunction, negative habits, destructive thought patterns, hopelessness, and fear. You may have produced a prison record or a bad reputation. The *good news* is that *you* are a producer and can change the *seed* you're sowing to *produce* a different harvest and a different future.

Galatians 6:7 says, *"Do not be deceived, God is NOT mocked, whatever a man sows that he shall also reap!"*

In other words, God doesn't determine the harvests of your life. *You do*! How? By the seeds you sow! You won't enjoy your harvest if you sow seeds of hate, animosity, negativity, infidelity, and iniquity!

*"He who sows iniquity will reap sorrow, And the rod of his anger will fail."*
*Proverbs 22:8*

## A LESSON FROM THE LIFE OF SAMSON

One of the guarantees you can take to the bank on the Bible's authenticity is its transparency and honesty. I mean, no other literature throws its own people under the bus and tells on itself, spilling the most embarrassing and shameful details as the Bible does on its people. Even the most famed heroes are not exempt. Moses was a murderer. Abraham lied when it served him and was willing to trade his wife's virtue and safety to benefit his own neck and prosperity. Noah got drunk. David committed adultery and then had the woman's husband killed in battle. The Bible can be trusted because it doesn't airbrush out our humanity but conversely exposes it and reveals to us a God who can move mightily through even the most flawed among us!

## CHAPTER TEN: **PRODUCER**

One of those folks is Samson, the only son of Manoah and his wife. Samson was a powerful, mighty deliverer and judge of Israel who had a fetish for the forbidden. As a Nazarite, he had three rules:

1. No wine or intoxicating drink.
2. He could *not* touch anything unclean or dead.
3. He was *not* allowed to cut his hair.

Sadly, Samson has done all three over his life, and he does them spectacularly among the Philistines and not even his own people. He loved Philistine women, and even his father was puzzled, asking him if there were no attractive Israelite women. Why would he go to the Philistines to find love and a helpmate? It seems that the old adage is true. *"That which we are deprived of, we strive for!"* It certainly was in Samson's case.

Samson was anointed by God to be a judge in Israel. He was anointed to produce certain results—freedom from tyranny, liberty from oppression, and justice where there was injustice. However, he got entangled with a gal named Delilah! For time's sake, I'm not going to retell the story (But I encourage you to read it for yourself in Judges 13-16.) The story culminates with Samson giving Delilah access to the innermost secrets of his heart, not because she *loved* him but because he *lusted* after her beauty. *Lust* is a thief and a robber. It will steal your strength, vision, purpose, and destiny if you don't put it in its place!

> *"When Delilah saw that he had told her all his heart, she sent and called for the Lords of the Philistines, saying, "Come up once more, for he has told me all his heart." So the Lords of the Philistines came up to her and brought the money in their hand. Then she lulled him to sleep on her knees, and called for a man and had him shave off the seven locks of his head. Then she began to torment him, and his strength left him. And she said, "The Philistines are upon you, Samson!" So he awoke from his sleep, and said, "I will go out as before, at other times, and shake myself free!" <u>But he did not know that the Lord had departed from him. Then the Philistines took him and put out his eyes, and brought him down to Gaza. They bound him with bronze fetters, and he became a grinder in the prison. However, the hair of his head began to grow again after it had been shaven."</u>*
> *Judges 16:18-22*

## EMERGE

Samson is a powerful picture and example of what the spirit of this world seeks to do to all of God's men. Did you see what I underlined?

- Samson lost his strength (the Spirit of the LORD departed from him).
- Samson lost his vision (they gouged out his eyes).
- Samson lost his freedom (they put him in bronze fetters and took him to Gaza).
- Samson lost his purpose (they *made him* a grinder in prison).
- Samson lost his honor (they would bring him out to entertain them when they were drunk).

Samson was *never* meant to grind grain for the Philistines. He was meant to produce for the Kingdom of God. *You* are not meant to grind for the empty spirit of this world; rather, you are meant to produce wealth, blessings, and resources that have eternal impact.

## ISN'T THAT A PROSPERITY GOSPEL?

Jesus taught us to "beware of false teachers. You shall know them by their fruit!" Then he said, "Beware of false prophets you shall know them by their fruit, for a tree is known by its fruit." (Matthew 7:15).

Notice He doesn't say, "Beware of false teachers and false prophets. You shall know them by their false teaching and their false prophesies!" He says instead, *"You shall KNOW THEM BY THEIR FRUIT!"* (Emphasis mine)

What does that mean? It means you will know them by what they *produce*! In an orchard, it's easy to discern and distinguish what tree is what. You look at the *fruit* the tree is producing. The fruit tells you what kind of *tree* it is! When you see peaches hanging on the branches, you know it's a peach tree. When you see apples, it's an apple tree. The same goes for oranges, figs, pomegranates, nectarines, lemons, etc. What the tree produces *identifies* the tree!

Read what Jesus said about wisdom:

> *"But wisdom is justified by all her children."*
> Luke 7:35

Did you see that? Wisdom is justified (proven right) by all her children—in other words, what she (Wisdom) produces. God made you a producer, but what you pro-

## CHAPTER TEN: **PRODUCER**

duce is up to you! If you don't like what your life is producing, you can change your seed today, set it in motion, and be different tomorrow. Maybe your life has produced divorce, dysfunction, betrayals, strained relationships, bankruptcy, brokenness, and so on. God has bestowed upon us one of the most magnificent gifts called *repentance*!

*God* created you to produce. You are designed, created, and commissioned to produce *more* than you need because you are *called* to be your brother's keeper and a *blessing* to others. A Spirit of Religion robs men everywhere of this truth. Don't let it rob you. You can never have too much money, but you can certainly *not* have enough to pay the bills. The main spirit behind most child sex trafficking is poverty in the parents. Poverty is wickedness. If someone tries to argue with you and says, *"You certainly can have too much money!"* Please correct them and tell them you cannot have too much money, only too little *kingdom vision!*

If you have millions sitting around and don't know what to do with it, it's not a "money" issue." It's an issue of a lack of vision for the purposes of God! Deuteronomy 8:18 tells us that *God gives us the power to get wealth so that we may establish His covenants on the earth!* If you've come under this deceptive teaching and lie from the pit of Hell, simply repent! It's that easy!

The word *"repent"* literally means to change your thinking, change the direction of your thoughts and mind. "Repent" comes from the Greek word "MetaGnoia"—Meta: to change or transform, Gnoia: knowledge/thinking. I have been a pastor for over thirty years now, and there is *not* a week that goes by where I am not in church or at a conference where I hear a word and realize I need to *repent*. I have seen untold blessings and breakthroughs follow every time I have had the opportunity to genuinely repent.

At the beginning of my ministry, while living in New Zealand, a prophetic individual called me out for having a "second best" mentality and needing to repent of it. The *fruit* that followed spoke for itself. Wisdom was justified by her children!

I had to repent of small-mindedness. BOOM. I began to *see* further and grander than I ever had before. The *fruit* was beyond exceptional! When I repented of hatred toward my father, joy, love, compassion, and freedom began to flow into my heart and life. These things were noticeably absent prior and had to be found in a temporal 'fix' via alcohol or drugs. Many people who have substance abuse addictions are people

**EMERGE**

carrying *hatred, bitterness,* and *unforgiveness* toward a parent or loved one. Joy and peace only come fleetingly when alcohol or drugs are present. If these people would just *repent* and *forgive*, they would produce peace, joy, love, and compassion. The addiction to the artificial and temporal happiness that comes from a substance would be broken!

REPENT. CHANGE YOUR SEED. PRODUCE A DIFFERENT HARVEST AND A DIFFERENT FUTURE!

## AMERICA'S FOUNDING FAITH

The UNITED STATES of AMERICA makes up just under 5% of the world's population, yet is responsible for almost 50% of the *wealth* generated in the world.

America is often the first to send aid or relief when other nations are in crisis. She is the largest funder of missions and world evangelism. She created the middle class and pioneered "consumer culture," so we don't fix our old stoves, fridges, washing machines, phones, or cars when they break down; we just replace them with new ones. By "new," I mean upgraded and greatly improved.

America has become the world's breadbasket, producing foods and resources that are imported by practically every nation in the world today! This is a Herculean feat for a nation that began in 1776. Just two hundred years ago, thirteen colonies formed the UNITED STATES of AMERICA—the *only superpower* ever to exist that did not use its military might to dominate and enslave other nations. Instead, she has "at her own expense" fought wars on foreign soil to topple dictators and fascist tyrants for nothing in return.

America put the first man on the moon, and an American said, *"One small step for man, one giant leap for mankind!"* - *Neal Armstrong, Astronaut.* We have put a rover on Mars and satellites into orbit. We mapped the ocean floor. We put planes into the sky, commuting people across the globe at their leisure. We have built giant ships that travel the seas, carrying cargo, resources, and exotic material goods to lands far away. We have mastered communication, not just with Alexander Graham Bell's invention of the telephone. Now, a child can FaceTime, Skype, or Zoom Grandma in real-time from the other side of the world.

The world has been around for much longer than just two hundred and forty-seven years, yet all of the above has been the *product* of this great land. In fact, America

## CHAPTER TEN: **PRODUCER**

sets the new measure for a nation's health, wealth, and well-being by the term GDP (Gross Domestic Product)—how much wealth each individual living in a nation can produce personally. What made America the superpower producer she is today, and can that help you become a more fruitful producer?

In the book *The 5000 Year Leap*, W. Cleon Skousen cites twenty-eight fundamental ideas unique to the United States of America that literally changed the world and made this nation perhaps the greatest nation to ever exist! All twenty-eight ideas flow from the *undeniable* Judeo-Christian faith that the founding fathers possessed, cherished, endeared, and espoused! I believe these ideas will bless you immensely, and you will discover the "genius" of our founding fathers and the power behind their devotion to the Creator of the universe!

These twenty-eight ideas fly in the face of every globalist dictator and fascist communist who has sought and seeks to plunder and impoverish the citizenry so they can rule over them. These ideas are under attack today. The *Left* has tried to deny them, rewrite them, slander, and vilify them. They have done everything they can to remove them, but these ideas are still held dearly by all who have put on the uniform, fought for the flag, fled a communist regime, and found refuge and asylum from socialist dictators. Despite the Left's assault on America's foundations, these twenty-eight principles form the backbone of our Constitution, which was written to protect and secure our freedoms. These principles and ideas caused a bunch of pilgrims, who fled here on board the Mayflower to escape religious persecution in England, to form the world's greatest and wealthiest superpower! America is a miracle in motion, and the devil is trying everything he can to take her down. But warriors like *you* will not let that happen on our watch! Amen!

Here are the principles:

| | |
|---|---|
| 1 | The Genius of Natural Law |
| 2 | A Virtuous and Moral People |
| 3 | Virtuous and Moral Leaders |
| 4 | The Role of Religion |
| 5 | The Role of the Creator |
| 6 | All Men Are Created Equal |
| 7 | Equal Rights, Not Equal Things |
| 8 | Man's Unalienable Rights |
| 9 | The Role of Revealed Law |

## EMERGE

| | |
|---|---|
| 10 | Sovereignty of the People |
| 11 | Who Can Alter the Government? |
| 12 | Advantages of a Republic |
| 13 | Protection Against Human Frailty |
| 14 | Property Rights Essential to Liberty |
| 15 | Free-market Economics |
| 16 | The Separation of Powers |
| 17 | Checks and Balances |
| 18 | Importance of a Written Constitution |
| 19 | Limiting the Powers of Government |
| 20 | Majority Rule, Minority Rights |
| 21 | Strong Local Self-government |
| 22 | Government by Law, Not by Men |
| 23 | Importance of an Educated Electorate |
| 24 | Peace Through Strength |
| 25 | Avoid Entangling Alliances |
| 26 | Protecting the Role of the Family |
| 27 | Avoiding the Burden of Debt |
| 28 | The Founders' Sense of Manifest Destiny |

God created *you* and then commissioned you to be fruitful and multiply. However, being "productive" is *your* choice.

*"The wealthiest places in the world are not Gold, mines, oil fields, diamond mines, or banks. The wealthiest place is the cemetery. There lies companies that were never started, masterpieces that were never painted. In the cemetery there is buried the greatest treasure of untapped potential. There is a treasure within you that must come out. Do not go to the grave with your treasure still within you."*
- Myles Munroe

## SCRAPING THE SKIES

Today, our modern cities all over the world boast the most magnificent skylines, with the most stunning skyscrapers, lit up like Christmas trees piercing the darkness of night, giving one solace, awe, and wonder as we gaze open them. None of what we see and experience would have been possible without the existence of an amazing Chris-

## CHAPTER TEN: **PRODUCER**

tian man; Elisha Graves Otis. He is the man who patented the look and operation of the modern-day elevator. It was the 'invention' of the elevator, that allowed us to build structures right up into the sky, where you can now travel from the ground floor to the 161st floor without losing your breath or even breaking a sweat!

Elisha Otis was born on August 3, 1811, in Halifax, Vermont, USA. Although he loved tinkering and had a talent for craftsmanship and inventions, he moved from job to job, without ever finding any real success or satisfaction. His first successful invention happened in New York where he worked in a bed frame factory. He devised a solution that helped him to automate the production of bed frames and make four times more material than with manual work.

With the $500 he earned from that invention he started his short-lived company where he tried to manufacture automatic breaks for trains. That also neither took off nor garnered any attention or respect. At the age of 40, while working at the Bedstead company, he was cleaning up the factory floor and wondered how he could get all the old debris up to the upper levels of the factory. He had heard of hoisting platforms, but these often broke, and he was unwilling to take the risk in case it came crashing down upon himself or some other unlucky employee. But like a stone in your shoe, the question lingered and bothered him each day.

After months of contemplation, Elisha Otis and his sons, who were also tinkerers, designed their own "safety elevator" and tested it successfully. He initially thought so little of it he neither patented it nor requested a bonus from his superiors for it, nor did he try to sell it. After having made several sales, and after the bedstead factory declined, Otis took the opportunity to make an elevator company out of it, initially called Union Elevator Works and later Otis Brothers Co.

In 1845 he first came to the idea of making an elevator with an automatic break. In the beginning no one took notice of this invention, but he gained much publicity when in 1854, at the "New York World's Fair" at Crystal Palace (now Bryant Park) in New York City. He gathered a crowd and then proclaimed he would do something that defied gravity! As the crowd gathered to watch the spectacle he boasted of, Elisha Otis rode the platform, high into the air, and once up high enough, gave the order to have the rope holding and hoisting the platform to be cut. An Axeman cut the rope, and the platform immediately dropped several feet, only to come to an immediate halt.

The crowd gasped in shock and then cheered as Otis' invention of a special brake

# EMERGE

kicked in, stopping the elevator from falling any further. The crowd cheered in marvel and amazement. That day, Elisha Otis "produced" more than an elevator or a safety brake device. He produced "confidence" that people could get into a steel box, in a hollowed-out shaft and travel against gravity, up and down, to great heights without fearing death or calamity. The modern elevator was born that day!

"A model of engineering simplicity, the safety device consisted of a used wagon spring that was attached to both the top of the hoist platform and the overhead lifting cable," wrote Joseph J. Fucini and Suzy Fucini in Entrepreneurs: The Men and Women Behind Famous Brand Names and How They Made It, as quoted by The American Society of Mechanical Engineers. "Under ordinary circumstances, the spring was kept in place by the pull of the platform's weight on the lifting cable. If the cable broke, however, this pressure was suddenly released, causing the big spring to snap open in a jaw-like motion. When this occurred, both ends of the spring would engage the saw-toothed ratchet-bar beams that Otis had installed on either side of the elevator shaft, thereby bringing the falling hoist platform to a complete stop."

Today, something like three hundred and twenty-five million people per day ride an elevator, thanks to Elisha Otis. At the time of Otis' invention, there were very few buildings above five stories. Because of the invention of the Elevator, by 1899 the Park Row Building of New York boasted 30 floors. Then, just nine years later, the Singer Building in New York was forty-seven stories high. The very next year the MetLife building went to fifty floors high. Then just four years later in 1913, the Woolworth Building opened a sky scraper with fifty-seven floors. By 1931, the Empire State Building was the awe of skyscrapers, even making itself the feature piece in the Hollywood blockbuster King Kong! The Empire State was one hundred and one floors high. Nobody thought this was possible at the time, but today there are buildings that reach up to one hundred and sixty-three floors in Dubai. Elisha Otis changed the landscape, to be more accurate the "SkyScape," of the world in which we live today!

## AMERICA, THE GREAT INVENTOR NATION

The number of patents in the USA Today is staggering. America boasts something like 3,350,000 patents in force as of 2020. The lightbulb was invented by Thomas Edison. Wilbur and Orville Wright put man into the sky when they invented flight in Kitty-hawk, North Carolina. Willis Carrier, in 1902, invented the air conditioning unit, allowing us to tame the extremes of temperatures across the nation and world, making habitable places previously deemed too harsh for human dwelling.

# CHAPTER TEN: PRODUCER
## UNITED WE STAND
## THE POWER OF WORKING TOGETHER

### AN AESOPS FABLE

*There is a classic Aesop's fable about a father whose sons were always fighting. In order to show them the value of working together, the father had one of the sons bring him a bundle of sticks. He gathered his sons around him, and one at a time, he asked each young man to take the bundle of sticks and try to break it. None succeeded. He then split open the bundle and handed each son one or two sticks, asking them once again to try to break them. This time, the sons did so easily. "You see, boys," he said, "Individually, these sticks do not have much strength, but when you combine their individual might, they form something of much greater power. Separately, you can be broken, but together, you are stronger."*

### MORE THAN A WORKER ANT

*"Go to the ant, you sluggard! Consider her ways and be wise, Which, having no captain, Overseer or ruler, Provides her supplies in the summer, And gathers her food in the harvest."*
*Proverbs 6:6-8*

God commanded man to be fruitful and multiply. He then placed the man he had formed into the Garden to tend and keep it! God gave Adam a job before the fall, and he also gave Adam a job before he gave him a wife!

God created you to produce and reproduce. *You* were created and designed to be productive. Man's self-worth is tied to his ability to reproduce. Take away a man's productivity, and you take away his very meaning for existence.

### NEVER RETIRE, ONLY REFIRE!

Many years ago, I heard a preacher at our EMERGE men's conference ask the audience: "Who invented retirement at age sixty-five?" The audience pondered and stuttered a few varying answers, but the preacher was not asking because he didn't know. The question was rhetorical. The answer, he said, was "Hitler and the Nazis!" The audience gasped in disbelief. Surely not! However, he went on to tell us that it wasn't Hitler's benevolence and kindness that motivated the invention of "retirement at sixty-five;" it was something far more dark and sinister.

## EMERGE

He explained how the Nazis studied what causes men to die off quickly, and they found that if you take away a man's productivity, you take away his purpose and the meaning for living.

> *"Moses stripped Aaron of his garments and put them on Eleazar his son; and Aaron died there on the top of the mountain. Then Moses and Eleazar came down from the mountain."*
> Numbers 20:28

Hitler discovered that removing a man's meaning and purpose, removing his productivity, would cause him to die within a decade. Hitler had already been implementing his eugenic agenda, eliminating those he deemed to be *"useless eaters!"* Originally, this term was confined to the mentally and physically disabled, but seeing its immediate success in the economy, Hitler expanded it. He saw an aging population as a burden on society and the economy because they contributed less with each passing year. He decided they were no longer of value and no longer deserved to live. Hitler deduced that these feeble, aging folks needed more resources to assist them and more personnel to "care" for them, personnel who could otherwise be used to help him conquer the world. He had no time for these "useless eaters!"

So, he invoked his solution: make man retire at sixty-five. Flanked by his chief psychologists and so-called "medical experts"—scientists (they used the terms "trust the science" and "don't be a science denier." Sound familiar?)—he told a cheering, naively trusting nation he was benevolently looking after the German people and instituting mandatory retirement for anyone sixty-five years of age!

Research to confirm this has not been easy to gather, but there are almost limitless writings on the insanity of Germany's Fuhrer and the mournful blind trust of the German citizenry. All you need to do is look at the average lifespan of a male in America today (74.3 years) and then correlate that to when men traditionally retire (which, again, in America, is at age sixty-five). Simple math tells you they "died within ten years!"

On a recent trip to Israel, I was profoundly impacted when I overheard our Jewish guides, who were just chatting simple trivia, say, *"Did you know that in Hebrew there is no such word as retirement? It doesn't exist in our language!"*

## CHAPTER TEN: PRODUCER
# THE 40/40 FACTOR!

*Never* retire, only re-fire! What does that mean? To put it simply, you should divide your life into two halves. For the *first* forty years, you work for money. For the *next* forty years, you should make that money *work for you*! In the first forty, you produce with your hands, labor, and time. In the next forty years, you use your head, wisdom, and knowledge to *produce* wealth.

*"A good man leaves an inheritance to his children's children, But the wealth of the sinner is stored up for the righteous."*
Proverbs 13:22

## CAN I BE PRODUCTIVE IF I'M POOR AND FROM A POOR COUNTRY?

"He was cast out by his fellow villagers, who believed he had gone mad. But now, Arunachalam Muruganantham is pioneering a positive change in women's health," read the headline in an article in *The Independent UK*. The article was about India's inventor of the modern-day maxi pad for women during their menstrual period.

When Arunachalam spotted his wife gathering dirty rags in the home one day, he asked what they were for. He was shocked by her response. She was using them for her monthly period. He was even more taken aback by her reply when he asked why she was not buying sanitary napkins in the shop. She responded, "If I buy sanitary napkins, it means I can't afford to buy milk or bread for the family."

The conversation spurred him into an inventing frenzy to try and produce an affordable napkin for women, such as his wife, to help them during their monthly menstrual cycle. Rumor has it that he once wore a football bladder filled with animal blood to test his prototype. However, he was forced from his home by the villagers, who thought his methods had become too crass and perverse. After this, he started collecting used napkins from medical students and storing them in his home. Even his mother and his wife abandoned him, believing he had gone temporarily mad. Fourteen years later, the forty-nine-year-old who never finished school has fewer regrets. His award-winning napkins have been produced on simple machines by groups across rural India, helping to revolutionize women's health right across the continent. He has now been dubbed the "tampon king," and he is replicating his model all over the world[1].

**EMERGE**
# FROM ENGINEERING TO MINISTRY

You don't have to be an inventor to be productive. You just have to be engaged— engaged in activity, engaged in work. Nothing is better than for a man to work hard and enjoy the rewards of his hard work and labor. In a free market economy, the marketplace will remunerate you for your time, labor, expertise, and the value you add to the company/market.

> *"Here is what I have seen: It is good and fitting for one to eat and drink, and to enjoy the good of all his labor in which he toils under the sun all the days of his life which God gives him; for it is his heritage. As for every man to whom God has given riches and wealth, and given him power to eat of it, to receive his heritage and rejoice in his labor—this is the gift of God."*
> Ecclesiastes 5:18-19

Wealth is not something that is found or transferred. It is produced. You can produce wealth. You can flourish. You can prosper.

> *"And you shall remember the Lord your God, for it is He who gives you power to get wealth, that He may establish His covenant which He swore to your fathers, as it is this day."*
> Deuteronomy 8:18

## THE MEANING OF LIFE IS TO GIVE LIFE MEANING!

I can still remember the long drive up the escarpment. My heart was trembling; nausea dominated my stomach and emotions as I reflected openly on the decision I just made to attend full-time bible college at Power Ministry School in Baulkham Hills, Sydney. Had I just made the greatest mistake of my life? I left a career in engineering, a safe job with guaranteed income for the rest of my life, to throw caution to the wind and attend Bible school with no guarantee that there would be a job for me as a pastor in a church after I graduated. What had I done? Looking back now, it was perhaps the most significant decision I could have made, one that blessed me and aligned me with God's destiny for my life.

When I was an engineer, we built products out of steel only to place them into cargo containers. These would then be loaded onto giant cargo ships that would sail away from our shores to foreign and distant lands, never to be seen again. I remember standing at the dock asking myself, "Is this what the rest of my life looks like?" Would I be engaged in toil and labor on products I would never see again?

## CHAPTER TEN: **PRODUCER**

Despite all the advice I got from the "play it safe" crowd, I did leave an engineering career. I didn't realize it then, but attending Bible College was God's calling upon my life. I knew I loved to entertain people and would always tell stories (most of them not true or embellished—never let the facts get in the way of a good story), making people laugh. I loved to joke and had no problem at all with public speaking. In fact, I thrived on it! At my high school, we won the talent quest every year with a comedy skit I wrote. At Bible College, I was quickly thrust into the *head* of the *drama* department and re-wrote all the skits we used to open high school students' hearts to receive the Gospel.

Using comedy, drama, and public speaking, we saw the most amount of high school students come to Christ than the college has ever seen. We had a massive impact everywhere we went and even had many groupies who eventually came to bible college and are serving God today. Some of our innovations included "The Zarzoff Brothers," "King Gees," "Ford Pills, They Really Work," and "Cornflakes" (plus other rip-offs of current-day TV commercials). I had a genuine love and care for people, and looking back, I can see why God called me to be a pastor.

I'm no longer a cog in the wheel of some big company where I am only a number, and a replaceable one at that. I'm doing what I was always born to do. I am living in line with God's wiring of my life, doing that which I was gifted to do. They say that once you find your purpose in life and start to do it, not only will you love what you do, but "you'll never work another day in your life" because you're doing what you were created to do!

You were created with all kinds of gifts and talents, wired with skill sets, and infused by God with desires in your heart that, like stars in the night sky to a sailor, guide you into your calling and destiny! Don't settle for a job or a career. Don't fall into the *nimrod* spirit of the world with its "reduce you to cattle" plan comprising of finishing school, going off to college, graduating and getting a job, then buying a house, paying taxes, and then retiring to die! Life is too short. God is too good, and your life is *too important*! Find your calling and align your vocation with your gifting and desire. You'll never work another day in your life; you will be infinitely more productive and fruitful and live the most bountiful and blessed life.

### BLESSED TO BE A BLESSING!

Adam was given the Garden to tend and to keep! Had anyone, upon entering, praised Adam, saying, "Nice Garden you've planted here! WOW! I like what you've done with those date palms!" Adam would have been taking credit where it was not

## EMERGE

due. *Stewardship* is the key to producing powerful results in your life. While Adam did not plant the garden, he was certainly responsible for its maintenance and upkeep. In fact, he was responsible for its increase and global expansion. The small paradisiacal garden was meant to "fill the entire earth!" That was Adam's calling and Adam's destiny! Adam obviously blew it when he stole from the boss.

God raised up a man named Abraham. God blessed Abraham for the sole purpose of blessing the nations.

> *"Now the Lord had said to Abram: "Get out of your country, From your family And from your father's house, To a land that I will show you. I will make you a great nation; I will bless you And make your name great; And you shall be a blessing. I will bless those who bless you, And I will curse him who curses you; And in you all the families of the earth shall be blessed."*
> *Genesis 12:1-3*

> *"There is NOTHING wrong with creating wealth It is ONLY wrong when you don't use it to help other people!"* - Jeff Hoffman, CEO

Your life has meaning when you see yourself as "blessed to be a blessing," when you are productive, and when you live for more than yourself.

## CHALLENGE

There was a man in the Bible who failed miserably on this very issue:

> *"And He said to them, "Take heed and beware of covetousness, for one's life does not consist in the abundance of the things he possesses." Then He spoke a parable to them, saying: "The ground of a certain rich man yielded plentifully. And he thought within himself, saying, 'What shall I do, since I have no room to store my crops?' So he said, 'I will do this: I will pull down my barns and build greater, and there I will store all my crops and my goods. And I will say to my soul, "Soul, you have many goods laid up for many years; take your ease; eat, drink, and be merry."' But God said to him, 'Fool! This night your soul will be required of you; then whose will those things be which you have provided?' "So is he who lays up treasure for himself, and is not rich toward God."*
> *Luke 12:15-21*

# CHAPTER TEN: **PRODUCER**

The man lost his life when he lost sight of what his life was all about. He was blessed to be a blessing. Instead, his *only* focus was on himself. When you *only* think of yourself and don't see the brotherhood of humanity, don't see how you're meant to be your brother's keeper, don't see how *you* can and should make a difference in the world, you're breathing, but you're not living. You have a pulse, but you no longer have a heart! Be *productive* so you can be God's instrument in making the world a better place!

# CHAPTER ELEVEN
# LEADER

## גיהנמ

*(Manehig)*
*Leader, chief, Head.*

"*Leadership is example.*"

*Leadership is the capacity to translate vision into reality.*
—Warren Bennis, Leadership consultant

*The first responsibility of a leader is to define reality. The last is to say thank you. In between, the leader is a servant.*
—Max DePree, Businessman, Writer

## CHAPTER ELEVEN: **LEADER**
# WHAT DOES IT MEAN TO BE A LEADER?

Many years ago, I heard the story of a lighthouse keeper and his young apprentice. Lighthouses are often portrayed as artistic architectural pieces perched high on a headland above craggy rocks and sheer cliff faces. A lighthouse, however, is not built to be an artistic ornament or an architectural aesthetic. They are built for one purpose and one purpose alone: to guide ships safely into the harbor and away from the dangerous rocks and reefs of a headland.

One evening, a fierce storm produced raging waves, some up to forty feet high, crashing into the rocks and pounding the lighthouse. At every thundering crash of a wave, the entire lighthouse shook violently. The young apprentice would immediately look at the lighthouse keeper's face, searching his eyes for fear and concern or calm and resolve. In his short life, he had never experienced a storm like this but was sure his much older master had at some point in his life. There were always the stories. They seemed like possibly exaggerated legends, but now the young apprentice pondered, *"What if they were true?"*

With every shuddering crash of these massive waves, the apprentice would look immediately to the lighthouse keeper. Should they abandon the structure? Was it safe? Was this old lighthouse sound enough to withstand this violent tempest? All these thoughts ran through the young apprentice's mind. However, the lighthouse keeper remained poised, fixed with a steely calm amid the raging wind and waves.

Just then, a giant wave crashed into the lighthouse with such impact that it shook the entire structure and extinguished the light. Grappling in the dark, the lighthouse keeper frantically fumbled through the cupboards and drawers, striking a match and lighting a small glass-encased oil lamp. The young apprentice could see both concern and resolve on the lighthouse keeper's face. The apprentice watched helplessly as the keeper tried, again and again, to reignite the lighthouse lamp from inside the lighthouse, but the more he threw the switches backward and forwards, the more dead the light seemed. The young apprentice thought perhaps the lighthouse keeper would say, "Abandon ship!" He thought of the safety of being inland in his warm bed, away from the crashing waves, and a sudden sense of relief washed over him.

Instead, the lighthouse keeper turned to the young apprentice and said, *"Get your hat, coat, and the toolbox. We have to go out and try to relight the lamps manually!"* Terror washed over the young apprentice. Swallowing hard, he looked at the lighthouse keeper. Using all the self-control he could muster to keep his little lip from stammering, he said,

**EMERGE**

*"But sir, if we go out, we may not come back!"* In response, the lighthouse keeper said, *"We have to go out. We don't have to come back!"*

Leadership is doing what's right with no guarantees of survival. Leaders think of themselves last. They put duty, honor, and the mission above their personal benefits. That's what separates leaders from hirelings. Jesus said the hireling flees when the wolf comes for the sheep. The hireling doesn't stay. He doesn't fight. He doesn't risk his life against the wolf. His heart was never *for* the sheep. It was always for the benefit. There are many people with dazzling resumes. They have amazing credentials, diplomas, degrees in leadership, and impressive plaques adorn their walls. Over the years, however, I have seen many with those credentials seek and crave position, power, and privilege only to leave when the going gets tough—whether from an organization, a battle, or responsibility.

> *"I am the good shepherd. The good shepherd sacrifices his life for the sheep. A hired hand will run when he sees a wolf coming. He will abandon the sheep because they don't belong to him and he isn't their shepherd. And so the wolf attacks them and scatters the flock. The hired hand runs away because he's working only for the money and doesn't really care about the sheep."*
> John 10:11-13 NLT

Leadership finds a way to make a comeback when you're down. It finds ways to win and turns each humiliating defeat into a powerful, educational lesson. When they asked Thomas Edison how it felt to fail a thousand times before he got the lightbulb invention correct, Thomas Edison responded, "Oh, I didn't fail a thousand times; inventing the light bulb was a 1001 step process!"

Leadership is when the captain of a sinking ship ensures his passengers and crew are safely off the vessel before he moves to safety, even if it means he goes down with the ship. That's what leaders do. Today, it's a forgotten truth, lost in the tumultuous seas of entitlement and self-aggrandizement!

Leadership is first accepting responsibility and blame when things go wrong and being the last to receive praise when things go well. Leadership thanks and praises the team, giving credit to them for the victory. You will never be a great leader if it's all about you and your delicate ego. *Great* leaders produce other leaders even greater than themselves. These leaders are not threatened by the greatness in those around them. Instead, they celebrate, champion, and develop it!

# CHAPTER ELEVEN: LEADER

How do you know if a vine is a great vine? Simple. By the *fruit* it produces. Not the leaves it displays, not the color or thickness of the trunk. The fruit. The fruit speaks for the vine. You cannot fake fruit. You can tell a lot about a leader by the "fruit" of the leaders they raise up and develop around them!

## THE BIBLICAL LEADERSHIP ENIGMA

There is a wonderful (you may call it strange) enigma in the Bible. In the New Testament, Moses is mentioned ninety-nine times, while Joshua is only mentioned twice. Elijah is mentioned some twenty-seven times, while Elisha is only mentioned once.

We know that Joshua succeeded where Moses failed—namely, bringing the children of Israel into the promised land and dispossessing the nations occupying their God-given territory. Yet he's only mentioned twice in the New Testament, while Moses is mentioned ninety-nine times. Likewise, Elisha, the servant of Elijah, did *twice* the amount of signs and miracles Elijah did, yet he's only mentioned once in a brief passage. In contrast, Elijah is mentioned some twenty-seven times. *Why?*

Here is the enigma.

Heaven doesn't have the same value matrix as Earth. On Earth, we measure a man by *his* accomplishments. This is not the case for Heaven. If it were, the Bible would be full of Joshua and Elisha, but instead, it's full of Moses and Elijah.

> *"Because every tree is known by its fruit!"* - Luke 6:44

God sees the accomplishments of Joshua and Elisha as the *fruit* of Moses' and Elijah's leadership. Your greatest accomplishments are achieved through those you have developed around you—beginning with your bride and your children.
No vinedresser or vineyard owner will ever cut down a vine that produces better fruit and vines each season. Great leadership is determined not only by what it accomplishes but also by the level of quality it produces!

## HEAVY IS THE HEAD THAT WEARS THE CROWN

Throughout history, particularly in medieval times, the sword of Damocles has been a popular story illustrating the duality of being a ruler and the immense responsibility accompanying that power. The sword of Damocles was a sword, hung over the head of Damocles in the king's palace.

# EMERGE

The story goes something like this:

Dionysius was so concerned about his life that his bedroom had a moat surrounding it to thwart potential assassins, and he only allowed his daughters to shave his beard. One day, Damocles, a member of the ruler's court, complimented Dionysius a bit too profusely. Damocles complemented the tyrant on his riches and power and even speculated how easy and wonderful his life must be!

Being as anxious and paranoid as he was, Dionysius was taken aback by the comments. He decided to teach Damocles a lesson about the weight of power. The ruler asked the subject if he would be interested in trading places with him only for a single day. Damocles could not believe his luck and enthusiastically took Dionysius up on his most gracious offer. Dionysius ordered his many servants to wait upon Damocles, who was seated on the ruler's luxurious, golden couch. He was fed countless gourmet delicacies by the most beautiful of servants and the most gifted chefs. He was covered in all kinds of expensive lotions and perfumes. The humble courtier was basking in the luxury of being a king. Dazzled by the sumptuous throne room, the beauty of Dionysius' servants, and the countless sparkling, opulent objects surrounding him, Damocles hardly noticed the sharp blade hanging just inches above his head. Dionysius had strung up a razor-sharp sword above Damocles's head by using a single hair from a horse's tail that could snap at any moment, bringing the blade down upon him and ending his life. When Damocles noticed the sword, he couldn't focus on anything else. Damocles quickly became overwhelmed with fear and anxiety. No longer able to enjoy the luxuries of his newfound power, he got up and ran from the room, begging to be freed from his position as king for the day, the position he had so coveted just moments earlier.

According to Cicero, the tale was the ultimate example of the danger, pressure, and paranoia that inevitably come with yielding immense power. He also claimed that those in power were in constant fear of dying and, therefore, could not be truly happy.

> *"With great power comes great responsibility!"*
> *- Uncle Ben Parker*

Most folks covet leadership for the position and the perks. Few, however, realize that leadership is all about *responsibility*! The Bible teaches that a person's level of authority is directly attributed to the level of responsibility he assumes. When we abdicate taking responsibility, we lose authority.

CHAPTER ELEVEN: **LEADER**
# THE AUTHORITY RESPONSIBILITY CONNECTION

*"For the kingdom of heaven is like a man traveling to a far country, who called his own servants and delivered his goods to them. And to one he gave five talents, to another two, and to another one, to each according to his own ability; and immediately he went on a journey. Then he who had received the five talents went and traded with them, and made another five talents. And likewise he who had received two gained two more also. But he who had received one went and dug in the ground, and hid his Lord's money. After a long time the Lord of those servants came and settled accounts with them. "So he who had received five talents came and brought five other talents, saying, 'Lord, you delivered to me five talents; look, I have gained five more talents besides them.' His Lord said to him, 'Well done, good and faithful servant; you were faithful over a few things, I will make you ruler over many things. Enter into the joy of your Lord.' He also who had received two talents came and said, 'Lord, you delivered to me two talents; look, I have gained two more talents besides them.' His Lord said to him, 'Well done, good and faithful servant; you have been faithful over a few things, I will make you ruler over many things. Enter into the joy of your Lord.' "Then he who had received the one talent came and said, 'Lord, I knew you to be a hard man, reaping where you have not sown, and gathering where you have not scattered seed. And I was afraid, and went and hid your talent in the ground. Look, there you have what is yours.' "But his Lord answered and said to him, 'You wicked and lazy servant, you knew that I reap where I have not sown, and gather where I have not scattered seed. So you ought to have deposited my money with the bankers, and at my coming I would have received back my own with interest. Therefore take the talent from him, and give it to him who has ten talents. 'For to everyone who has, more will be given, and he will have abundance; but from him who does not have, even what he has will be taken away. And cast the unprofitable servant into the outer darkness. There will be weeping and gnashing of teeth.'"*

*Matthew 25:14-30*

In this magnificent parable, Jesus illustrates the correlation between authority and responsibility. The two stewards who fully accepted responsibility for their master's money were rewarded with authority and given rulership over regions. The one steward who *failed* to accept responsibility lost not only authority but also respect and opportunity.

Responsibility and authority are two sides of the same coin.

You cannot possess one without the other.

## THE DEVIL'S VICTIM CULTURE AGENDA

The devil has been working overtime in our age to create a "victim culture." Today,

**EMERGE**

the most oppressed, or in layman's terms, the *biggest victim*, is given the loudest voice. However, while the Earth amplifies their voice, Heaven diminishes their authority. The devil wants it this way because he enjoys his most dominant rule over those who abdicate responsibility for their lives.

A few weeks ago in church, one of my campus pastors mentioned how the devil has no authority over our lives. One person commented, *"Yeah, then how come he can do so much damage in my life and others in our city through addiction, anxiety, and depression?"* The answer came immediately: *the devil only has as much authority in our lives as we give him!*

As it was in Eden, so it is today! Jesus stripped the devil of all his authority; however, many men gave him authority over their lives by abandoning responsibility.

When we "blame others" for our woes, we abdicate responsibility and lose authority. When we claim victimhood, we declare that someone else has authority over our lives, and we do not. The Bible says this about Jesus Christ:

> *"Let this mind be in you which was also in Christ Jesus, who, being in the form of God, did not consider it robbery to be equal with God, but made Himself of no reputation, taking the form of a bondservant, and coming in the likeness of men. And being found in appearance as a man, He humbled Himself and became obedient to the point of death, even the death of the cross. Therefore God also has highly exalted Him and given Him the name which is above every name, that at the name of Jesus every knee should bow, of those in heaven, and of those on earth, and of those under the earth, and that every tongue should confess that Jesus Christ is Lord, to the glory of God the Father."*
> Philippians 2:5-11

Do you see this?

Jesus Christ received all <u>authority</u> *because* he accepted all <u>responsibility</u>. He died upon the cross for the sins of the world. He was crucified between two thieves, numbered with the transgressors, yet was innocent of all sin and wrongdoing. He came and took responsibility for "our sins" upon Himself, and because He accepted total responsibility, God gave Him total authority.

In every area of your life where you have *not* accepted total responsibility, you have given up authority.

## CHAPTER ELEVEN: **LEADER**

*Repentance* is God's gift toward empowerment.

Repentance has received a bad label as of late. Most see it as solemn weeping born out of shame and hopelessness. It's actually one of the greatest empowerment gifts God has given us. Whenever we repent of a sin or transgression, we are accepting responsibility for our actions. Whatever we accept responsibility for, we receive authority over! The most powerful way to overcome sin is to repent and accept responsibility for it.

When my daughter asks if a friend of hers can sleep over on the weekend and we say, "Yes," we are accepting responsibility to care for that young lady. This means we now have the authority to lay out "the rules"—bedtime, mealtime, no boys, wearing a helmet while riding an electric bike, and so on.

Imagine if I am now at our local Target and see a girl my daughter's age. If I start telling her what time she should switch off her lights and go to sleep and that she must wear a helmet when riding her electric bike, I will be arrested for being a weirdo. It's not that there was anything wrong with the curfew times or the safety instructions for riding an electric bike, but because I have *no authority* to tell her these things, I have *no responsibility* for her.

## **REPENTANCE BRINGS POWER**

You cannot be delivered from something you won't repent of!

I have been in pastoral ministry for over thirty years. It's become evident to me that it is near impossible to deliver someone from demonic bondage when they are unwilling to repent of the transgression causing the bondage in the first place. Why?

Because until you repent (accept responsibility), God's authority cannot flow toward you. *If* you repent, you receive authority and power to drive out the demonic.

> *"Therefore submit to God. Resist the devil and he will flee from you."*
> James 4:7

The scripture above is one of the most popular verses quoted for resisting the devil. But did you see the first part of the verse? "Submit to God!" Then you can successfully resist the evil one and drive him out! When we repent, we accept responsibility. When we accept responsibility, we receive authority. When we receive authority, we are *empowered* to drive out the demonic and have victory over the situation.

# EMERGE

## LEADERS LEAD

Leaders go first. Nothing will change in your marriage while you play the "blame game" and make everything about your spouse's faults. Nothing will change financially, emotionally, economically, and spiritually, while you blame others for your lot in life. If you are still blaming your parents, your absent father, your football coach, your college professor, a teacher, or an abuser... *nothing* will change. I'm *not* saying that they were *not wrong*. I am also *not* saying you weren't cheated, abused, or ripped off. I am saying that while you adopt the position of "victim," you place the authority on your abusers and will remain oppressed (and most likely depressed).

This is where we need to learn from the leader of leaders Himself, Jesus Christ. Upon the cross, Roman guards gambled for His clothing right beneath His feet. Having just been nailed to the crucifix, Jesus lifted His voice to heaven and said, *"Father, forgive them, they know not what they do!"* (Luke 23:34)

Please note they were *not asking* for forgiveness, nor were they *deserving* of it, yet Jesus forgave them. Why? Because He was not going to give up authority. He was about to die on the cross for man's sins so He could have the authority to forgive all sin and transgression. He also was going to have authority over death and the grave.

When you forgive them, you are not condoning what they have done, and you are not permitting them to keep doing it. You are simply telling them their sinful behavior and abuse are not the highest authority over your life. By choosing to forgive, you make the statement that God and His law reign supreme over your life! As soon as you do that, authority, power, and freedom flow toward you!

Leaders lead. They go first. They don't wait for perfect circumstances. They don't wait for everyone around them to do the right thing before they start doing it. They are the first to forgive. They are the "bigger" person in the room.

## LEADERS PAY FIRST AND PLAY LATER

*A wild donkey who was wandering idly about one day came upon a pack donkey lying at full length in a sunny spot, thoroughly enjoying himself. Going up to him, the wild donkey said, "What a lucky beast you are. Your sleek coat shows how well you live. How I envy you!" Not long after this, the wild donkey saw his acquaintance again, but this time he was carrying*

## CHAPTER ELEVEN: **LEADER**

*a heavy load, and his driver was following behind him and beating him with a big stick. "My friend," said the wild donkey, "I don't envy you anymore, for I see you pay dear for your comforts."*
*- AESOP FABLE*

Nothing in life comes free. In fact, if it does come to you free, it will leave you just as quickly. Everything has a price tag on it—marriage, family, success, influence, everything. That's what gives life value and meaning. If it were all free, like the socialists and communists want you to believe, then socialism and communism would have worked by now. However, the exact opposite is true after six thousand years of recorded history. Why? Because you don't *value* anything that comes to you for free or without a price. Human beings are creatures of reward. We judge things according to their perceived value and worth to us. Jesus told several parables demonstrating this:

*"Again, the kingdom of heaven is like treasure hidden in a field, which a man found and hid; and for joy over it he goes and sells all that he has and buys that field. "Again, the kingdom of heaven is like a merchant seeking beautiful pearls, who, when he had found one pearl of great price, went and sold all that he had and bought it."*
*- Matthew 13:44-46*

The "meaning of life" could be described as "to give life meaning." If there is nothing to hunt, nothing to fight for, nothing of impeccable beauty and value to pursue, nothing to sacrifice for, life will quickly lose its meaning. In the Aesop Fable above, the wild donkey envies the coat of the pack donkey until he realizes that "he pays for his dear comforts!"

When you go to the mall or walk into a store, there are price tags on everything you see. Why? Because they carry value. Value to the merchant/seller. Value to the manufacturer. Value to the designer and creator. Therefore, a value/price is attached to it. One of the greatest lessons we can teach our children is to save up for something they desire. If they save for it, we teach them there is a price tag for what they value. Nothing comes free. We also teach them their life has a value attached to it. They are remunerated for hours spent on chores or work. They may have worked one hundred hours around the home, and now all the sweat and pain of the labor is forgotten as the new X-Box is opened before them.

**195**

## EMERGE

As leaders, we must understand that we "pay first," and then we get to play later, whether that's in education, marriage, family, or investments. Jesus Christ, the leader of leaders, came and died upon the cross while we were still sinners!

> *Before there was one iota of repentance or personal benefit to Him, He paid the ultimate price, giving His life in exchange for ours upon the cross. "But God demonstrates His own love toward us, in that while we were still sinners, Christ died for us."*
> *- Romans 5:8*

Jesus paid first and then reaped later. For almost two thousand years, people have come to Him daily and been born again into His family and kingdom. He paid first and then received it later. He didn't wait until a billion people were guaranteed to come into the kingdom before He died for them. Leaders always pay first. If you want things to change in your life, *pay first*!

If you want friends, pay first. Do you want your marriage to flourish? Pay first! How? You initiate taking responsibility to provide what your bride desires—date nights, flowers, gifts, time, kindness, and forgiveness.

"But hang on," some may say, *"What if there's no change? What If I do all that and they don't change? What if..."* Contracts predetermine outcomes and secure guarantees. Never reduce your marriage to a "contract!" Your spouse is not a partner or "other entity." She is your gift from Heaven, your helper, sent you from God. Everything changed in my marriage when I *stopped* seeking my own desires and requiring guarantees. As soon as I threw caution to the wind and accepted God's challenge to *lead* in my home, everything changed.

As I met and sought to "exceed" her expectations, the selfish "my needs versus your needs" war ended. My bride is magnificent, and I lack for nothing. It all changed when I began to *lead* sacrificially and upfront—going first. After all, that's what *alpha's* do, but that's another chapter!

## CYNICISM IS THE DEVIL'S SNARE

It has been said, "A cynic is someone who knows the price of everything but the value of nothing!"

## CHAPTER ELEVEN: **LEADER**

Cynicism is cancer. Never allow yourself to fall into the devil's trap of making you cynical. We all know someone who is now a cynic. Are they happy? Nope, the exact opposite. They are bitter, miserable folks. If you listen to them, they will declare they are victims of someone else's wrongdoings, that life is cruel, unfair, and of little or no value. Long ago, they gave up authority, power, and freedom, adopting the position of victimhood. Being a victim is not static. It is not a final destination. It breeds cynicism in the hearts of men.

Don't allow yourself to become a cynic. Almost all the persecution we endure as we grow Awaken church comes from those who have descended into the victim seat and speak out of souls poisoned by toxic cynicism. Leaders *refuse* to allow defeats, betrayals, hardships, or failures to develop a victim mentality, which then breeds cynicism! Leaders remain hopeful. They bounce back. They are optimists. They are conquerors. They are overcomers!

> *"The godly may trip seven times, but they will get up again. But one disaster is enough to overthrow the wicked."*
> *- Proverbs 24:16 NLT*

Many of you have probably seen the famous advertisement that Ernest Shackleton ran in the newspaper to try to recruit men for his *Endurance* expedition:
*"Men wanted for hazardous journey. Low wages, bitter cold, long hours of complete darkness. Safe return doubtful. Honour and recognition in the event of success."* - Ernest Shackleton

This advertisement is one of the most famous in history. It is frequently quoted as one of the best examples of copywriting. It has been used many times in books covering topics ranging from *Introduction to Evangelism* to *Web Application Defender's Cookbook*, and it's even been printed on tee shirts.
*Why?* Because it touches the core of every man's heart—to live an adventure, risk it all for something of value and worth, be heroic, be a champion, build a great name, and leave a legacy!

## VISION IS THE PREREQUISITE FOR LEADERSHIP

> *"Let them alone. They are blind leaders of the blind. And if the blind leads the blind, both will fall into a ditch."*
> *Matthew 15:14*

## EMERGE

When Jesus spoke about leadership in Matthew chapter 15, He discussed the essentiality of vision. If the blind are leading the blind, disaster awaits, and both will fall into a ditch. The leader *must* see! The leader *must* have *vision*!

Vision is what you *see* when your eyes are closed. Sight is what you have when your eyes are open. Sight sees what's directly in front of you; vision sees what's ahead of you! Sight can see out several miles, depending upon your elevation and vantage point, whereas vision can see years ahead into the future and doesn't require geographical advantage. Joseph saw the sun, moon, and stars bowing down to him while sitting in prison, abandoned by his family, and sentenced for a crime he did not commit.

*If you are to lead, you must see!*
*All leaders see a way!*

When Leanne and I moved to San Diego, we were immediately met with what "could not" be done here in this city. The locals were too enthusiastic to tell us about the difficulties and the challenges restricting the churches from flourishing. My assignment before the God of Heaven who called me was *not* to give him a report of the "giants" occupying the promised land. I was supposed to describe the challenges of the "fortified cities," the difficulty of the terrain, and the impossibilities of the environment. This would be "repeating" the report the ten spies gave Moses in Numbers chapter 13.

> *"Then they told him, and said: "We went to the land where you sent us. It truly flows with milk and honey, and this is its fruit. Nevertheless the people who dwell in the land are strong; the cities are fortified and very large; moreover we saw the descendants of Anak there. The Amalekites dwell in the land of the South; the Hittites, the Jebusites, and the Amorites dwell in the mountains; and the Canaanites dwell by the sea and along the banks of the Jordan." Then Caleb quieted the people before Moses, and said, "Let us go up at once and take possession, for we are well able to overcome it." But the men who had gone up with him said, "We are not able to go up against the people, for they are stronger than we." And they gave the children of Israel a bad report of the land which they had spied out, saying, "The land through which we have gone as spies is a land that devours its inhabitants, and all the people whom we saw in it are men of great stature. There we saw the giants (the descendants of Anak came from the giants); and we were like grasshoppers in our own sight, and so we were in their sight."*
> *Numbers 13:27-33*

## CHAPTER ELEVEN: **LEADER**

Many people refer to the men who brought the negative report as the *"ten spies,"* but they were, in fact, *leaders* in Israel. Moses had selected twelve leaders, each one to represent their tribe. They were meant to be the best of the best. Their mission was to spy out the land, but even though their mission was spying, they were not spies. They were selected to be leaders.

This tells us you can have the title of *leader*, be recognized by the world around you as a leader, and even be accepted by your peers as a leader but *still not* function as a *leader* in the God-ordained sense.

*Leaders always see a way. (Vision)*
*That's the job of a leader.*

When I was confronted with all the "difficulties and the impossibilities" of building a city-changing church in San Diego, I knew the God I serve doesn't respect excuses. He is looking for leaders with faith and vision.

Years later, Joshua would be confronted with the monolith structure of Jericho's walls. It was a wonder to behold. The best of human engineering at that particular time. Walls so high and thick that chariots could race around on top, and real estate could be sold as sound structures within the walls. It was, by all appearance, deemed to be an impregnable fortress. However, God speaks to Joshua in Joshua 6:2:

*"And the Lord said to Joshua: "See! I have given Jericho into your hand, its king, and the mighty men of valor."*
*Joshua 6:2*

God expected His leader to *see*!

Everyone else saw the impossibility, the difficulty, and the structural challenges. But God commanded Joshua to *see* the defeat and demise of this city that had reinforced its rebellion and resistance to the things of God. Joshua knew his assignment. *See*. Vision.

The key to vision is where you spend your time. The ears open the eyes. Faith comes by hearing and hearing the word of God (Romans 10:17). Fear comes through negative reports. Doubt and unbelief are the product of our audible exposure. Joshua is with the angel of the *Lord*, the commander of the armies of Heaven. He commands Joshua to *see* that God has given Jericho into his hand along with its king (authority) and its "mighty men of valor" (strength).

## EMERGE

When you, as the leader, cannot see, when you are overwhelmed by the enormity of what stands before you, when you feel dwarfed, or when hopelessness has set in, get with God. He is the source of all vision and hope. Each time I would get overwhelmed, I would bring the reports of man and lay them before my God. Each time, I would hear the words of Christ:

> *"But Jesus looked at them and said, "With men it is impossible, but not with God; for with God all things are possible.""*
> *Mark 10:27*

The gift Jesus Christ has given us is that we are *not* abandoned to the limitations of human strength, capability, reason, or intellect. Rather, we have access to the very power of God and can live in the "All things are possible with God" zone!

I was told we should not hope to get a permanent church building here in San Diego. There was "No Zoning" here for churches, and San Diego was the fifth most expensive city in the USA. Even if we could find a building, there was an overwhelming chance we would *not* be able to get the finances to secure it. I had a choice—be one of the ten spies whose names are pretty much forgotten by almost all but the most astute biblical scholars, or be a Joshua and Caleb. I chose the latter, mainly because *life* is too short *not* to trust God and throw all caution to the wind. Seventeen years later, we own eleven church properties and lease another three.

Impossible is reserved *only* for the leader who doesn't walk with God. Don't live in the prison of the "impossible." Draw near to God so His word can fill you with *faith* and bring the *vision* to see through the *walls* of your Jericho into victory. Leaders *see*.

Leaders and prophets *see*. Another word for prophet is a seer (see-er). Every leader should have a prophetic edge, declaring that "through our God, we shall do valiantly, for it is He who treads down our enemies!" (Psalm 108:13).

See breakthrough in your marriage, see your children flourishing, see yourself possessing God's promises, see yourself holding the title to your own piece of real estate in your city, see yourself flourishing and prosperous.

If you don't see it, you cannot possess it!

## CHAPTER ELEVEN: LEADER

*"And the Lord said to Abram, after Lot had separated from him: "Lift your eyes now and look from the place where you are—northward, southward, eastward, and westward; for all the land which you see I give to you and your descendants forever."*
*Genesis 13:14-15*

The inference in this passage of scripture is that Abraham can have "everything" he sees. What he cannot see, he cannot have! The biggest battle of every leader is to *see*.

God is a promise-making God.
God is a promise-keeping God.
He is looking for promise-believing people.

*You* and I are called to be that person—a believer. This will automatically catapult you to leadership. The world is desperate for leadership, especially in these uncertain and challenging times. Seers are unparalleled and prized at this time. Leaders who see are the leaders who will get to lead.

**SEE!**

## CHAPTER TWELVE
# CHAMPION

## חולא

*(HEB)*

"It's what we OVERCOME that makes us MEN!"
"Victory has a thousand fathers, but defeat is an orphan!"
- John F Kennedy

"It's not the mountain that we conquer, rather it is we ourselves!"
- Sir Edmund Hillary

# CHAPTER TWELVE: CHAMPION
## HOW TO BECOME A CHAMPION

*"The Philistines now mustered their army for battle and camped between Socoh in Judah and Azekah at Ephes-dammim. Saul countered by gathering his Israelite troops near the valley of Elah. So the Philistines and Israelites faced each other on opposite hills, with the valley between them. Then Goliath, a Philistine champion from Gath, came out of the Philistine ranks to face the forces of Israel. He was over nine feet tall! He wore a bronze helmet, and his bronze coat of mail weighed 125 pounds. He also wore bronze leg armor, and he carried a bronze javelin on his shoulder. The shaft of his spear was as heavy and thick as a weaver's beam, tipped with an iron spearhead that weighed 15 pounds. His armor bearer walked ahead of him carrying a shield. Goliath stood and shouted a taunt across to the Israelites. "Why are you all coming out to fight?" he called. "I am the Philistine champion, but you are only the servants of Saul. Choose one man to come down here and fight me! If he kills me, then we will be your slaves. But if I kill him, you will be our slaves! I defy the armies of Israel today! Send me a man who will fight me!" When Saul and the Israelites heard this, they were terrified and deeply shaken."*
1 Samuel 17:1-11 NLT

The above passage is from the famous story of David and Goliath. Notice it says Goliath was the "Champion" of Gath. That means he had defeated, and probably killed, all his opponents and challengers.

We *become* a champion when we overcome and by what we defeat in battle. A champion is someone who has conquered his opponents and challengers.

Romans 8:37 tells us, *"Yet in all these things we are MORE than CONQUERORS through Him who loved us!" (Emphasis mine)*

You may not realize it now, but you and David have something in common. You are both more than conquerors through Christ! Just as David struck down the giant and then used the giant's sword to cut his head off, so too the Spirit in you is that of a conqueror, nay, *more* than a conqueror. Whatever giants you are currently facing (or will face in the future), *know* that the Same Spirit who rested upon David now rests upon you!

203

## EMERGE

You may be addicted to pornography, lust, anger, fear, insecurity, or some sort of substance. Whatever you face, as a born-again man of God, you possess a Spirit that has already designated you to be more than a conqueror! If you say, *"Well, I tried and thought I had won my battle with pornography, but I fell right back in!"* or *"I was sober for all these years, and then I had a relapse. I don't think I'll ever be free!"* please understand the devil wants you to believe your temporary setbacks and failures are permanent. They are *not*! The Spirit upon you will not quit or depart *until* you have defeated every enemy daring to try to dominate you!

> *"I will be with you, even to the end of the age!"*
> *- Jesus to us in Matthew 28:20*

You may say, *"But if that's true, why do I keep failing?"* Let me tell you a story that may help you.

Harry Houdini was known as a great escape artist. It was said he could escape from anything. He would often be placed in a straight jacket designed to restrain the most crazed and violent of human beings, then be extra secured with several chains and padlocks. To raise the stakes, he would also be submerged in a water tank. Onlookers would cover their mouths at the impossibility of escaping, *only* to find Houdini would surface each time. In utter bewilderment and awe, the crowd would erupt into applause. Both fans and skeptics alike would scratch their heads and wonder, "How did he do it?"

Harry Houdini possessed the incredible ability to dislocate his shoulders, allowing him to free himself from the restraint of the straight jacket. Then, he would regurgitate a previously swallowed hairpin and use it to pick the locks. He had trained his body to hold his breath underwater for at least five minutes.

Harry Houdini studied locks his entire life. He was an expert locksmith and boasted he could pick any lock. There was no prison or cell he could not break out of. The crowds would gather in the tens of thousands to see his marvelous and stunning escape feats.

Until one day...

A sheriff took Houdini up on a bet that he could break out of any cell, so the sheriff put him into one of his cells. After freeing himself from the straight jacket, in routine form, Houdini regurgitated the hairpin and began to pick the lock. He picked, and he picked. An hour passed. Then another. Houdini began to sweat profusely. What trickery was this?

# CHAPTER TWELVE: **CHAMPION**

He picked and picked, waiting to hear the "click," indicating his victory over the lock and his freedom from the cell. Sadly, after six hours of trying everything, the great escape artist, who boasted no cell or restraint he could not escape from, surrendered and admitted defeat. He had met his match. He had been conquered by a lock he couldn't pick.

The Sheriff walked over to the humiliated Houdini and, with his left hand, pushed upon the cell door, swinging it wide open. The cell door was already unlocked! The *only* prison Houdini couldn't escape was the one already opened. All he had to do was push it open, and he could have walked out. Instead, he worked and worked to open it.

Jesus has already defeated every enemy and destroyed the works of the devil. In Christ, *you* are more than a conqueror because *He* has won the war and defeated the enemy. The prison cell door is *unlocked, the chains are broken, and the enemy is defeated. You are not so much trying to "defeat" your giant* as you are called to walk in the victory Christ has wrought for you!

The spirit of pornography is already defeated.

The spirit of fear, anger, addiction, rejection, and bondage is *already defeated*!

Champion is in your DNA now that you are born again! Champion is the anointing that rests upon you.

> *"Greater is He that is in you than he that is in the world!"*
> 1 John 4:4

> *"He who sins is of the devil, for the devil has sinned from the beginning. For this reason Christ was manifest, to DESTROY the works of the devil!"* 1 John 3:8

*A champion* is who you are. Champion is your identity. Champion is your modus operandi. What are you living *under* that God has set you *over*? God said to Joshua in the sixth chapter of the book of Joshua:

*"Joshua, SEE I have given Jericho into your hand. Its king and its mighty men of valor!"*

In other words, God was saying to Joshua, *you cannot* defeat something you don't *see* God has given you *victory over*!

**EMERGE**
## IF THEY HAD QUIT, NO ONE WOULD HAVE BLAMED THEM. BUT THEN AGAIN, NOBODY WOULD HAVE REMEMBERED THEM EITHER!

Woody Allen—Academy Award-winning writer, producer, and director—flunked motion picture production at New York University and the City College of New York. He also failed English at New York University.

Leo Uris, the author of the bestseller <u>Exodus</u>, failed high school English three times.

When Lucille Ball began studying to be an actress in 1925, the head instructor of the John Murray Anderson Drama School told her, "Try any other profession. Any other."

In 1959, a Universal Pictures executive dismissed Clint Eastwood and Burt Reynolds at the same meeting with the following statements. To Burt: "You have no talent." To Clint: "You have a chip on your tooth. Your Adam's apple sticks out too far, and you talk too slow."

In 1944, Emmeline Snively, director of the Blue Book Modeling Agency, told modeling hopeful Norma Jean Baker (Marilyn Monroe), "You'd better learn secretarial work or else get married."

Liv Ullman, who was nominated two times for the Academy Award for Best Actress, failed an audition for the state theater school in Norway. The judges told her she had no talent.

Malcolm Forbes, the late editor-in-chief of Forbes magazine (one of the most successful business publications in the world), failed to make the staff of the school newspaper when he was an undergraduate at Princeton University.

In 1962, four nervous young musicians played their first record audition for the executives of Decca Recording Company. The executives were not impressed. While turning down this British rock group called the Beatles, one executive said, "We don't like their sound. Groups of guitars are on the way out."

Paul Cohen, Nashville Artist and Repertoire Man for Decca Records, while firing Buddy Holly from the label in 1956, called Holly "the biggest no-talent I ever worked with." Twenty years later, Rolling Stone called Holly, along with Chuck Berry, "the major influence on the rock music of the 60s."

## CHAPTER TWELVE: **CHAMPION**

In 1954, Jimmy Denny, manager of the Grand Ole Opry, fired Elvis Presley after one performance. He told Presley, "You ain't goin' nowhere...son. You ought to go back to drivin' a truck." Elvis Presley went on to become the most popular singer in America.

When Alexander Graham Bell invented the telephone in 1876, it did not ring off the hook with calls from potential backers. After making a demonstration call, President Rutherford Hayes said, "That's an amazing invention, but who would ever want to use one of them?"

Thomas Edison was probably the greatest inventor in American history. When he first attended school in Port Huron, Michigan, his teachers complained that he was "too slow" and hard to handle. As a result, Edison's mother decided to take her son out of school and teach him at home. The young Edison was fascinated by science. At the age of ten, he had already set up his first chemistry laboratory. Edison's inexhaustible energy and genius (which he reportedly defined as "1% inspiration and 99% perspiration") eventually produced more than one thousand three hundred inventions. When Edison invented the light bulb, he tried over 2,000 experiments before he got it to work. A young reporter asked him how it felt to fail so many times. He said, [3]"I never failed once. I invented the light bulb. It just happened to be a 2,000 step process."

In the 1940s, another young inventor named Chester Carlson took his idea to twenty corporations, including some of the biggest in the country. They all turned him down. In 1947—after seven long years of rejections—he finally got a tiny company in Rochester, New York (the Haloid Company) to purchase the rights to his electrostatic paper-copying process. Haloid became Xerox Corporation. Both it and Carlsn became very rich.

John Milton became blind at age forty-four. Sixteen years later, he wrote the classic Paradise Lost.

When Pablo Casals reached ninety-five years old, a young reporter asked the following question: "Mr. Casals, you are ninety-five and the greatest cellist that ever lived. Why do you still practice six hours a day?" Mr. Casals answered, "Because I think I'm making progress!"

After years of progressive hearing loss, by age forty-six, German composer Ludwig van Beethoven became completely deaf. Nevertheless, he wrote his greatest music, including five symphonies, during his later years.

## EMERGE

After losing both legs in an air crash, British fighter pilot, Douglas Bader, rejoined the British Royal Air Force with two artificial limbs. During WWII, he was captured by the Germans three times—and three times, he escaped.

After having his cancer-ridden leg amputated, young Canadian, Terry Fox, vowed to run on one leg from coast to coast the entire length of Canada to raise $1 million for cancer research. Forced to quit halfway when cancer invaded his lungs, he and the foundation he started raised over $20 million for research.

Wilma Rudolph was the twentieth of twenty-two children. She was born prematurely, and her survival was doubtful. When she was four years old, she contracted double pneumonia and scarlet fever, which left her with a paralyzed left leg. At age nine, she removed the metal leg brace she had depended on and began walking without it. By thirteen, she developed a rhythmic walk, which doctors said was a miracle. That same year, she decided to become a runner. She entered a race and came in last. For the next few years, in every race she entered, she came last. Everyone told her to quit, but she kept on running. One day she actually won a race. And then another. From then on, she won every race she entered. Eventually, this little girl, who was told she would never walk again, won three Olympic gold medals. "My mother taught me very early to believe I could achieve any accomplishment I wanted to. The first was to walk without braces." - Wilma Rudolph

Franklin D. Roosevelt was paralyzed by polio at the age of thirty-nine, and yet he became one of America's most beloved and influential leaders. He was elected president of the U.S. four times.

Sarah Bernhardt, who is regarded as one of the greatest actresses to ever live, had her leg amputated as a result of an injury when she was seventy years old. She continued to act for the next eight years.

Louis L'Amour, the successful author of over a hundred Western novels with over two hundred million copies in print, received three hundred and fifty rejections before he made his first sale.

General Douglas MacArthur might never have gained power and fame without persistence. When he applied for admission to West Point, he was turned down not once but twice. The third time, he was accepted and marched into the history books.

# CHAPTER TWELVE: **CHAMPION**

Abraham Lincoln entered the Blackhawk War as a captain. By the war's end, he had been demoted to the rank of private.

In 1952, Edmund Hillary attempted to climb Mount Everest, the highest mountain then known to humans—twenty-nine thousand feet straight up. A few weeks after his failed attempt, he was asked to address a group in England. Hillary walked to the edge of the stage, made a fist, and pointed at the picture of the mountain. He said in a loud voice, "Mount Everest, you beat me the first time, but I'll beat you the next time because you've grown all you are going to grow...but I'm still growing." On May 29, only one year later, Edmund succeeded in becoming the first man to climb Mount Everest.

After Fred Astaire's first screen test, the memo from the testing director of MGM, dated 1933, said, "Can't act! Slightly bald! Can dance a little!" Astaire kept that memo over the fireplace in his Beverly Hills home.

An expert said of Vince Lombard: "He possesses minimal football knowledge. Lacks motivation."

Socrates was called "An immoral corrupter of youth."

When Peter J. Daniel was in the 4th grade, his teacher, Mrs. Phillips, constantly said, "Peter J. Daniel, you are no good. You're a bad apple, and you're never going to amount to anything." Peter was totally illiterate until he was twenty-six. A friend stayed up with him all night and read him a copy of "Think and Grow Rich." Now he owns the street corners he used to fight on and published his latest book, <u>Mrs. Philips, You Were Wrong</u>!

Louisa May Alcott, the author of Little Women, was encouraged by her family to find work as a servant or seamstress.

Beethoven handled the violin awkwardly and preferred playing his own compositions instead of improving his technique. His teacher called him hopeless as a composer.

The parents of the famous opera singer, Enrico Caruso, wanted him to be an engineer. His teacher said he had no voice at all and could not sing.

Walt Disney was fired by a newspaper editor for lack of ideas. Walt Disney also went bankrupt several times before he built Disneyland.

Albert Einstein did not speak until he was four years old and didn't read until he was seven. His teacher described him as "mentally slow, unsociable, and adrift forever in his foolish dreams." He was expelled and refused admittance to the Zurich Polytechnic School.

Louis Pasteur was only a mediocre pupil in undergraduate studies and ranked fifteenth out of twenty-two in chemistry.

Isaac Newton did very poorly in grade school.

The sculptor Rodin's father said, "I have an idiot for a son." Described as the worst pupil in the school, Rodin failed three times to secure admittance to the school of art. His uncle called him uneducable.

Leo Tolstoy, author of *War and Peace*, flunked out of college. He was described as "both unable and unwilling to learn."

FW Woolworth's employers at the dry goods store said he didn't have enough sense to wait upon customers.

Henry Ford failed and went broke five times before he finally succeeded.

Babe Ruth, who is considered by sports historians to be the greatest athlete of all time and is famous for setting the home run record, also holds the record for the most strikeouts. He struck out one thousand three hundred and thirty times, yet he hit seven hundred and fourteen home runs.

Winston Churchill failed 6th grade. He did not become Prime Minister of England until he was sixty-two.

Eighteen publishers turned down Richard Bach's ten thousand word story about a "soaring" seagull, *Jonathan Livingston Seagull* before Macmillan finally published it in 1970. By 1975, it had sold more than seven million copies in the U.S. alone.

Richard Hooker worked forty-seven years on his humorous war novel, *M*A*S*H*, only to have it rejected by twenty-one publishers before Morrow decided to publish it. It became a runaway bestseller, spawning a movie and a highly successful television series.

# CHAPTER TWELVE: ONE MAN

Johann Sebastian Bach's life was full of tragedy. By the age f ten, both parents had died. He was raised begrudgingly by an older brother who resented another mouth to feed. As an adult, his life was also difficult. His first wife died after thirteen years of marriage. Of twenty kids from two marriages, ten died in infancy, one died in his twenties, and one was mentally handicapped. Eventually, he went blind and then was paralyzed from a stroke. Yet he wrote great music. He was a Lutheran and perhaps the world's greatest composer of church music.

Abraham Lincoln didn't quit; he is probably the greatest example of persistence. The sense of obligation to continue is present in all of us. A duty to strive is the duty of us all. I felt a call to that duty. Born into poverty, Abraham Lincoln was faced with defeat throughout his life. He lost eight elections, failed in business, and suffered a nervous breakdown. But he didn't quit.

1816 His family was forced out of their home. He had to work to support them.
1818 His mother died.
1831 Failed in business.
1832 Ran for state legislature—lost.
1832 Also lost his job—wanted to go to law school but couldn't get in.
1833 Borrowed some money from a friend to begin a business, and by the end of the year, he was bankrupt. He spent the next seventeen years of his life paying off this debt.
1834 Ran for state legislature again—won.
1835 Was engaged to be married. His fiance died, and his heart was broken.
1836 Had a total nervous breakdown and was in bed for six months.
1838 Sought to become speaker of the state legislature—lost.
1840 Sought to become elector—lost.
1843 Ran for Congress—lost.
1843 Ran for Congress again—this time, he won. He went to Washington and did a good job.
1846 Ran for re-election to Congress—lost.
1849 Sought the job of land officer in his home state—rejected.
1854 Ran for Senate of the US—lost.
1856 Sought the Vice-Presidential nomination at his party's national convention—got less than a hundred votes.
1858 Ran for US Senate again—again, he lost.
1860 Elected president of the U.S.

"The path was worn and slippery. My foot slipped from under me, knocking the other out of the way, but I recovered and said to myself, 'It's a slip and not a fall.'" -Abraham Lincoln, after losing a senate race.

## EMERGE

# CHAMPIONS ARE FORMED BY WRESTLING WITH GOD

I love the Bible. It is so colorful yet so powerful. It has the most amazing and intriguing stories, with the most profound truths embedded within them.

As a father of three sons, I had a good decade of enjoying wrestling with my boys. Coming home from work, my sons, Jordan, Ashley, and Tommy, would get wrestled to the ground. We would destroy the living room, much to Mom's chagrin. They looked forward to it as much as I did, and I noticed their strength and confidence increase as they got older. After they hit their teenage years, I would intentionally make excuses *not* to wrestle with them as much because they would often put some serious "hurt" on me. I didn't want to show weakness or drive to the chiropractor for a late-night adjustment to reset ribs that had been popped out!

The Bible has an incredible story where God (the Father) comes down to wrestle with Jacob (His son).

> *"And he arose that night and took his two wives, his two female servants, and his eleven sons, and crossed over the ford of Jabbok. He took them, sent them over the brook, and sent over what he had. Then Jacob was left alone; and a Man wrestled with him until the breaking of day. Now when He saw that He did not prevail against him, He touched the socket of his hip; and the socket of Jacob's hip was out of joint as He wrestled with him. And He said, "Let Me go, for the day breaks." But he said, "I will not let You go unless You bless me!" So He said to him, "What is your name?" He said, "Jacob." And He said, "Your name shall no longer be called Jacob, but Israel; for you have struggled with God and with men, and have prevailed." Then Jacob asked, saying, "Tell me Your name, I pray." And He said, "Why is it that you ask about My name?" And He blessed him there. So Jacob called the name of the place Peniel: "For I have seen God face to face, and my life is preserved." Just as he crossed over Penuel the sun rose on him, and he limped on his hip. Therefore to this day the children of Israel do not eat the muscle that shrank, which is on the hip socket, because He touched the socket of Jacob's hip in the muscle that shrank."*
> *Genesis 32:22-32*

This was the moment when Jacob was "born again." He was no longer Jacob (heel grabber/usurper) but Israel (prince with God). There is something even more profound in the story.

## CHAPTER TWELVE: **CHAMPION**

When Jacob, excuse me, Israel realizes he wrestled with God, he calls the place *"Peniel,"* saying, *"I have seen God face to face, and my life is preserved!"* The Bible then says that as he crossed over *Peniel*, the sun rose on him, and he limped on his hip.

It may look like a small and perhaps insignificant typo or even a misspelling, but the Hebrew language doesn't contain clear vowels like the English language. The difference here is not only intentional but extremely *powerful*!

*Peniel* literally means "Place of Champions" or, even more accurately, "Place of God's Champions."

Every warrior in the Bible had *one* thing in common. You may say they were experts with swords and spears. Nope. There's something else. David was a warrior. Moses was a warrior. Abraham was a warrior. Joshua was a warrior.

What was the *one thing* they all had in common?

Like Jacob, they all had intimacy with God. They were *all* worshippers.

The devil has sold the men of this generation a *lie*! He's told them it's *not* masculine to be a worshipper, that worshipping is a feminine action. But the exact opposite is true, and the devil knows it. He knows those who *"kneel before the Almighty can stand up to anything!"*

When you worship, it is more than singing songs to God. Worship is the entrance into *seeing* just how *big* and *awesome* God is! When you *see* the *size* of your God, you begin to realize nothing can stand before you all the days of your life!

When David walked into the valley to face Goliath, the Bible described Goliath as "The Giant" and even recorded his height at six cubits and a span (9'9" tall). But what the writers missed was what David saw. They saw the Giant as the 'big man' on the battlefield. David saw HIS GOD as the REAL INSURMOUNTABLE UNDEFEATED CHAMPION GIANT!

> *"Then David said to the Philistine, "You come to me with a sword, with a spear, and with a javelin. But I come to you in the name of the Lord of hosts, the God of the armies of Israel, whom you have defied. This day the Lord will deliver you into my hand, and I will strike you and take your head from you. And this day I will give the carcasses of the camp of the Phi-*

# EMERGE

*listines to the birds of the air and the wild beasts of the earth, that all the earth may know that there is a God in Israel. Then all this assembly shall know that the Lord does not save with sword and spear; for the battle is the Lord's, and He will give you into our hands."*

*I Samuel 17:45-47*

David SAW that his God was the REAL giant, and that day, he prevailed over the Philistine. When you SEE your problems bigger than your God, it's a simple issue. You've stopped worshipping. When you enter into praise and worship, you will SEE how Big and Awesome He is and how NOTHING can defeat or oppose him!

## WHENEVER YOU OVERCOME SOMETHING, YOU DON'T JUST CONQUER IT; YOU PROCURE AUTHORITY OVER IT!

In the battle where David defeated Goliath with a stone and a sling, he didn't just knock out the giant. He didn't race up and stab him through the heart. He didn't cripple him or leave him brain-damaged in a vegetated state. At the end of this battle, Goliath wasn't sitting in a nursing home, being spoon-fed mushed vegetables, wetting his pants every hour.

David *cut off* Goliath's head!

Why? Well, there's the obvious lesson of finality that we learn from zombie warfare. Shooting or stabbing a zombie only temporarily keeps them at bay because they are the walking dead. To defeat them, you have to remove their heads!

I am using a little humor here, but *yes,* beheading Goliath definitely meant David wouldn't have to face a rematch with this giant ogre. There's also something more powerful at play here. In the Bible, *the head* speaks of authority—as in "the head of the house" or the "head of the church!" Kings wear crowns upon their heads, identifying them as the authority or potentate over that kingdom/region.

When David cut off the "champion's" head, he didn't just defeat and eliminate the threat; he procured authority over the Philistines. That's why when they saw David presiding over the giant's dead carcass, raising up into the air Goliath's head, the Philistine warriors fled in terror. They knew, as does the devil, that the spiritual authority resided in their champion. Now that he was defeated, that spiritual authority belonged to David.

## CHAPTER TWELVE: **CHAMPION**

This is what the Bible calls "principalities and powers, thrones and dominions" in Ephesians 6:12.

It's a similar principle to combat sports. When the champion is defeated, a new champion receives the *belt*, title, and prestige that goes along with it. All the perks and accolades of being the *new* champion belong to the victor. As the old adage states, *"To the victor go the spoils!"*

*"How does that apply to me?"*

I'm glad you asked.

Don't be content to just "knock down" your giant. To gain authority over him, you *must cut off his head*!

That means:
- Erasing and eliminating all porn.
- Canceling all subscriptions to dark sites.
- Canceling memberships to strip clubs and seedy houses.
- Getting to a Bible-based rehab and completing all twelve steps in the recovery process. Don't leave before because you're feeling better! I'm sure David felt a sense of relief and victory when he saw Goliath stagger like a drunkard, clutching his head while blood poured down his face, pooling in his beard and spilling onto his armor, feet, and the ground. David watched as the almost ten-foot-tall behemoth of a man stumbled and dropped to his knees. The Philistine warriors' shouts turned to a deafening hush as the giant crashed face-first into the dirt, blood pooling around his abnormally gargantuan-sized head. Finish all 12 steps. Have a sponsor to whom you can submit and be accountable.
- Forgiving your father. Don't just move away, cut him off, or ignore him. You have to *forgive* him to cut off the giant's head.
- Forgiving your *ex*. You can't just numb the pain, ignore the pain, or even bury the pain. You have to *cut off the head* and forgive them. That does *not* mean you condone or accept their betrayal or behavior. It also doesn't mean you are letting them "get away" with injustice. It means you're forgiving them so that *you* can be free. It means you trust a *holy, righteous,* and *morally perfect* God to execute justice in this situation. Trust me. He will.

# EMERGE

> *"Unforgiveness is like drinking poison in the Hope that the person who hurt you will DIE!"*
> *- Joyce Meyer*

Alcohol and drugs temporarily numb our pain or even cause us to feel temporary reprieve as we momentarily forget the wounds of injustice and betrayal. They do not fix the problem. They cannot. They are not designed to. In over thirty years of outreach to the homeless, I have never met someone who said that turning to alcohol or drugs to numb the pain in their lives has been a wonderful blessing and allowed them to thrive victoriously. Sadly, it's been the exact opposite.

You need to *"cut the head off the snake,"* so to speak. Satan is the snake. He is the master architect of evil in this world and our lives. That's why Jesus calls him *the* Evil One!

In the movie *The Equalizer*, Denzel Washington plays a retired special forces agent who, upon seeing the evil and corruption around him, can no longer just sit by and do nothing. When he sees young girls robbed of their innocence and trafficked to meet the lusts of wicked and perverted men, he cannot help but get involved. However, he soon realizes that evil *cannot* be negotiated with, nor can it be appeased. *Evil* refuses to coexist with the righteous. It seeks to dominate and destroy them. In the movie (a *must-watch*), Denzel realizes he has to "cut the head off the snake" and take out the Russian Mafia's leader.

Upon doing this (in spectacular form, I might say), the movie ends with the young girl free to make something of herself, using her musical and academic gifts to live a life of freedom, function, and purpose!

> *"God doesn't give the hardest battles to his toughest soldiers. He creates the toughest soldiers through life's hardest battles"*
> *– Warrior Saying*

## CUT THE HEAD OFF THE SNAKE

My final point on this topic is:

I have found that the location where David defeats Goliath is intentionally included in the Bible and carries a very powerful secret to being victorious and free!

## CHAPTER TWELVE: **CHAMPION**

*"Now the Philistines gathered their armies together to battle, and were gathered at Sochoh, which belongs to Judah; they encamped between Sochoh and Azekah, in Ephes Dammim."*
*I Samuel 17:1*

Notice that the location is in Judah. David is fighting an enemy that has placed himself inside of David's territory. He was from the tribe of Judah.

The hardest battles I have fought are the battles within and against myself. There is another saying we repeat at EMERGE, and I have no doubt you have probably heard it: *"My biggest ENEMY is actually my INNER-ME!"*

The enemy locates himself inside the safety of our walls and works from within. The Trojan Horse was a successful warfare strategy because the city of Troy was unbreachable from the outside. The city was located high on the cliff tops above an exposed beach. It had fortified walls with archer towers, complimenting the uphill rugged terrain that any army would have to negotiate to make it to the gates. However, we know from history that the city of Troy fell and fell permanently. How? By a flattering gift supposedly sent by the gods (as the sensually indulgent elders deemed.) They considered the giant horse a monumental gift and blessing, honoring their superiority and prowess. They promptly brought it into the city gates while they decided where best to place this wonderful "work of art!"

History recalls that upon the fall of midnight, a select band of warriors (not unlike SEAL Team 6), who were carefully hidden inside the monument, climbed out, opened the gates, and signaled to the armies hidden in the safe harbor on the other side of the cliffs that the city was *ripe* for the taking! Meanwhile, the inhabitants of Troy were oblivious to any sense of danger as they slept or staggered home drunk and inebriated from their late-night carousing. They had no idea this would be their last night enjoying the freedoms and protections of this once magnificent city!

The slaughter was immense and final.

> *"Your mind is a battlefield. Be its commander, not its soldier."*
> *- Warrior Quote*

Jesus, who espoused all the magnificent traits of a warrior champion, told us the following; *"If your eye causes you to sin, pluck it out. If your hand causes you to sin, cut it off!"*

## EMERGE

In other words, once you have dealt with the external, understand that the *true champion* must ruthlessly address our sinful nature within. Notice that He (Jesus) doesn't advocate that if your eye causes you to sin and lust, you should *force* all women to wear a burqa. He locates the real source of the problem and then gives us a remedy.

Please do *not* misread Jesus as wanting to create blind and maimed followers with missing eyes and hands. Jesus was speaking figuratively and using strong hyperbole to get the point across. *You* are the issue. It's *not* the strip club, the internet, the liquor stores, or the marijuana dispensaries. It's *you*. It's your inner sinful nature that needs to be defeated.

Repentance, discipleship, prayer, and His word are the instruments of cutting off the head of the enemy within or our "inner me!"

## BUT HOW DO I DEFEAT MY INNER ME?

This is a brilliant question and brings us to the crux of personal freedom, deliverance, and breakthrough. How do I defeat myself?
Isn't that an oxymoron?

Isn't that the enigma that has puzzled and plagued the most outstanding leaders of mankind over the millennia?

Plato once said, *"For a man to conquer himself is the first and most noblest of all victories!"*
Thank you, Mr. Plato, but *how*?

The answer is prayer and fasting. In my life, there has been *no substitute* for this. When Jesus confronted a powerful spirit of self-destruction in a young boy, he remarked, *"This kind only comes out through prayer and fasting!"* (Matthew 17:21).

I have found that "the flesh" (Bible terminology for the human condition) is weak and, therefore, susceptible to becoming addicted to all kinds of vices and proclivities. It *loves* pleasure and *hates* pain and discipline.

Every time we fast, we deny the flesh and its cravings, breaking bondages and addictions and resetting our heart and spirit on the things of God. Psychologists will tell you it takes about twenty-one days to form a habit but forty days to break one. When you fast, the breakthrough and freedom you receive in every area of your life are amazing. It's so much deeper than overcoming food cravings.

# CHAPTER TWELVE: **CHAMPION**

*Wine* became a big "go-to" for me during 2020, with all the lockdowns and the hate we were getting for keeping our church open during those tyrannical times. I noticed myself looking forward to more than one glass each evening after work and found I struggled to sleep if I didn't drink at least two glasses. We are not legalistic about such things—we are biblical!

> *"All things are lawful for me, but not all things are helpful; all things are lawful for me, but not all things are beneficial."*
> 1 Corinthians 10:23

Cutting out wine was the greatest way to *reset* my flesh and break its "need" for it. At the same time, I decided to stop drinking coffee. It was powerful. I also found my red meat craving subsided! During this time, I ate healthier, had more energy and focus, didn't crave wine, and drank more *tea* than coffee!

I would say that it's good to do this at least *once* a year! We do it every January. It's the best way to keep conquering yourself!

## **ENCOURAGEMENT AND EMPOWERMENT**

Here are some of my favorite quotes to inspire you to be the *champion* you are called to be!

> *"Let your plans be dark and as impenetrable as night, and when you move, fall like a thunderbolt."*
> – Sun Tzu

> *"The Spartans do not ask how many are the enemy but where are they."*
> – Plutarch

> *"Victory is reserved for those warriors who are willing to pay its price."*
> – Sun Tzu

> *"He who sweats more in training bleeds less in war."*
> – Spartan Warrior Creed

> *"A true warrior fights not because he hates what is in front of him, but because he loves what is behind him."*
> – G.K. Chesterton

# EMERGE

# CHAPTER THIRTEEN

# ALPHA

א

ALEF

Strength / OX

*"Lesser men believe in luck or in circumstance, but the ALPHA Male believes in cause and effect!"*
*- Ralph Waldo Emerson.*

*"A Lion does not concern itself with the opinion of sheep!" - C S Lewis*

*"If you don't play to win, don't play at all!" - Tom Brady*

*"If Nobody HATES you, nobody knows you!" - Grant Cardone*

*"Haters are all failures. It's 100% across the board. No one who is truly brilliant at anything is a Hater!"*
*- Joe Rogan*

*"Whoso would be a MAN, must be a non-conformist!"*
*- Ralph Waldo Emerson*

*"We must DARE to be great, and we must realize that greatness is the fruit of toil and sacrifice and high courage!"*
*- Theodore Roosevelt*

*"I am the ALPHA and the OMEGA the first and the last, the beginning and the end!"*
*- Revelation 1:8*

## EMERGE
# WHAT IS IT TO BE A REAL MAN?

Our society continually says to become "a real man," yet it does so without actually defining what is meant by a "real man." Should a young man who aspires to live up to society's expectations of becoming a "real man" become a samurai, a knight, or perhaps a Navy seal? Would a Mafia Don be acceptable? What about an artist, a rockstar, or an actor? Perhaps it requires bravery and sacrifice. Maybe a firefighter or a policeman? Is a "real man" a CEO like Elon Musk? Someone who doesn't settle to be one of the workers in a factory? The definition is as vague as the choices are endless.

When I was young, I was grateful for "pre-woke" Disney back when it had inspiration, morals, and family values. I was convinced that to be a "real man" when I grew up, I had to be willing to fight a great fight against evil to rescue the beautiful princess trapped in the tower, suffering gross injustice. I would have to defeat witches, warlocks, and fire-breathing dragons who would burn any would-be heroes to a crisp if they dared to approach to rescue her.

I learned that evil forces in the world threaten my future and the future of the princess who would instantly fall in love with me, sighing, *"My hero,"* as she sank overwhelmingly into my arms. Obviously, we'd be getting married after I triumphantly conquered the dragon and any other foe in my wake! I knew it was noble to protect my village, my town, my family, my community, and yes, even my country.

The graduation ceremony from "real man" to "hero" would require the appearance of a fire-breathing dragon, threatening to end the lives of innocent people and all those near and dear to me. Without the dragon, how could I be a hero? Once the dragon appears, I would have to be the first to respond. After all, the one who slays the dragon receives all the accolades and glory and the love of the most beautiful girl in the land. The dragon could *not* be shot by Farmer Joe while he was out on his walk. No. I had not only to respond, but I also had to be the one to defeat the dragon, vanquishing it with my heroic bravado!

Interestingly, the word "hero" is derived from the root "ser," from which we also get the word servant (as well as slave and protector). In Chinese and Japanese, the word for "hero" is also derived from the words "slave" and "protector." The word "samurai" is also derived from the word for servant. Throughout the centuries, young boys from all walks of life have embraced the opportunity to serve and protect their villages, families, loved ones, and even their countries with the hope of being seen and herald-

## CHAPTER THIRTEEN: **ALPHA**

ed as a hero. It's almost like this desire is "hardwired" into our souls. Often, it seemed that the greater the chance of death, the more zealously our young men embraced the opportunity to fight and prove themselves—sometimes just for the honor of being remembered posthumously as a hero!

*You* were born to be a *hero* to somebody!

Yes, *you!*

Please, let that sink in.

It may be your son, your daughter, your wife, your team, your village, or your community. *Heroism* is in your DNA. *You* are an *alpha*. That makes you the "go-first" pioneer, dragon slayer, beautiful princess rescuer, wicked witch defeater, against-all-odds conqueror, noble, lionhearted *hero*! What is the pay and reward for our heroes who volunteer to fight fires and crime to keep society safe? It's praise, respect, and purpose.

## WHAT IS SO IMPORTANT ABOUT THE ALPHA?

A friend recently told me he purchased a German shepherd dog to guard their smaller dog and family pet because of increased coyote sightings near their estate. This German shepherd is a protector because of its training and also because of its DNA. I was fascinated to hear that this lone dog would scare off and intimidate an entire gang of coyotes. The family had seen the coyotes staring at their small dog on many occasions and recounted how wily and opportunistic coyotes are when they are hungry. They will stop at nothing to feed their craving bellies. The addition of this German shepherd was at the suggestion of a man who was once a special forces marine and now trains these dogs to protect homes from all kinds of predatory evils. Since the presence of this *alpha* shepherd, the coyotes have yet to be sighted on or anywhere near the property.

This is *alpha* on display. This is how *alphas* work. Sometimes, just the presence of an *alpha* is enough to deter evil and wickedness! My friend went on to tell me how this former military Special Ops individual has developed a company that goes into areas where dangerous wild animals threaten the lives of the people living in certain villages and towns.

He told me of a recent contract this man had undertaken in a region of Africa. A pack, perhaps more accurately, a "gang" of wild baboons, was coming down from the jungle into the village. They would harass the villagers, steal their food, and threaten

# EMERGE

their lives. The chaotic damage was only increasing, as were the gang's numbers. The baboons grew more and more brazen every day. The villagers posed little to no resistance and were filled with all kinds of delectable food and other amenities. After the death of several of their goats and pets, as well as a nearly fatal attack upon a young child, the villagers had enough. They knew if they didn't take immediate measures, a small child or elderly person might become a fatality!

My friend contacted this man's office after hearing he specializes in situations like this. The tribal chiefs of the village were put through to speak directly to him. They asked him in no uncertain terms if he could actually help them. Apparently, after hearing his guarantee that he could easily fix the situation, they promptly contracted with him.

Years of Special Ops training made him an expert in dealing with violent thugs and pests. Upon his arrival at the village, the village chiefs and elders gathered around and asked him how difficult this task would be. They told him of the swelling number of baboons in the nearby jungle. It was almost reaching plague proportions, and they had given thought to relocating their village. These baboons were growing in their brazenness. They would walk through the village unafraid, hissing at people, stealing food, and damaging small businesses in the village square.

The man replied that it would not be that difficult of a task. All he had to do was find the *alpha* male and take him out! He told the elders that as soon as he took out the alpha male, everything would return to being peaceful and normal. It took under a week for him to locate the alpha and then take him out! Since then, the village has had no more trouble with baboons.

In Chapter 3 of this book, we saw that the Hebrew word for "father" is בא—the Alef and the Beit. It literally means "the strength or the ox of the house." Statistics have shown that when there is no father/alpha present, there is no strength in the home to drive away pests or those seeking to harm, hurt, or take advantage of those living in the villages.

From teen suicide to poor SATs, violent crime, incarceration, early death, disease, divorce, promiscuity, and vulnerability to sexual assault, abuse, and rape. Whenever the APLHA is taken out of the home, the house suffers. Where FATHERS are missing, society falls apart. The ALPHA is indeed the strength of the house. Masculinity is the safeguard of the house. The evidence is indisputable. Take out the ALPHA, and the house is crippled.

## CHAPTER THIRTEEN: ALPHA
# AN EMERGE MOMENT

Many years ago, in the early days of our EMERGE conference, God gave me the most profound and prophetic revelations on the alpha and the beta. He showed me that so many men present had lost their alpha roar due to a lethal combination of life's overwhelming struggles and challenges, personal failures, and transgressions. God wanted to bring it back!

We were at standing-room-only capacity in our Bressi Ranch campus, where we held the conference sessions. Over four hundred men shouted a prophetic warfare declaration to break the devil's lies and re-attain their God-given *alpha* status! It was nothing short of supernatural and powerful! Men wept on the altar. Testimonies flooded in from not just the men but also their wives and many of their children.

I had recently returned from South Africa, where we visited a wild animal park. At this park, we saw a pride of lions that had brought down a zebra. We got to pull up and watch as the pride arranged themselves to heartily feast on their newfound prey. I noticed there was more than one adult male in the pride. I asked my hosts, *"How do you know which one is the alpha?"* They responded, *"You see the one that's eating? The one with blood around his mouth and face? That is the alpha. The others won't eat until he is done. He's the alpha, make no mistake!"*

Just then, one of the other male lions, who looked as big and strong as the alpha, approached the carcass to fill his hungry belly. Suddenly, the lion feasting on the plumpest part of the zebra let out a ROAR that literally caused the van in which we were safely sitting to shake! The other male lion promptly scampered off. The answer to my question was illustrated before me. The alpha had *roared*, and the other lions backed off in submission.

The Bible can also (crudely) be reduced to the battle between two lions. Jesus is the *lion* of the Tribe of Judah (Revelation 5:5), and Satan is also portrayed as a "roaming lion, seeking whom he may devour" (1 Peter 5:8). Make no mistake. There is *only one* alpha. Satan is the defeated beta. He is "Scar" from *The Lion King*.

Jesus said, *"I am the ALPHA and the OMEGA, the beginning and the end!"*

When *His roar* is present, the enemies and inferior lions back off! There is a scene in *The Lion King* where Scar has duped Simba and Nala into going to the forbidden realm—the elephant's graveyard, which is the domain of predatory hyenas who would

# EMERGE

love nothing more than to feast upon the flesh of two young lion cubs. As hungry hyenas surround Simba and Nala, Simba tries to be brave and protect Nala. He musters all his strength to let out a *roar*! Unfortunately, his little frame has yet to fully develop, so instead of a commanding roar, a pitiful squeal gushes forth to the amusement and laughter of the hyenas. Not to be deterred, and seeing no other option, Simba fills his young lungs with breath again. As he attempts to let out a roar toward the approaching, now emboldened hyenas, a booming *roar* shakes the cave. But it's *not* from his mouth. It was Mufasa, his father, coming to rescue them. When he roared, the hyenas retreated in fear, and he proceeded to give them a thrashing!

God showed me the devil had stolen the *alpha* roar of our men.

Of all men.

*Alpha* is *pure* masculinity. Masculinity is *alpha*.

When the devil *attacks* masculinity through the cultural "toxic masculinity" agenda, you can be sure he is *not* out to purge the abuses of masculinity but masculinity altogether. A beta's agenda can only be fulfilled when the *alpha* is no longer present.

## DISCOVER AS YOU GO

God was instructing and shaping our EMERGE men's ministry philosophy and strategy as each year came and went. Each year, our mission became a little more clear and powerful. I knew I didn't want to emasculate men, which, if I was being honest, was my experience at most men's events prior. We would sit in a room and be berated for the very things that made us male—a propensity to enjoy battles and competition, a love of the aesthetics of the female form, testing our strengths, not apologizing for our ego, desiring to *win* and not just be about "how we play the game," etc. God wired us this way, and I knew He didn't make a mistake. That is *not* to say that these attributes have not been badly affected (or infected) by our sinful nature.

They have. Most certainly, and most definitely.

However, the attributes themselves are not to be dismissed or discarded but rather redeemed! You are meant to *fight*, so "put on the whole armor of God" (Ephesians 6:10) and fight the evil one and his demonic hordes. Fight sin. Fight temptation. Fight evil wherever it rears its ugly head.

# CHAPTER THIRTEEN: **ALPHA**

You were created to *see* the female form and be attracted to it. The Bible says, *"As a loving deer and a graceful Doe, let her breasts satisfy you at all times; and always be enraptured with her love!"* It's *not* the desire and delight to look upon beautiful breasts that are evil. It's the devil using them to draw you away from always being enraptured with your wife! Enraptured can also be translated as "intoxicated." The devil knows there is *nothing* more powerful than a man enraptured by the gift of his God-given bride! You were created to *win*. The devil has perverted this to mean "defeating and humiliating others" to make yourself feel like the big man. You can win, however, without being a jerk and without having to humiliate others. I love watching title fights. After the fight, there is a winner and a loser. The commentator will interview the two fighters, first the winner and then the loser. It's always so magnificent to see these fighters begin by giving praise and honor to their opponent's warrior heart and prowess, giving them credit for the battle they brought that evening and how it brought out the best of them!

## MY PERSONAL BATTLE WAS THE JOURNEY SHAPER

The *one* ministry I felt completely inadequate in and disqualified for was men's ministry. I did not *feel* alpha. I felt beta at best! I grew up in a home where my father struggled with being a father—troubled and tormented by the demons of his past. As he struggled, so did his two sons.

He ran away from his home and his father when he was just fourteen. His mother died of tuberculosis when he was just three years old, and his father remarried when he was five years old. His stepmother already had two children of her own and naturally favored and protected them. World War II left a lot of widows and caused a lot of tragedy, trauma, and pain. I no longer judge my father, but we all have to live with the consequences of our choices.

After running away from his family, he met my mother while attempting to buy a pair of shoes. My mother was a shoe clerk in her little town, nestled upon the edge of the remarkably beautiful Black Forest in Baden Wurttemberg, Germany. Unfortunately, he got my mother pregnant before they were even engaged to be married, and he had now added the dishonoring of my Opa, his future father-in-law, to the mix. As children, my brother and I would ask my father about his family, especially our grandfather. He would gnash his teeth with fetid anger and curse his father. He hated his father. That was all there was to it, and to this day, he still carries a deep, deep resentment toward him.

You have probably heard the statement, *"Hurting people, hurt people!"*
Because my father never dealt with his childhood injustices, abuses, traumas, and issues, he simply carried them and inflicted these upon his own children. It's a fixed law of divine justice;

> *"If you forgive anyone's sins, they are forgiven.*
> *If you do not forgive them, they are not forgiven."*
> John 20:23 NLT

This verse, in the original Greek, can also be read as, *"If you forgive someone's sins, they are forgiven, but if you retain their sins, they are retained!"*
Your life produces from the inside out.

When you were formed in the womb, you were formed from the "inside out"—first, your internal organs and, lastly, your skin, hair, eyelashes, fingernails, and so on. You were formed from the inside out because all life flows from the inside out.

Our childhood was the direct result of the inner carnage of my father's heart.

Because I was the eldest, I was subject to the most ridicule and the most abuse from my father's self-loathing. Nothing I did was ever good enough, and he ensured I was aware of all my shortcomings and failures, constantly reminding me what a disappointment I was and how I didn't have what it took to make it in the world.

We are all programmed to believe words. Whether those words are the truth or not is another matter. We all believe words. Contracts are formed using words. When we marry, we exchange vows, which are simply words spoken in the form of promises that we declare before God and witnesses, vowing that we will be in this marriage "until death do us part!" The *most potent* and powerful word is the word of God. It's pure power and pure truth. It brings deliverance and healing. It shapes and forms the future. Jesus said in John 15:3, *"You are already clean because of the WORD that I have spoken to you!"* The word of God cleanses and transforms.

When you grow up in a home without God, however, the words most predominant-

# CHAPTER THIRTEEN: ALPHA

ly shaping your worldview and your self-image come from the *alpha* in your home—your father. I look back, and I see the belief I had formed about myself not having "what it takes to be a man" or to lead and find a productive place of influence in this world came from the continual repetition of these belittling, demonic, angry, hate-filled words.

Thank *God* for His *word*! Feed upon it. Let it wash you, cleanse you, heal you, and restore you!

## ALPHA IS NOT SOMETHING YOU NEED TO BECOME BUT SOMETHING YOU NEED TO RESTORE!

I wrote about the original Hebrew word for "man" in the first chapter of this book, but I want to explore another aspect for this chapter. Below is the Hebrew word for man, ADAM.

## מדא

It has the Alpha (Alef) followed by the Dalet and the Mem.
The Alef (ALPHA) is always representative of God throughout scripture.
Dalet Mem is the Hebrew word 'Dam' which means 'Blood!'

Man (Adam), broken down to its crudest definition, could be understood as the being who "*is the blood of God's strength and leadership.*" Even more simply put, MAN is the bearer and possessor of divine "*Alpha Blood.*" Just as blood is passed down from the father, not the mother, in vitro, so the scriptures make it clear that Adam is the son of God—literally, the blood of the Alef/Alpha. The Bible goes on to proclaim that *all men*, despite skin color, ethnicity, demography, social status, and birth origins, are made of "one blood!"
Acts 17:26 "*God has made of one blood, all the peoples of the earth!*"
This obviously stands in direct opposition to the current narratives of our time, which seek to divide men according to ethnicity, melanin content, and social status. We, however, know who is the author and architect of such lies and misinformation—Satan, the devil, the dragon, the deceiving serpent of old! According to the holy

# EMERGE

scriptures, the created makeup of man is of one who is infused with "Alpha-Blood!" When God said to Adam in Genesis 1:28, *"Exercise dominion and subdue..."* it was in total alignment with his wiring.

*You* were created to be *alpha*, not beta, gamma, or anything less. You were created to have dominion, not to be dominated. You were created to master, overcome, subdue, overthrow, and conquer. Much of the various extreme sports we witness today are just a crude outworking of this intrinsic, internal wiring—men finding a euphoric escape from the mundane day-to-day grind. We get a euphoric high from risking our very lives should something go wrong. We want to defy nature's laws, even gravity itself, just to "feel alive" and not feel like we've become "just another brick in the wall!" Our current educational system is more akin to creating "worker bees" who subsist only to serve a queen's agenda in the banality of the hive.

Individual expression, creativity, and autonomy are all frowned upon by the mainstream machine, which, in an eerie, somewhat prophetic reflection of the movie The Matrix, has designated human beings as nothing more than batteries, supplying power and resources to the system's masters.

*"I'm one of these people that likes adrenaline and new things, like extreme sports. It makes me feel alive."* Gisele Bundchen

In Genesis 11, Nimrod, the great "hunter" before the *Lord*, finds his agenda is diametrically opposed and thwarted by Almighty God. Why? What's wrong with a tower? We have skyscrapers today. Was God against skyscrapers or towers? No. Nimrod was not a hunter of wild beasts but of men. He wanted to conquer them and strip them of all individuality and self-autonomy, which is reflected in the quote, *"Come let us bake bricks and let us bake them thoroughly"* (Genesis 11:3). The replacement of stone was indicative of a top-down enforced uniformity of thought, opinion, narrative, adherence, and even worship. Nimrod in the Bible is also referred to as Gilgamesh in the ancient Sumerian texts. It is the "spirit" behind the systems of communism and socialism. It seeks to remove all individuality and reward for personal achievement, enslaving all into an egalitarian "equality of outcome" myth. This allows the lazy, indolent, corrupt, and reprobate to be rewarded equally with the entrepreneurial, hardworking, risk-taking innovators.

Perhaps the meteoric rise of extreme sports experienced in the last two decades is nothing more than a cry from the multitudes of their desire to break free from the pressure to conform to a regimented birth-to-death cycle. A glance at some of the extreme sports phenomenons includes free solo climbing (rock climbing without safety ropes where line slip can end in a fatality), or the craze throughout Russia, and now some other parts of the world, of hanging without harnesses from tower-

# CHAPTER THIRTEEN: ALPHA

ing skyscrapers. Some people even jump from one to another. Then there's Bungee jumping into crocodile-infested waters, volcano boarding, and extreme dinghy racing, where motorized high-speed dinghies race through crocodile-infested waters in Australia's Murray River basin. Add to that poisonous snakes, sharp jagged rocks, and high speeds, and you can see the appeal (or not)! Is it the discovery of new adrenaline highs? Or is it more about the "recovery" of innate wiring to dominate, overcome, subdue, and live rather than be tied down to a regimented system seeking to reduce us from human beings to human doings?

> *"Then God blessed them, and God said to them, "Be fruitful and multiply; fill the earth and subdue it; have dominion over the fish of the sea, over the birds of the air, and over every living thing that moves on the earth."*
> *Genesis 1:28 NKJV*

How do I know God's will for my life? It's actually quite easy. Simply look at your wiring. Everything is designed and created (shaped/manufactured, if you will) for a purpose. A knife is created to cut things. A chair is designed to allow people to sit. A bed is for sleeping and rest, and a light bulb is for seeing when the sun has set. Air conditioning controls the temperature to maintain maximum comfort. Genesis 1:28 clearly describes that man was created to be *fruitful, multiply,* and *fill the earth, subduing it to exercise dominion over it!*

In other words, *you* were created to *thrive, multiply,* and be *fruitful* (expressive, creative, colorful, inventive, productive, and prosperous) to *subdue* and exercise *dominion*! I could have written this entire book just on those five things. Five, incidentally, is the number for grace. One meaning of Grace is "divine empowerment." God has graced (divinely empowered) you and me to *thrive, multiply, flourish, subdue,* and *dominate*!

> *"Strength, Courage, Mastery, and Honor are the alpha virtues of men all over the world."*
> *–Jack Donovan.*

# EMERGE

## CHAPTER FOURTEEN
# DISCIPLE

# דימלת

*(Talmud)*

"Then He said to them, "Follow Me, and I will make you fishers of men.""
Matthew 4:19

"It is enough for a disciple that he be like his teacher, and a servant like his master. If they have called the master of the house Beelzebub, how much more will they call those of his household!"
Matthew 10:25

"You are becoming somebody, but WHO you are becoming is not determined by your desire or vision. It's determined by the loudest and most influential voices you allow to speak into your life!"
- Jurgen Matthesius

'Tell me, and I forget. Teach me, and I remember. Involve me, and I learn.'
—Benjamin Franklin

'The illiterate of the 21st century will not be those who cannot read and write, but those who cannot learn, unlearn, and relearn.'
—Alvin Toffler

'The more I read, the more I acquire, the more certain I am that I know nothing.'
—Voltaire

# CHAPTER FOURTEEN: DISCIPLE
## TALMUD—DISCIPLESHIP

What is the Talmud? "According to Jewish tradition, Moses received the Torah as a written text alongside a commentary: the Talmud. The Talmud is the oral tradition that coincides with the Torah. It is a depiction of the primary codification of the Jewish decrees. It explains the written texts of the Torah so that people know how to apply it to their lives."[1]

What does that mean? It means that the Talmud is the divinely inspired instruction of how to live out and apply the Torah, the laws and commandments of God, received by Moses. It's a wonderful thing to behold. God didn't just give a ransom list of demands as a burden humanity has to attempt to figure out how to practice. The Talmud suggests that God gave us accompanying instructions to go along with the magnificent Ten Commandments. The biggest battle in your life (and my life) is *not* the knowledge of *"what's right and what's wrong!"* I don't have any issue *knowing* what's right. My struggle is *doing* what's right! That's discipleship! That's the Talmud!

## DISCIPLESHIP BY WHOM?

We've all heard the saying, *"He's a chip off the old block!"* or *"The apple doesn't fall far from the tree!"* When people say these things, they are saying they can discern and detect someone else's influence and DNA in our lives. When Jesus challenged the disciples with the mantra, *"Follow me, and I'll make you fishers of men"(Mark 1:17),* He wasn't hiring staff or building a team. He was making a commitment to make these men something they could never have become on their own!

Discipleship is the reproduction method of the kingdom.

What *most* people don't realize is that they *are* being discipled already. It's not a question of "if" you're being discipled, but rather by who and by what! If the culture, the media, your friends at the bar, and Hollywood celebrities are the loudest and most influential voices in your life, then you will espouse their values and parrot their beliefs. What most folks don't realize is that the devil works through these mediums to influence people away from God. It's prolific, persistent, and perpetual.

Whenever you turn on the nightly news, they follow an agenda. They see you as sheep. Knowing that most people don't like to think for themselves, they get you to leave the "thinking" to the newscasters and anchors. After all, we have had to think all

# EMERGE

day at school, at work, with the kids, and on the sports field. We often want someone to tell us what's happening and what to believe about it. Why do you think so many "news stations" advertise their anchors, attempting to solicit your loyalty and audience, proclaiming sainthood upon their station and anchors with *"A News Anchor YOU can trust!"*

Trust? With what? With telling you the truth? That's what they're saying. Whether they really are committed to it or not is arguable. We live in an era of fake news. Many of the beautiful and talented faces on our nightly screens have been seduced and bought with money, fame, and success. Any resistance they might have is pacified by what they would stand to lose if they push back or question the narratives being handed down to them by their executives.

God created our world and the universe around us with *words*. Words frame worlds.

Your world is framed by the *words* you hear, believe, and *amen* in your heart (by "*amen*," I mean come into agreement with). Your life is governed by words. When you buy a house, a title deed is signed, and mortgage papers are drawn up using words. All business deals are written using words. When you got married, you exchanged vows before God and man using words.

## DISCIPLESHIP POWER

I remember when I was graduating from Bible college, there were two job offers on the table—one in New Zealand and the other in Australia. I desperately wanted to stay in Australia and was definitely leaning on that offer. This way, I could marry my Leannie, stay close to friends and family, and enjoy the beautiful Aussie lifestyle. However, my Bible college dean decided to take me out for a coffee and help me process my decision. Being young and somewhat immature, I immediately gushed about how I wanted to stay in Australia and get married and how the Australian job came with a part-time salary. The New Zealand job, however, had no salary offer whatsoever. What the dean said next rocked me to the core and changed the course of my destiny!

He said to me, *"Jurgen, you need to choose wisely. Whoever you serve, you will become in five years!"* It gave me a completely different perspective on the decision before me. One choice was a beautiful and kind pastor. The other was an unconventional apostolic leader who would carry a national influence. Sadly, the latter was the one with no

## CHAPTER FOURTEEN: **DISCIPLE**

salary and no immediate comfort or gratification. God was *testing* me, and I knew which one the Holy Spirit was trying to get me to choose. I would have to swallow my pride further when I told my father that, after leaving a career in engineering and attending Bible college, I was now embarking on working for a church for *free* in another nation. I knew he would certainly not approve. To be fair, he hadn't approved from the start and told me in no uncertain terms that he would *not* give me *"Vun Cent, Not Vun Cent of support!"* True to his word, he didn't. I had chosen to go with God, who had miraculously provided for my two years at Bible college. This same God showed no signs that He was about to quit now. I chose the more difficult path, and God was there the entire way.

Five years later, I had indeed attained national influence and became one of the most sought-after speakers at youth conferences and youth events in New Zealand. Everybody must serve somebody. You must *choose wisely* whom you will serve because you will become just like them in five years!

> *"It is enough for a disciple that he be like his teacher, and a servant like his master. If they have called the master of the house Beelzebub, how much more will they call those of his household!"*
> *- Matthew 10:25 (NKJV)*

## **THE PSYCHOLOGY OF DISCIPLESHIP**

Psychology began when therapists realized that our lives, struggles, issues, and successes stem from one thing—our *"psyche-ology."* What does that mean?

Psychology comes from two root words[2]:
1. Psyche - Soul
2. Logos - Word(s)

Psychologists deal with the "soul words" that dominate our inner thought life. The Bible classifies this as the "issues of the heart!"

> *"As a man thinks in his heart, so is the man!"*
> *Proverbs 23:7 (NKJV)*

If you deep down tell yourself, *"I'm no good. I'm a failure. I'm useless. I will always un-*

# EMERGE

*derachieve and disappoint!"* your life will reflect all of those statements. That's why the Bible challenges us to *"Above all else, guard your heart for out of it flows the issues of life!" Proverbs 4:23 (NKJV).* Jesus came to interrupt the negative words that govern your life and replace them with words that will elevate and empower your life! When Jesus called the disciples to follow Him, He knew they could become extraordinary if they adopted His words over their current soundtrack.

## THE INTERRUPTER

Jesus is the ultimate interrupter. I mean, the man who was quietly born in a tiny little village in one of the world's smallest nations ends up splitting *time in half*—BC/AD. In the opening stanza of the gospel of John, Jesus is the word become flesh—not "a" word becoming flesh, but *the* word!

> *"In the beginning was the Word, and the Word was with God, and the Word was God. He was in the beginning with God. All things were made through Him, and without Him nothing was made that was made. In Him was life, and the life was the light of men."*
> John 1:1-4

Discipleship is the process by which Jesus interrupts our entire lives through His word! Our thoughts, dreams, desires, value system, virtues, and morality. His word delivers us, heals us, transforms us, elevates us, invigorates us, comforts us, empowers us, and cleanses us.

> *"You are already clean because of the word which I have spoken to you."*
> John 15:3

A disciple (of Christ) has submitted themselves to the elevation of God's word above their own thoughts, opinions, values, and beliefs. Their beliefs become shaped by the words of Christ. *No human* can reach their fullest potential without the word of God interrupting and reshaping their lives. None. Whenever you face a crossroads between what God's word says and what your preferences are, choose God's word!

> *"Therefore whoever hears these sayings of Mine, and does them, I will liken him to a wise man who built his house on the rock: and the rain descended, the*

# CHAPTER FOURTEEN: **DISCIPLE**

*floods came, and the winds blew and beat on that house; and it did not fall, for it was founded on the rock. "But everyone who hears these sayings of Mine, and does not do them, will be like a foolish man who built his house on the sand: and the rain descended, the floods came, and the winds blew and beat on that house; and it fell. And great was its fall." And so it was, when Jesus had ended these sayings, that the people were astonished at His teaching, for He taught them as one having authority, and not as the scribes."*
*Matthew 7:24-29*

Wow! Did you *read* what Jesus just said? Your ultimate destiny and life success are determined by what you do with His word. Notice that both the wise man and the foolish man heard the word, but only one acted upon it—only one heard and *did* the word! When you *do* the word, you set its power in motion in your life!

Many years ago, the Holy Spirit posed a question to me. He asked, *"When is the word of God most powerful? When it is spoken or when it is believed/applied?"* I wanted to say, *"When it is spoken!"* but the beautiful helper, the Holy Spirit, made it very clear that the word of God is *most potent* when it's heard and *applied*. Discipleship is the helping and empowering of ordinary humans to apply the divine supernatural word of God to their lives! When we do, our lives are forever changed. Literally! You receive eternal life!

Discipleship is the most important and most neglected mission on the planet. Most churches believe the most important mission is to "save lost souls!" However, Jesus didn't say to go into all the world and save lost souls. He commissioned us to *"Go into all the world and make disciples."*

*"And Jesus came and spoke to them, saying, "All authority has been given to Me in heaven and on earth. Go therefore and make disciples of all the nations, baptizing them in the name of the Father and of the Son and of the Holy Spirit, teaching them to observe all things that I have commanded you; and lo, I am with you always, even to the end of the age." Amen."*
*Matthew 28:18-20*

"Baptizing them, teaching them to observe all the things that I have commanded you," Jesus was showing that the most powerful mission of the church is the discipleship of nations and their adherence to observe and keep His teaching and commandments!

**EMERGE**
# DISCIPLESHIP IS EMPOWERMENT

The level of *power* in your life directly correlates to the level of God's *word* in your life! God's word is power. God has embedded His power into His word. Just like every seed has the power to reproduce a life-giving plant after its kind, so too does every word of God! God's anger burned against Moses when he was commanded to *speak* to the rock to bring forth water, but instead *struck* the rock (*twice*), disqualifying him from leading the people into the promised land (Numbers 20:11).

Why? Because Moses was meant to mature the children of Israel from dependency upon an anointed man of God to the *power* of obedience to God's word. The serpent attacked God's word in the garden by the serpent and has created all the chaos and disorder in the world since then. Wherever God's word is applied and obeyed, nations, families, communities, and individuals *flourish*. Wherever it is discarded or dismissed, chaos and destruction ensue.

God gives *powerful* insight into what He desires in His promise-taking leaders and people:

> *"This Book of the Law shall not depart from your mouth, but you shall meditate in it day and night, that you may observe to do according to all that is written in it. For then you will make your way prosperous, and then you will have good success. Have I not commanded you? Be strong and of good courage; do not be afraid, nor be dismayed, for the Lord your God is with you wherever you go."*
> *Joshua 1:8-9*

Moses had a staff that performed miracles. A "magic stick" that did "supernatural tricks." I'm intentionally being a little indelicate and irreverent. When Joshua was appointed to succeed Moses as Israel's leader, God did *not* ask Moses to pass the "magic stick" to Joshua. Instead, He tells Joshua, "*Do not* let my law/word depart from your mouth!" (Joshua 1:8, NKJV). In other words, "to inherit the promised land and take down the giant, enemy opposition stacked against you, you don't need a "magic stick" so much as you need My word on your mouth!" The highest objective of being a disciple is to live with such devotion that God's word/law *never* departs from your mouth. It cannot be replaced by self-help motivational pomposity, social "justice" claptraps, fear, hopelessness, or negativity. God's *word* in your mouth makes you powerful.

God's word/law in your mouth should be echoed by its application in your life! When these two are in alignment and operation, your life will flourish. When these are not present or are out of order, your life will be fraught with dysfunction, limitation, and forfeiture.

# CHAPTER FOURTEEN: DISCIPLE
## CAN I DISCIPLE MYSELF?

Sadly, you cannot disciple yourself. That doesn't mean you can't choose to be discipled or even choose the strength and depth of that discipleship. What do I mean by that? I'm glad you asked. One of the interpretations of the word "disciple" literally means "disciplined one.³" While I can undoubtedly value and apply discipline to my life, I have discovered that I get much more significant results in the gym when I hire a trainer because, naturally, I am more committed to my comfort than my progress! When pain and exhaustion set in during a repetition of an exercise, I want to stop and quit, but the trainer will yell, *"Give me three more!"* I felt like I didn't have *one* more in me, but he was demanding three more. Reluctantly, I press on, not wanting to disappoint or appear to lack in my masculinity. After two, I need his assistance to get the third repetition out. Gains are made in this zone. They say *all gain* happens at the point of *failure* in the gym!

You need someone speaking into your life who is committed to seeing God's word in your mouth and congruently in your life. You cannot disciple yourself because *"the deceitfulness of sin"* is so crafty, *"crouching out the door, with its desire for you"* (Genesis 4:7). We need an outside voice, one that deeply cares for us, our betterment, and our future enough to call us out and keep us accountable. Blessed is the man who has this; poor is the man who doesn't. Sometimes, the discipline we lack needs to come from the leader we are being discipled by. To discipline, call out a foul, call out transgression, and rebuke (in love) are some of the greatest acts of love.

> *"Let the righteous strike me; It shall be a kindness. And let him rebuke me; It shall be as excellent oil; Let my head not refuse it. For still my prayer is against the deeds of the wicked."*
> Psalms 141:5

These are the words of King David, who was rebuked and corrected by Nathaniel, the prophet when David sinned with Bathsheba and arranged to have her husband Uriah conveniently killed in battle to cover his adultery and sin.

> *"Because I think I am making progress!"*
> - Pablo Casals[4]

Take a leaf from Pablo Casals' playbook and be a lifelong learner!" Pablo Casals was considered the best cellist. At age ninety-five, he could have easily rested on his laurels and accomplishments. Instead, he continued learning and developing, practicing six hours a day.

# EMERGE
# THE WILD ASS, THE PACK ASS, AND THE LION

*"A wild ass saw a pack ass jogging along under a heavy load, and he taunted him with the condition of the slavery in which he lived with these words, 'What a vile lot is yours compared with mine. I am as free is the air, and I never do a stroke of work, and as for fodder, I have only to go to the hills and there I find far more than enough for my needs, but you, you depend on your master for food, and he makes you carry heavy loads every day, and he beats you unmercifully!' At that moment, a lion appeared on the scene. He made no attempt to molest the pack ass owing to the presence of the driver, but seeing the wild ass with no protection, promptly fell upon and attacked the wild ass, with no one to protect him, and without more ado made a meal of him."*

The Bible tells us Satan roams around like a roaring lion seeking whom he may devour. Like this magnificent fable potently illustrates, those who are not being discipled and are not accountable to anyone but themselves appear free. They look like their life is the more desirable. However, they are the ones I have seen again and again get devoured by the wicked lion, Satan.

## THE BENEFIT OF BEING A DISCIPLE

You may be asking, "What's the benefit of being a disciple?" What's the gain? What advantage does it give me in life?

The answer is straightforward. God speaks through His word. When God's word is in your life (both in your mouth and in your life), you will begin to hear clear direction from God. His voice will come to you easily and clearly.

> *"Now Samuel said to Saul, "Why have you disturbed me by bringing me up?" And Saul answered, "I am deeply distressed; for the Philistines make war against me, and God has departed from me and does not answer me anymore, neither by prophets nor by dreams. Therefore I have called you, that you may reveal to me what I should do." Then Samuel said: "So why do you ask me, seeing the Lord has departed from you and has become your enemy?"*
> *I Samuel 28:15-16*

In the above story, Saul has become incongruent with God's word. He has not only stopped obeying God, but he has also willfully entered into rebelling against God's word and will promote self-preservation over the purposes of the God of Israel.

God does *not* have to speak to you simply because you call upon Him. He does, how-

# CHAPTER FOURTEEN: DISCIPLE

ever, "draw near to those who draw near to him" (James 4:8). If you obey God's word and exalt it above every other voice in your life, you will hear His voice when you need it. The lesson here is: If you prioritize God's word when you don't need it, it will come to you when you do!

## IS ANYBODY LISTENING?

The great Methodist Missionary, Dr E Stanley Jones, told this story: Jones spent two weeks each year traveling from city to city in India to raise funds for his Mission. He would schedule up to three talks per day with prominent citizens in an attempt to gain their financial support. He would address one group at breakfast, the second at lunch, and the third at dinner. The next day, he would repeat his appeals to three groups in another city. One night, after his third presentation, he rushed to the airport where he had booked the last flight of the day to his next day's destination. As he stood in line, they announced that his flight was oversold and requested that passengers give up their seats in return for an additional free round-trip ticket to the city of their choice.

When he heard the announcement, Jones thought he heard the Lord whisper to him, "Step out of the line." He hesitated—doing so would mean missing at least two meetings the next day. He stayed in line.

When he was nearly at the podium, he again felt God urging him to step out of line and give up his seat. Again, he hesitated, unsure whether it was God or only his imagination. But when he was just one person away from the airline agent, he again heard God speak, this time in no uncertain terms: "STEP OUT OF THE LINE!" Jones obeyed, and someone else took his seat on the plane.

The following day, Dr. E Stanley Jones awoke to the tragic news that the airliner he was meant to travel on had crashed, and all the passengers aboard were killed. There were no survivors. As he scrambled to let his family know he was not on board and was still alive, the media had also learned that Dr. Jones had not been aboard as scheduled and rushed to interview him. When told why he had not been aboard the ill-fated flight, they were incensed.

"Do you mean to tell us that you were the only one God loved enough to warn?" they frenetically asked.

"Oh no!" came Jones' quick reply. "I don't mean that at all! I know God loved every person aboard that plane at LEAST as much as He loves me. But, you see, I was the only one who was listening."

**241**

## EMERGE

From Kung Fu masters to samurai warriors to marketplace mentorship programs, *discipleship* is the choice medium for imparting values, developing strengths, and ensuring that next-generation leaders are raised to carry on the legacies. *You* are most potent when you are being discipled. According to scripture, you are then required to "make disciples," imparting to others the life lessons, values, and word of God *you* have been taught!

The Hebrew word for *disciple* is "Talmud," which literally means "the traditions and laws of the Israelites." A disciple is someone who procures not only the law and knowledge of Israel and her God but also the traditions and values that flow from this law. In other words, your entire lifestyle reflects the *laws* in your heart!

## BE A DISCIPLE

The Bible teaches a powerful principle espoused by the Aesop Fable mentioned above. When we are submitted under authority, that authority becomes a covering over our lives. The great news about discipleship is you get to choose whom you submit under to be discipled. Jesus invited His disciples, saying, *"Follow me, and I'll make you fishers of men!"* He put the ball in their court. They had the option to say yes or no. They could have walked away. But they said, "*Yes!*" What lies on the other side of your *"yes"* to God is beyond comprehension. I'm sure these fishermen and tax collectors didn't expect that they would become a central part of the best-selling book of all time, the Bible. They had no idea their lives would inspire billions for all eternity. They just said yes.

Say *yes* to becoming a disciple and watch what God does with and through your life. Now, a little caveat. When I say you get to choose who disciples you, you don't get to decide *how* they disciple you. Jesus *never* checked in on them for a consensus or made them a committee to determine the vision, mission, and strategy. In fact, He would get up in the morning and depart for the next assignment, and it was up to them to follow Him (hence "follow me"). It was not a one-off request but a "for the rest of their lives" command!

*"I never learned from a man who agreed with me."*
*–Robert A. Heinlein*
*"It is what we know already that often prevents us from learning."*
*– Claude Bernard*

# CHAPTER FOURTEEN: DISCIPLE
## MAKE DISCIPLES

You will enjoy peace, power, prosperity, and great success. You will be protected from the evil one seeking to devour your life. You will hear God clearly in times of trouble. You will flourish in this life. You will ensure that legacies are carried forward in strength and power by a new generation!

A disciple is *not* just a disciplined follower of Jesus Christ, which is what I was taught at Bible college. If that were true, you could be a disciplined follower of Christ in a cave or a monastery and *never* reproduce yourself. The church would have died out in the first century and wouldn't be here today. To me, a disciple is a *"passionate pursuer of Christ and a purposeful reproducer of Christ-followers!"*

People will often comment at funerals, *"You can't take anything with you into eternity!"* As far as material things are concerned, this is true, but there is something we can take with us into eternity. It is the *only* thing we can take. Disciples. The people we led to Christ. The people we taught how to obey His word over the world's domineering pressures. The people we played a part to form Christ in. They will be with us for all eternity! Discipleship is the engagement of labor that will last for eternity! No other industry, organization, or corporation can promise you that only Christ and His great commission! Go and make disciples! Effect eternity. Plunder Hell. Populate Heaven! Amen!

## A FEW CLOSING DISCIPLESHIP THOUGHTS...

*"It takes more courage to reveal insecurities than to hide them, more strength to relate to people than to dominate them, more 'manhood' to abide by thought-out principles rather than blind reflex. Toughness is in the soul and spirit, not muscles and an immature mind."*
– Alex Karras

*"There is nothing noble in being superior to your fellow man; true nobility is being superior to your former self."*
– Ernest Hemingway

*"Judge a man by his questions rather than by his answers."*
-Voltaire

# EMERGE

# REFERENCES

### Chapter 1
1. Watson, Paul Joseph. "What is 'toxic masculinity'?" March 3, 2023. Video, 0:57. https://www.youtube.com/shorts/7Hb2o82eMp0

### Chapter 3
1. Harper, C., & McLanahan, S. (2004). Father absence and youth incarceration. Journal of Research on Adolescence, 14, 369-397
2. Farrell, Warren, and John Gray. The boy crisis: Why our boys are struggling and what we can do about it. Dallas, TX: BenBella Books, 2019.

### Chapter 9
1. Weintraub, Karen. "Sperm counts are decreasing, study finds. What might it mean for fertility?" USA Today. November 15, 2022. https://www.usatoday.com/story/news/health/2022/11/15/sperm-counts-decrease-men-health-exposure-fertility/10668233002/

### Chapter 10
1. Buncombe, Andrew. The Independent Friday, June 29, 2012

### Chapter 14
1. Evans, Ashley. "Talmud Vs Torah." Bible Reasons. February 27, 2024. https://biblereasons.com/talmud-vs-torah/
2. Online Etymology Dictionary. "Psychology." October 13, 2021. https://www.etymonline.com/word/psychology
3. Onoriobe, Israel. "Build Your Character." World Vision Crusade Outreach Ministires. August 7, 2020. https://www.wvcom-international.org/build-your-character/
4. Green, Cheryl. "Why Did Pablo Casals Practice at Age 90?" The Age Coach. August 11, 2017. https://theagecoach.net/2017/08/11/why-did-pablo-casals-practice-at-age-90/
5. Dorner, Nancy L. God's Vitamin C for the Spirit. (Starburst Publishers, 1996), 176

**EMERGE**

# CHAPTER TEN: **PRODUCER**

Made in the USA
Monee, IL
26 April 2024

57548716R00138